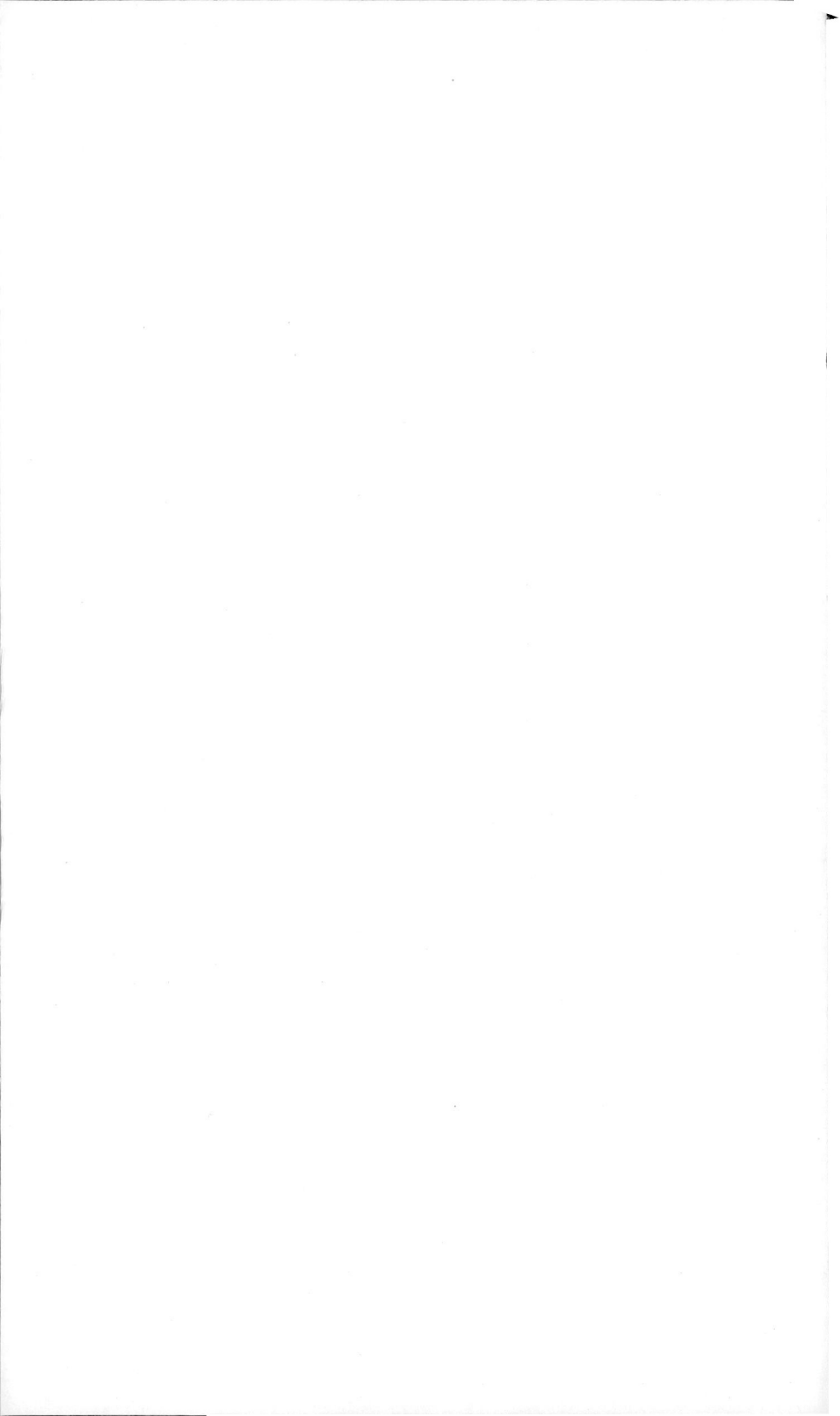

WE LED IN
MUNICH

Steven Lawther

WE LED IN
MUNICH

The unlikely adventures of
Raith Rovers in Europe

pitch

First published by Pitch Publishing, 2025

1

pitch

Pitch Publishing
9 Donnington Park,
85 Birdham Road,
Chichester, West Sussex,
PO20 7AJ
www.pitchpublishing.co.uk
info@pitchpublishing.co.uk

A CIP catalogue record is available for this book
from the British Library.

ISBN 978 1 83680 193 1

Typesetting and origination by Pitch Publishing

MIX
Paper | Supporting
responsible forestry
FSC™ C016779
FSC
www.fsc.org

Printed and bound on FSC® certified paper in line with
our continuing commitment to ethical business practices,
sustainability and the environment.

Printed and bound in India by Replika Press Pvt. Ltd.

Contents

This book is dedicated to every Raith Rovers supporter who, if only for a moment, believed that the impossible was possible.

You'll Never Beat Shaun Dennis

As this book was being finalised, supporters received the news that former captain Shaun Dennis had passed away. Throughout the period that this book covers, Shaun was the unyielding heart of the Raith Rovers defence, relentlessly competitive on the field, quietly contemplative off it – characteristics which made him a favourite of supporters. He is the most decorated player in the club's history and one of our most loved. Our thoughts go out to his friends and family. Shaun was, and always will be, a true Rover.

Acknowledgements

THIS BOOK could not have been possible without the help of a significant number of people who generously gave up their time to be interviewed. In particular, I would like to express my sincere gratitude to Jimmy Nicholl, Ian Murray, Julian Broddle, Colin Cameron, Stephen Crawford, Jason Dair, Gordon Forrest, Ally Graham, David Kirkwood, Danny Lennon, Stephen McAnespie, Robbie Raeside, Graham Robertson, Anthony Rougier, Alex Taylor, Scott Thomson, Barry Wilson, Jim Clark, Scott Davie, Grace Fowlie, John Greer, Davie Hancock, Shaughan McGuigan, Graeme Meldrum, Gavin Quinn, Kenny Smith, Jonathan Tippetts-Aylmer, and Steve Wallace.

I would particularly like to thank the fans who agreed to be interviewed and shared their stories. There were many people who travelled to watch the side in the UEFA Cup, and unfortunately in a single book it is not possible to capture the story of everyone. I hope that in reflecting the recollections of the fans interviewed it gives a voice to every supporter on the journey.

Thirty years have passed since many of the events in this book. Where it has been possible, I have made every attempt to check the full accuracy of events but in many instances, I have had to rely on the memories and recollections of the people who were there. The stories contained within this book are therefore recounted on an as told to me basis and any errors, mistakes or inaccuracies are entirely unintentional.

Additional thanks go to the following people:

- Gordon Brown for generously agreeing to provide the foreword to this book and continuing to raise the profile of the club at every opportunity

- All at Pitch Publishing for their support and assistance in bringing this book to publication

- Raith Rovers' club photographer Tony Fimister for providing access to his personal collection of European photos

- John Greer, Phil Nicholson, Steve Wallace, Susanna Freedman, Ray Browne, and Kristín Hauksdóttir of Reykjavík Photography Museum for help on photographs

- Ruaridh Kilgour for contacts in the Faroe Islands

- John Petersen for providing the Gøtu Ítróttarfelag perspective

- Brynjólfur Þór Guðmundsson for his unrivalled knowledge on Akranes and revisiting an unfortunate defeat so graciously

- John Litster, author of *Always Next Season* and Bill Gilby, editor of *Europe Blinked*. Both books provided excellent background information

- Elaine Lawther for her support, encouragement, and role as unofficial editor

Steven Lawther

Foreword by Gordon Brown

I HAVE been at Stark's Park when Raith Rovers have emerged triumphant victors, those unforgettable days when we have achieved promotions. And I've been there when we have lost badly, as that day a few years ago when we were relegated by Brechin City to League One. But nothing matches the sense of pride that I and thousands of Rovers fans shared more than 30 years ago when we won the Scottish League Cup and then qualified for European football.

I have followed Raith Rovers all my life and been attending matches since before the Jim Baxter time and remember how he humiliated Rangers with a display of skill that made them buy him for £16,000. I still remember the names of those in the first team I saw play in the late 1950s – Drummond, Polland, McNaught, Leigh, McEwan, Copland, Kelly, Williamson and Urquhart. I've cheered the team at Stark's Park and at away games when players such as Jocky Richardson, Gordon Wallace, Gordon Dalziel, and more recently Dylan Easton and Lewis Vaughan were scoring with ease.

And it's the thought of repeating the famous victories like winning that 1994 League Cup against Celtic, getting into Europe and then getting into the second round of the

UEFA Cup that keeps you going. Games played abroad have often been treacherous for Raith. The story of a trip where players were shipwrecked is part of Rovers folklore. In 1923, the team had been en route to play friendly matches on the Canary Islands when their ship the SS *Highland Loch* ran aground off the coast of Spain. The players were rescued by local fishermen and survived, not only to tell the tale, but to win all four of those games.

When I was a schoolboy in the 1960s, Raith brought Israeli side Petah Tikva to Kirkcaldy, which I was told was the first foreign team to play at Stark's Park – the first ever foreign team I'd ever seen. I remember that day, Raith Rovers playing a European match. But nothing comes close to taking on Bayern Munich in 1995. I could not be present – I was in parliament at the time and was instructed not to leave. But I will for ever hold in my mind that photograph – the one on my wall at home – of the scoreboard showing Bayern Munich 0 Raith Rovers 1. And Danny Lennon will be remembered for ever as the goalscoring hero. I'm told that when Jimmy Nicholl, the great manager, entered the dressing room in the Olympiastadion with his team in a shock 1-0 lead, he was in fits of laughter having overheard the Bayern squad being chastised by their manager.

Nothing can really match this feeling of being up against the biggest clubs, making us believe that Kirkcaldy could be a match for Europe's finest. And while we lost the tie overall, we could hold our heads high. Bayern might have gone on to win the European Cup on many occasions, and we might have been – for a few seasons – in Scotland's third league, but the thought that we could get back to those glory days of matching Bayern Munich and their internationalists will never leave us. To this day the story of that first half in Munich encourages the players, excites the supporters, inspires our newest fans and keeps me hoping Raith Rovers will get into Europe again.

The Right Honourable Gordon Brown
Former Prime Minister of the United Kingdom and
lifelong Raith Rovers supporter

Prologue

RAITH ROVERS' assistant manager Colin Cameron emerged from the tunnel in Dingwall and glanced towards the large travelling support who had arrived in the Highlands for the second leg of their Scottish Premiership play-off. The fans had snaked their away up the A9 that morning for a noon kick-off, their yellow away strips matched by the early sunshine on their journey. Although trailing Ross County 2-1 from the first leg at Stark's Park, optimism was high. Throughout the 2023/24 season they had watched their side defy the odds and gain a reputation for stunning comebacks and last-minute winners. A one-goal deficit, even against strong opposition, was recoverable and there was still belief that they could secure promotion to the Scottish Premiership for the first time in over 25 years.

As Cameron walked towards the dugout, a familiar refrain could be heard from the away end. 'We led in Bayern Munich, beat Celtic in the cup' sang the support. The song had emerged a few seasons earlier and gained traction among fans of the Kirkcaldy club as they chased promotion. Those lyrics held a particular significance for Cameron. Thirty years earlier, as a young, elegant midfielder bursting with energy, he had featured in the Jimmy Nicholl side of the early 90s that swept to success on a blend of fearless enthusiasm and sheer belief. He had helped Raith defeat Celtic to lift the League Cup, qualifying for the UEFA Cup, and graced the pitch in the Olympiastadion when Danny Lennon's free kick deflected off the head of Bayern defender Andreas Herzog to give Rovers a 1-0 lead over the German giants.

The large electronic scoreboard showing Raith leading Bayern is now etched into the consciousness of every supporter. It is saved on hundreds of phones and adorns the walls in the houses of supporters, former players, and former prime ministers. When the Raith Supporters Trust commissioned a series of large posters in the South Stand concourse at Stark's Park celebrating key moments in the club's history, there was never any doubt that a picture of that historic Munich scoreboard would be included. As a moment in time, leading Bayern in the Olympiastadion was arguably one of the most surreal moments in the club's 142-year history, but it also represents the highest level Raith have ever reached, making it a fitting accomplishment to celebrate in song.

If there was reference to leading Bayern in the pre-match singing in Dingwall, there was also an echo of that night in Munich at the conclusion of the match. Rovers lost, with their dreams of a return to the top flight extinguished. But at the final whistle supporters stayed in place to applaud their side. The team may have been defeated, but the mood remained celebratory with recognition of just how enjoyable the journey to the play-off final had been. 'The support we got that day up at Dingwall was fantastic,' reflects Colin Cameron. 'They knew we weren't going to get promotion, but I think the fans were showing their appreciation to the players about what they had done for them and the experiences and the joy they have given them that season. That was the fans' way of saying "thank you", and it wasn't missed by the players.'

Thirty years before, fans had also remained in the Olympiastadion long after the final whistle to celebrate the players and management that had taken them to unimaginable heights. 'When we were in Munich the fans stayed behind and you have that iconic picture of when the players came across to us,' says supporter Gavin Quinn. 'It was the same in Dingwall. The supporters stayed with them, and they deserved it.'

What supporters should or should not celebrate has been the subject of debate in recent years across Scottish football. A narrative has emerged that unless you have won a title, achieved promotion, or secured a cup, then to revel in anything else is somehow embarrassing or improper. Rovers' magical night in Munich has been caught up in that discourse.

The famous scoreboard image may show the side leading 1-0, but at the conclusion of the game, Rovers had lost the match 2-1, the tie 4-1 on aggregate, and exited the tournament. On paper, it could easily have been mistaken for failure, but everyone present knew that it was anything but. 'That scoreboard has to be iconic,' says long-time fan and club historian John Greer. 'OK, we lost the game ultimately, but we are not celebrating failure, we are celebrating a high point in Rovers' history. I'm going to get emotional here, but it really was incredible.'

John's emotion comes not only from the memories of that moment, but also from thinking of those who didn't get the chance to experience such a monumental high. 'My grandfather saw great players and great teams,' he continues.

'He saw James, McNaught, Leigh, Baxter, Young. He saw all these players and he saw the team that finished third in Scotland and the team that scored the most goals and set a British record. He saw all this, but he never experienced a cup win and anything as euphoric as a trip into Europe. We had that privilege.'

It was the unlikeliness of the journey that made it special. That a team like Raith Rovers was even playing in Europe, never mind progressing through two rounds and, for a brief moment at least, frightening one of Europe's greatest clubs seems outrageous, and it was. It remains one of the great football stories. Yet it is a story that might never have happened.

It is often said that football is a series of individual moments combined to make something spectacular. A touch, a pass, a flick-on, a run, a block – each connected and all essential to the ball ending up in the back of the net. Alter or remove just one and things can change or evolve differently. A pass doesn't reach a winger, a bad touch allows a defender to block, a poor connection and the ball glides inches outside the post. The conclusion shaped differently. The same is true of Rovers' journey to the Olympiastadion. A series of interconnected events led a small provincial club from Fife on to one of the greatest stages in world football to take on and lead one of Europe's elite clubs. Yet at so many stages on that journey there were moments which, if absent, could have set Raith on an alternative path.

If Glasgow Celtic hadn't sacked Frank Connor and, hurt and angry, he hadn't decided to take a chance on Raith Rovers.

If Connor had not reignited a youth system and blended the young talent it produced with experienced professionals to provide the core of Rovers' success for the next decade.

If his successor Jimmy Nicholl hadn't persuaded the board to gamble on going full-time, taking the club to unprecedented heights.

If 16-year-old Brian Potter hadn't seized his moment in the League Cup semi-final and saved from Airdrie's Alan Lawrence in the penalty shoot-out.

If Gordon Marshall had held the ball after Jason Dair's shot, rather than spilling it to veteran striker Gordon Dalziel to equalise in the dying moments of the League Cup Final against Celtic.

And, perhaps most importantly of all, if Scott Thomson hadn't saved the penalty from Paul McStay to win the League Cup and ensure European qualification.

If any of those milestones had been absent or unfolded differently, then there may have been no story to tell.

Rovers wouldn't have qualified to play in the 1995 UEFA Cup.

They wouldn't have drawn Gøtu Ítróttarfelag from the Faroe Islands.

Fans and players wouldn't have experienced a 25-hour ferry trip, or a terrifying flight to a rocky outcrop in the North Atlantic.

They wouldn't have been rewarded with a trip even further north to take on Icelandic champions ÍA.

They wouldn't have spent a surreal 24 hours in a magical landscape watching the most defensive performance in Rovers' history and witnessing countless heart-stopping moments, all threatening to erase the possibility of drawing Bayern Munich in the next round. And even at the decisive moment in the Olympiastadion, when Danny Lennon lined up to take his famous free kick, a different outcome was possible. His strike could have risen into the Munich air and sailed over the bar. It could have hit the German wall. It could have missed the head of Andreas Herzog and landed safely in the arms of goalkeeper Oliver Kahn.

But it didn't. It deflected past Kahn into the Bayern Munich goal, sending the supporters who had travelled to watch their side and those watching at home into rapture and delivering a stunning moment that still resonates 30 years on. It was a goal and a moment that made us believe, and still believe, that anything is possible.

This is a story that might never have happened, but it did.

We led in Munich, and this is our story.

1

The Special One

AS HE sits in the bar of the Balmoral Hotel in Edinburgh, 68-year-old Jimmy Nicholl still bristles with enthusiasm about Raith Rovers. The love and warmth he has for the Kirkcaldy club is unmistakeable. 'The six happiest years of my life were spent there,' says Nicholl. 'Of that there is no doubt.'

It is a remarkable assessment given his impressive resumé in football. His playing career took him to Manchester United, Sunderland, Glasgow Rangers, West Bromwich Albion, Toronto Blizzard and, whisper it quietly, Dunfermline Athletic. He featured in two World Cups for Northern Ireland, coming up against the great and good of world football. And for the last 30 years he has worked consistently in the game as manager and coach at several clubs including Rangers, Hibernian, Aberdeen, Dundee, Falkirk and Cowdenbeath, with his passion for football undiminished as he continues to assist Michael O'Neill in his role as Northern Ireland manager. He is one of the game's great characters, loved by fans throughout football, but nowhere is his legacy cherished more than in a small town on the coast of Fife.

The very mention of his name in Kirkcaldy brings a smile to the face of Raith supporters and evokes memories of the most successful period in the club's history. Nicholl achieved promotion to the Premier League not once, but twice, won the club their first national trophy and secured their first participation in Europe. Arguably the most defining moment of his time in charge was the October night in 1995 when he masterminded the trip to Germany, taking on the might of Bayern Munich in the Olympiastadion and having the audacity to take the lead. 'As an achievement, that was probably it,' he reflects. 'Getting Raith Rovers to that stage and that level and to give Bayern Munich a game. All these years later, you have got to feel proud.'

When Nicholl had first walked through the front door at Stark's Park in the winter of 1990, notions of taking the club to such heights seemed fanciful, yet he was not inheriting a club in crisis. Rovers sat fifth in the First Division table, just three points behind leaders Airdrie, and had a talented squad of players. His predecessor had made sure of that, having dragged the club up from the bottom of the old Second Division. 'Frank Connor laid the foundations,' says Nicholl. 'He did a great job. Some of those players had been struggling at the time and Frank brought them back so I inherited great players, a great squad, and a great team.'

Raith were in good shape, but Nicholl was untested as a manager and, at first, struggled. He would record only one victory in his first nine games in charge, a win percentage that in today's football might tempt some chairmen to reach for the panic button.

The board recognised that their new man needed time and allowed him the breathing space to settle into the job. Results improved but the remainder of the season unfolded in unspectacular fashion and Rovers finished seventh. Salt was rubbed into the wound of a disappointing finish when Airdrie came to Stark's Park for the last league game and clinched promotion to the Premier Division, their fans invading the pitch at the conclusion. 'We were sitting in the dressing room hearing all the noise and celebrations,' recalls former Rovers defender Robbie Raeside. 'Jimmy was annoyed. He sat there and gave us this speech that was, "Listen to that. Remember that feeling and use it. This time next year, that will be us."'

Nicholl's prediction would prove correct, even if the timescale was a little out. The following season Rovers finished fifth, but 12 further months on, with full-time funding secured, his squad swept to the title, securing promotion to the Premier League with five games left to play. The move from part-time to full-time football had been instrumental to the success. It afforded Nicholl the opportunity to add mercurial talents like Craig Brewster and Peter Hetherston and assemble a strong collection of young apprentices who quickly injected raw and exciting talent into the first team. 'We had young players coming through that weren't scared,' says former Rovers player Davie Kirkwood. 'We had the likes of Jason Dair, Colin Cameron, and Stevie Crawford. Those guys were never frightened of a thing.'

Rovers' first foray in the Premier League proved short-lived and a combination of league reconstruction, inexperience and a lack of resources made it virtually impossible for them to avoid relegation. 'We fell short,' reflects former Raith defender Shaun Dennis. 'You have got to invest money to survive but then it's a risk. If you still go down and have players on two-year contracts on the same money as in the Premier League it cripples the club.

So, Jimmy just had to borrow and beg for what he could get.'

Despite the relegation, Rovers won praise for their fearless, attacking football. 'We were a great team,' says Ally Graham, a striker at Stark's Park from 1993 to 1996. 'A real good attacking team. People feared us. We went to Ibrox [in January 1994], drew 2-2 and we should have won. Some of the team goals we scored were top drawer. Absolute top drawer, and I think the fans appreciated our style of football.'

Back down in the First Division for 1994/95, the priority was to fashion a quick return to the Premier League, a feat easier said than done. Early results were less than impressive as Rovers felt the hangover of relegation. 'There was a lot of frustration at the start of that year,' explains former striker Stevie Crawford. 'We had got a lot of plaudits the previous year when we had gone up into the Premier League and there was probably the expectation that we would go on and win promotion again, but we weren't getting any momentum.'

Team-mate Stephen McAnespie provides a far blunter assessment. 'We were shite,' laughs the ex-Raith defender.

Rovers may have been temporarily toiling but Nicholl, along with assistant Martin Harvey, had created an environment at Stark's Park that was built for success. The young manager fostered a work hard, play hard ethos around the club, understanding implicitly that the greatest environment to perform in was one that was ruled by fun, not fear. 'All I ever wanted was them walking out their front door in the morning looking forward to training,' he explains.

Nicholl fashioned a workplace that players adored. 'There were managers who I played under who, to be honest, were fucking hopeless,' reflects former midfielder Alex Taylor. 'They were no fun to play for and the coaching police should have taken them away, but at Raith Rovers, Jimmy was the opposite. He was great fun, and his training sessions were always enjoyable. He wanted you to have fun, take chances and you never ever got bored.'

The team spirit at Stark's Park became legendary. 'It became like a club with your pals,' says Shaun Dennis. 'We were all desperate to get into training to see each other. Jimmy used to sit in the tearoom every day and would keep everybody entertained. Players started turning up half an hour early for training and staying behind for an extra hour at the end of the day. You didn't want to leave just in case you missed something.'

'What a carry-on we had,' adds Taylor. 'I used to travel up with the likes of Ronnie Coyle and there was a gang mentality. A lot of the guys were great storytellers. It didn't matter how many times you had heard a story it was great to hear it again because they always put a few extra lines on, added bits or exaggerated. I really enjoyed the laughs and the banter. I was often the butt of it, but I really didn't mind, because it was funny.'

Team spirit and fun was important, but it was underpinned by Nicholl's professionalism, tactical awareness, and football knowledge. 'People look at Jimmy and his personality and they think that he is just a laugh,' says Danny Lennon, 'but he knows the game inside out and because of that some of the football that we played was breathtaking.'

Jimmy Nicholl loved a joke, but he was a professional. He firmly believed there was a time to work and a time to play and it was important that players did not confuse the two. He was content to let his squad relax and bond on nights out, but demanded focus and determination when it came to training, playing, and working for the team. He also understood football. 'Training was different every single day and you did have a laugh,' says Davie Kirkwood. 'But it was his professionalism and knowledge of the game that stood out. Without that, Raith Rovers wouldn't have had the success they had, it was the perfect combination. It was having a bit of a laugh and a bit of fun, but when he came to the serious stuff, you switched on.'

'You go to events and reunions these days and Jimmy is very modest,' says Robbie Raeside. 'He says, "Aww, we just used to play five-a-sides and do this and that." But I remember Jimmy taking a bag of balls up to Randolph [Industrial Estate] and they were size two or three, tiny balls and he had us all practising passing and inside, outside foot and all sorts of different passing with these tiny balls. You go online now, and you have these laptop coaches coming out with the same as if it is the latest thing. Jimmy used to do that 30 years ago. He is a great tactician, and people need to know that.'

Nicholl took the vast experience he had gleaned throughout his impressive playing career and brought it to Raith, bringing a meticulous approach to every aspect of managing a football club. 'I would write everything down,' he recounts. 'From 1992 when we went full-time, I used to keep a wee diary of everything in notebooks. If a player was ill one Tuesday when we had a hard session, I would write it down. Then maybe three weeks later the same player is ill again and misses a Tuesday again, I would think, "There's a wee pattern developing here." I would also write wee notes on the games from the weekend in them.'

Those notebooks are an archive that would make for fascinating reading today, but they provided Nicholl with an understanding of his players that was unparalleled. He understood personalities and fashioned his squad with the right mix of character to make the team function, nurturing them to learn and grow as players using what he had learned throughout his own playing career. 'Managers can give players confidence in terms of playing you,' he explains. 'But also, in the way they talk to you and how they handle you. Experienced managers should know the different characters in each player and how to handle them.'

Nicholl's management of players was exemplary. He seemed to intuitively understand what players needed and how to get the best out of them. 'If he wanted to speak to you,' says former winger Barry Wilson, 'he would throw you a ball and you would take the ball and he would walk out on to the pitch with you. You would just sit on the ball at the centre circle and talk. No one was around. No one was listening through walls, and it never got heated. There was just respect.'

'He had patience,' explains Julian Broddle, a regular at left-back between 1993 and 1996. 'I struggled at first when I got to Raith, but Jimmy knew I could play. When I was going through a tough mental period at Partick Thistle, [manager] John Lambie took me to a hypnotist and all that sort of stuff. He gave me this cassette and said, "You have to listen to that before every game." Jimmy Nic just showed patience, stuck by me and played me most of the time. He understood that if I played, I would get confidence again.'

'He once left me out for a game against Dundee,' recalls Ally Graham. 'The boys couldn't wait to run down to the tearoom to tell me that I wasn't in the squad. We got beat and the manager pulled me into his office on the Monday morning and says, "See that game, you would have been perfect for that game. We would have won that game if you played. Next week you are playing." That was the way he worked. He was building my confidence up again to get the best out of me. He made you feel wanted and he gave you the confidence that you needed.'

That players talk with such warmth about a manager they have not worked with for decades, shows the strength of relationship that was built at Stark's Park during Nicholl's time in charge. Many still credit their most successful time in football or their future careers to what they learned under his guidance. 'There is a lot of stuff that Jimmy showed me on and off the park that I still carry with me,' reflects Stevie Crawford. 'When I played with Rovers, I went into games never frightened of trying to express myself and never being frightened of making mistakes. It was Jimmy who created that through natural enthusiasm and his energy.'

Nicholl's unique combination of enthusiasm, intelligence and tactical awareness had created the perfect conditions for success, but as Raith struggled at the start of the 1994/95 season, it would need a catalyst to jump-start their campaign. That would come in the shape of the League Cup which began on an August evening in the unlikely setting of Dingwall. It is an evening that fan Jonathan Tippetts-Aylmer recalls with fondness. 'I went up to Dingwall on the supporters' bus,' he says. 'My overriding memory of that game is that it was brand-new terracing we were on so there were no barriers and when Ally Graham scored a header, we were all on the pitch hugging him. We got dropped back off in Kirkcaldy outside the Novar Bar after midnight and as I was waiting on my dad coming to pick me up, Gordon

Dalziel and Ronnie Coyle ran past me saying, "Hurry up, we've still got half an hour until Jackie O's shuts!'"

In that slightly surreal moment, neither the young supporter waiting on a lift home or the Rovers players in a rush to get to the local nightclub were aware that they were about to embark on a journey that would lead them to unimagined success and unthinkable heights.

2

Unthinkable

THE PATH to becoming a Raith fan for Jonathan Tippetts-Aylmer was perhaps not a traditional one. He was not from Kirkcaldy and growing up had no family connection to the club. His father supported Montrose and Aberdeen and had occasionally taken him to Pittodrie to watch Alex Ferguson's side in action. Living in Lundin Links, many of his contemporaries supported East Fife, but early trips to watch the Bayview side with friends failed to fire his imagination. That privilege would be left to Raith Rovers.

'I remember my first game,' he recounts. 'It was 1984 and I was ten years old. My mum and dad were going through to Kirkcaldy shopping to get their messages and they asked if I wanted to go to the football while they did their shopping. I didn't really know anything about Raith Rovers as a club, but I loved football, so I thought, "OK, why not?" They dropped me off at the old turnstiles that used to be on the road, and I went into the main stand. I sat down and it was weird. I instantly thought, "This is my team." I can't explain it. It just happened.'

There was something about the quirky ground, the L-shaped stand and a stadium sandwiched between the road and the railway line that instantly appealed to the young supporter. 'I loved it,' continues Jonathan. 'I then started wanting to go to away games, so my parents phoned up and found out there was a supporters' club and the buses left from Volunteer's Green. It was Brian Fairful and Alan Melville that ran it in those days. East Stirling was my first away game and we won 5-0. There was an older guy, Drew, who made sure I got from the bus to the turnstiles and back to the bus.'

It was not exactly a glorious era to support Raith as they languished in the old Second Division, but there was enough to keep the young fan entertained and to nurture his growing affection for the club. An early standout memory was a chaotic Scottish Cup tie in 1985 against Aberdeen, where Rovers narrowly lost 2-1 and a group of Hibernian casuals pulled the emergency cord on a passing train and attacked Stark's Park from the railway line. Like many fans of his generation, one of Jonathan's favourite matches was the last day of the season in 1986/87. Rovers clinched promotion to the First Division in Stranraer in unlikely circumstances and along with the rest of the small but enthusiastic away support he invaded the Stair Park pitch to celebrate.

Fast forward to October 1994, and he was back on the pitch celebrating, this time at McDiarmid Park after 16-year-old reserve goalkeeper Brian Potter had saved the final penalty in the shoot-out to defeat Airdrie in the League Cup semi-final. The football club that he had fallen in love with as a ten-year-old while they were languishing in the bottom tier of Scottish football were now just one win away from a major trophy and European qualification.

After comfortably defeating Ross County 5-0 in their first tie, Rovers' 1994 League Cup run had been laced with magic. Premier League side Kilmarnock were dispatched 3-2 at Stark's Park with a Colin Cameron hat-trick. St Johnstone of the First Division were beaten 3-1 in the Perth quarter-final and then the teenage Potter had his moment in a tense semi-final, after regular goalkeeper Scott Thomson had been sent off for handling outside his box. 'You could feel the momentum building through the cup run,' reflects Danny Lennon. 'Ally Graham scoring hat-tricks, Colin Cameron scoring hat-tricks. We just kept going and enjoying it. A great quarter-final up at St Johnstone, a very close game and then into the semi-final against Airdrie. We lose Thommo and then young Potts comes on, and the wee man saves it, and you are into the final. It was fairytale stuff.'

It was the definitive moment of Brian Potter's career and one that is still fondly remembered around Kirkcaldy, earning him a deserved place in the club's Hall of Fame. Gordon Forrest, one of Potter's fellow apprentices at the time, recalls the elation of the moment. 'All of the apprentices were in the stand when Brian came on as a sub,' he recalls. 'To have one of your own, one of the other young kids doing that. It was amazing. We all jumped on the pitch at the end and joined in the celebrations.'

Also enjoying the celebrations in Perth that night was Robbie Raeside. The 22-year-old had featured in the first game of the League Cup against Ross County but had missed the remaining ties through injury. He had joined Raith as a 15-year-old schoolboy during Frank Connor's era and was one of the first wave of young players who went full-time at the club after the arrival of Jimmy Nicholl. The new manager was a familiar face for the defender. 'I had already met Jimmy Nicholl by chance,' explains Raeside. 'I was one of the local kids brought in to help on a coaching course when Jimmy was doing his [UEFA] A Licence at St Andrews University. I was one of the SFA runners and when the balls were scattered everywhere, I was the first one that ran to get them in. Jimmy commented on it and said I had great enthusiasm. For someone like him to pay me a compliment was great. I had no idea at that stage he was going to become my manager within a few months.

'When he got to Raith, he remembered me. He didn't even know my name at that point, but he just said to me, "All right big man, it is funny how football works, isn't it?" Straight away, I felt that we had a wee bond.'

Raeside was a tall, skilful centre-half. He had moved into that position from central midfield years earlier but credits Nicholl with successfully developing the defensive side of his game. 'It was Jimmy [Nicholl] who taught me how to become a proper defender,' says Raeside. 'Because I had been a midfielder, sometimes you didn't feel like you had enjoyed the game unless you dribbled into midfield and beat some boys. Jimmy taught me to enjoy defending and that stood me in good stead for the rest of my career.'

Raeside loved being at the Kirkcaldy club, getting the occasional start and being part of the full-time group of apprentices. The initial cluster included players such as David Sinclair and Philip Burn, with the exciting young talent of Stevie Crawford and Jason Dair added later. They would train during the day then return at night to train with the older part-time players.

Raeside progressed into the Raith first team and the Scotland under-21 squad before injuries started to unravel the impressive career that he was building. 'The only thing I regret now is that I let Jimmy down so much with injuries,' he reflects. 'I wish I could have played more for him, but my body let me down. I had bad injuries when I was 20 or 21 and it was tough. I was lucky that I had our physio Gerry Doherty to look after me, find surgeons and that, and Jimmy to stick by me and give me contracts or I wouldn't have got back playing at all.'

Injury removed any possibility of Raeside featuring in that historic League Cup Final, when after a pulsating 120 minutes of football, Raith defeated Celtic 6-5 on penalties to win their first national trophy. Sunday, 27 November 1994 is a date now etched into the collective consciousness of Kirkcaldy as the day they achieved the unthinkable. 'It was just a great thing, wasn't it?' beams Jonathan Tippetts-Aylmer. 'Probably the greatest thing to ever happen.'

It is a day that still brings a smile to the face of anyone of a Raith Rovers persuasion lucky enough to have been present. 'I was actually one of the young players to be selected to be on duty for cup final day,' recalls Gordon Forrest. 'I was the boot boy, and I was in the changing room. I even had to sing a song on the team bus on the way back from Ibrox. That was a moment I will never forget. At the front of the bus with a microphone singing and the trophy in my hand.'

Along with the silverware came a place in the UEFA Cup. Rovers had not only won their first major competition, but they had also qualified for European football for the first time in their history. 'Europe was a huge bonus for us,' says Jimmy Nicholl. 'I pushed that point before the final. I was saying, "Listen, as well as the chance to win a cup final, you have the chance to represent Scotland in European football. Raith Rovers in Europe! That will probably never happen again." I said to them, "You are 90 minutes away from Europe." That was basically it. That is all I used to say to them. That was a heck of a motivation for the players.'

Speaking to his squad now, their former manager is perhaps overstating the importance of the European place as motivation. 'None of us were thinking about Europe,' laughs Jason Dair. 'We were just trying to get as far in the cup as we could!'

'The fact that there was a European place didn't even feature,' agrees Stephen McAnespie. 'We never really focused on that side of it because we were just young and naive. Jimmy was maybe the experienced voice in the room who had been there, done that at Manchester United and Rangers. We didn't have a clue.'

It had been a magnificent achievement, but the start of the UEFA Cup was almost nine months away and after celebrations subsided, the task of getting Rovers back to the Premier League took precedence. Nicholl knew that failure to return to the top flight would have financial implications for the club and player contracts. Not even a trophy in the cabinet or the prospect of European competition could insulate Rovers from that financial reality.

A 2-1 defeat to league leaders Dundee a few weeks after their cup win made the prospect of promotion look increasingly remote, but the manager saw something in the performance that gave encouragement. 'We went to Dundee in the middle of December,' Nicholl recalls. 'We got beat but the performance that night was great. So, I said to them, "Let's see if we can keep that performance from here to the end of the season then we can win the league. All you need to do is win your next 21 games!"'

Nicholl's encouragement worked and a run of eight consecutive league wins and an unbeaten run that lasted until the middle of April carried them through the rest of the season. 'After we won the cup it all just clicked,' recounts Julian Broddle. 'We just started winning games and couldn't lose. The confidence we had was amazing. You go out and you know you are going to win. You just don't know by what score.'

Rovers had the chance to secure the title on the penultimate day of the season against rivals Dunfermline at Stark's Park, but a goalless draw left them needing a point away to Hamilton in their last game. A huge visiting crowd arrived at Firhill in hopeful mood, filling the whole of the Jackie Husband Stand. The two teams played out an uneventful 0-0 draw, enough to secure Rovers the First Division title and promotion. 'If you ever played a game of football and nothing happened, then that was it,' laughs goalkeeper Scott Thomson. 'I think there were about three shots at goal.'

It had been a remarkable season. A league and cup double secured and a cherished return to the Premier League. No one would have predicted that as the campaign had begun back in August. 'All my relatives had gone through on a supporters' bus to Firhill that last game,' says Robbie Raeside. 'My mum was even on the bus. After winning promotion and pipping Dunfermline, they had persuaded the bus driver to go back via Dunfermline. They were going through Dunfermline singing and banging on the windows. My mum still says that was the highlight of her day!'

The season concluded with striker Stevie Crawford being called into the Scotland squad for the Kirin Cup in Japan. There have been many former Raith players who have gone on to feature for their national side, but few had done so while playing for the club. It was a stunning achievement for the young forward. 'When you ask any young players now what their ambition is,' says Crawford, 'they say it is to go and play in the Champions League. For my generation, it was always to play for Scotland. That was my dream from an early age, pulling on the Scotland jersey. I felt like I was wearing the club badge at that point and not just going for myself or to represent my family, but also to represent Raith Rovers.'

In one final magical moment of a magical season, Crawford took to the field at the Toyama Stadium for his international debut and scored the winning goal in a 2-1 victory over Ecuador. Everything Raith Rovers touched seemed golden. Now, all that was left was to recharge over the summer and wait for the European adventure to begin.

3

In a Good Place

IF SUPPORTERS are the constant of any football club, then for Raith Rovers, Gavin Quinn is the constant of the supporters. 'Quinny', as he is affectionately known around Stark's Park, has been one of the most familiar faces on the terracing and in the stands for the best part of 40 years. Yet it could all have been so different if a Celtic-supporting uncle had gotten his way. 'My uncle had wanted to take me to Celtic games,' explains Quinn. 'But I was too young to get on the Celtic bus so that was knocked on the head.'

The Parkhead side's loss would be Raith's gain after a school friend encouraged him down to watch his local team. His first match was a forgettable midweek game against Arbroath which was lost 1-0, but for the Kirkcaldy youngster the connection was instant. 'I was hooked right away,' explains Quinn.

He would soon be travelling home and away to games, although following Raith Rovers in his early years required a degree of dedication. There were very few highs, but Quinn remained ever-present on the terracing as the club drifted towards the lower reaches of Scottish football. His loyalty was rewarded when Frank Connor arrived and started to turn Rovers' fortunes around. 'The crowds weren't very big when Frank came in,' says Quinn. 'So, you still used to swap ends. All the young lads like us used to stand outside the dressing room window and listen to Frank's rants at the players at half-time. Those were legendary. He did say when he came to the Rovers that we would get promoted within five years and that was exactly what happened.'

It was a special time at the club with the connection between fans and players in that period unique. The strong bond and togetherness of the players was picked up by supporters and taken into the pubs and nightclubs of Kirkcaldy. It is a time that many recall with fondness. 'We had a great connection with the team,' says Quinn. 'The players used to come back to the Abbotshall [Hotel], and we used to have parties on a Saturday night with them. It was unbelievable. There were also a lot of local guys in the side. Guys like Stevie Craw[ford], Jason [Dair], Shaun [Dennis] and Sinky [Davie Sinclair], which was great. So, to have Mickey [Colin] Cameron and all the Fife boys in the team was brilliant as well.'

It was an era that players also recall with fondness, even if the memories of certain nights out could become hazy. 'If there were camera phones back in Kirkcaldy in the 90s, then I'm sure a few of us would not have been allowed to play fitba',' jokes Stevie Crawford. 'Jimmy used to love us going out for a pint, because we would all go out together and you would mix with the fans. That was just how we were. It just felt real. When you were going through the harder times at the Rovers on the pitch, there was a togetherness between us, and the support and you felt protected.'

'The connection between the fans and the players was fantastic,' agrees Jason Dair. 'I mean I was local, Stevie

Crawford was local, Colin Cameron, Shaun Dennis, Davie Sinclair. There were a few from Glasgow, but they jumped into the whole thing. Most weekends the whole team were out in Kirkcaldy when we were playing at home and the Glasgow ones would stay up in the Abbotshall. We were out as a team together and we were quite happy to be out drinking with fans.'

***

With the club back in the Premier League and in the UEFA Cup, Jimmy Nicholl was focused on building a squad ready for the challenge. The success he had brought to Raith Rovers had always been built on a blend of experience and youth, but he had lost key senior players on the pitch in David Narey, Gordon Dalziel, and himself. 'I remember after the game against Hamilton,' he recalls. 'I thought, "That's me finished as a player. I can't go to the Premier League again." Then big Dave Narey came to me and said, "That's me finished, I can't do it," and I thought, "You are joking." That was me, David and Gordon Dalziel all gone. It was the spine of the team that had been there to help the younger guys.'

Nicholl knew that he had talented youngsters in his squad and had always been willing to afford them the chance to shine. He had been given his own opportunity early on in his Manchester United career and he had no hesitation in offering the same chances to promising youth players coming through in Kirkcaldy. 'Age didn't concern me at all,' explains Nicholl. 'For me, you shouldn't be hovering about a club waiting for a game aged 20 or 21. You should be pushing for the first team at 16, 17, or 18.'

Stevie Crawford, Jason Dair and Colin Cameron were all introduced to the squad at an early age and repaid the manager's faith with some exceptional performances. The older, experienced heads worked hard to nurture and develop the young players and ensure that they could hold their own, knowing that if they got stronger the team as a whole would benefit. The flood of talent into the first team energised the whole squad. 'I saw the young guys as established,' reflects Alex Taylor. 'They were right good, high-quality players. You could rely on them at any time, to control the ball, give it back to you. You could trust them with anything.'

Nicholl bolstered his side at the start of the season with two experienced professionals with knowledge of European competition. The first was Jim McInally, a £150,000 signing from Dundee United. 'I thought I would try and replace David Narey's experience with Jim McInally's experience,' explains the former Rovers manager. 'That was the idea.'

McInally was a Glaswegian, who had started out at a boys' club in the Gorbals. He had spent time at Celtic and Nottingham Forest before flourishing under Jim McLean at Dundee United. McInally had initially signed as a full-back but had been successfully converted by McLean into an elegant defensive midfielder. In his nine-year period at the club, the Tannadice side reached the UEFA Cup Final and won the Scottish Cup. With United relegated, McInally jumped at the chance to sign for newly promoted Raith as a player-coach. It offered not just a return to the Premier League, but a chance to reacquaint himself with the UEFA Cup.

The second arrival was Alex Taylor. The talented midfielder had been released by Partick Thistle after spending two years at the Glasgow club; his last kick of the ball had been a spectacular shot into the top corner late into a game at Ibrox to earn his side a point in their final match of the season. The strike silenced the home crowd, who were there to see their team awarded the league trophy, having already been crowned champions. Two days after the match, Taylor received a letter telling him that his services were no longer required at Firhill. 'Such is football,' he laughs.

It wasn't long before he was invited to Kirkcaldy to sign for Raith Rovers. 'Jimmy found out that I was available and asked me to come in,' explains Taylor. 'I didn't know too much about the club, but I knew that they had won the league and won the cup and were going to be playing in Europe, so it was an attractive offer, and I was happy to take it. I was just delighted that anybody wanted me at my age to be honest!'

Taylor was 33 years old and had amassed a wealth of football experience having started his career at Dundee United back in the early 1980s. 'I never really had that burning ambition to be a professional footballer,' he reflects. 'It just sort of happened. I just took every opportunity to play football. I went up to Tannadice and my dad came with me to negotiate my signing-on fee. Jim [McLean] asked my dad if I was fast. My dad replied, "Put it this way, if you send him up the shop to get a loaf, then you will be starving by the time he comes back." That probably brought my signing-on fee down a wee bit!'

Taylor experienced United in a golden era, when they won the championship at rivals Dundee's Dens Park and regularly played in Europe. He feels fortunate to have been around a United side packed with talent and who were achieving great success, but life under Jim McLean could be harsh and demanding and young players would frequently be locked into long contracts that benefited club more than player. 'Jim as an individual was very good at his job,' says

Taylor. 'But I think he took advantage of guys like me. He gave you nothing and he fined you constantly to get back even the wee bit he did give you. He was able to do that because that was just the way it worked then. I look back at it now and it wasn't a great way to treat young players.'

Taylor's time at United ended when he refused to sign an eight-year extension to his contract, resulting in him being frozen out of football for over 12 months as the club held on to his registration for the last year of his existing deal. 'Nobody would take a chance on me because United wanted a transfer fee,' he explains. 'They had these tribunals at the time and Jim had letters from clubs offering money for me, or apparently so anyway. He was trying to get a dossier to get my value up and as a result nobody would touch me.'

The Bosman ruling would eventually prevent clubs retaining the registration of players in this manner, but before its arrival, Taylor was left with no option but to leave football, missing a year of his development when as a player he should have been accelerating his career. Taylor's father had travelled up to Tannadice during his year out in an attempt to persuade McLean to release his son, but the discussion became fractious, and the United manager left the meeting with a black eye. 'I knew nothing about it at the time,' says Taylor. 'But word got around about what happened. A few years later, I was on a treatment table down at Lilleshall getting treatment for my knee and Alan Hansen was next to me. We got chatting and I told him who I was and that I had been at Dundee United. He said, "Wasn't it your dad that lamped wee Jim?" He then shouted across to Gary Gillespie, "Gary, come here. His old man was the one that hit wee Jim!" I was more famous for what my dad had done than anything I had done for a while!'

Taylor eventually returned to football and had successful spells at Hamilton, Walsall, Falkirk, and Partick Thistle. Having arrived in Kirkcaldy, he was eager to rekindle his relationship with the UEFA Cup. 'I think I took playing in Europe with Dundee United for granted because I was young,' he reflects. 'That was why I was excited when I got the chance again with Raith Rovers, I knew it was special and I knew I was going to enjoy it.'

There was anticipation all around the club about what was to come, with those already at Stark's Park equally keen to enjoy the experience of the UEFA Cup. 'I was on the last third of my career,' says Julian Broddle. 'The only way for me was downhill at that point so if I was sold, I knew there was no way it was going to be to anybody who would be playing in Europe. So, for me it was all about staying at the club and staying in the side so that you could play in the European campaign.'

Striker Ally Graham, by this point aged 29, was also keen to stay but agreeing a new contract would prove problematic at first. 'I have never really spoken about this,' he says. 'I went in and asked Jimmy for a new contract and he said, "No," that I wasn't getting it. I was in his office for two minutes and then I left. It was a bit frosty. It wasn't thousands of pounds a week or anything. It was £100 a week more and a couple of bob signing you were looking for. Nothing extravagant. I thought I was in a good position because of winning the cup and winning the league, but he told me "No."

'The way it eventually resolved itself was I got made an offer from the chairman and one of the board members. They jokingly told me that Jimmy had come in and told them that he needed money to buy a striker and that they'd concluded that the happy medium between us all was to offer me a contract!'

With the services of Graham secured, the rest of the squad relatively intact, and the addition of McInally, Taylor and Trinidadian player Tony Rougier, Jimmy Nicholl felt that the club was prepared. 'I never put too much emphasis on worrying,' reflects Nicholl. 'We were in a good place. Things were that good at the time and promotion was a massive thing. The young ones were there, and they were still learning, but they were becoming more mature, and it was great.'

The mood around the club and the support had grown feverish as they experienced success after success. For ever-present supporter Gavin Quinn, who had started following Rovers almost 20 years earlier, the club took him on a journey that he could never have anticipated. 'I was at the League Cup Final with my girlfriend Lorraine who's now my wife,' he recalls. 'The very first thing I said to her when we won the cup was, "That's us in Europe." It was unbelievable. I never thought for one minute that we would win a national cup and go and play in Europe. You just thought you'd be going to places like Stranraer, East Stirling, Berwick, Albion Rovers all the time – no offence to those teams!'

Rovers were in Europe and Gavin Quinn knew that he was definitely going. Now, he just had to wait to find out where.

4

Who?

THE LIST of clubs that would be participating in the UEFA Cup with Raith Rovers read like a veritable Who's Who of European football. Manchester United, Nottingham Forest, Leeds United and Liverpool from England. Lazio, Roma, AC Milan and Inter Milan from Italy. AS Monaco, Lens and Bordeaux from France. Real Betis, Sevilla and Barcelona from Spain. Werder Bremen and Bayern Munich from Germany. PSV Eindhoven from the Netherlands.

Throw in famous names from the smaller European nations such as Sparta Prague, Benfica and Malmö FF, and it was a stunning line-up. Rovers knew that they would not face any of these sides in the preliminary round and were boosted by the news that they would be seeded in the draw meaning that difficult opponents like Red Star Belgrade, Galatasaray, and Brøndby could be side-stepped.

Behind the scenes at Stark's Park, preparations for the tournament started. The club had received an early indication that their home ground may not be suitable for hosting larger European ties. Under UEFA rules, the crowd limit was set at the seated capacity plus half the overall capacity, significantly reducing the standard 9,200-capacity of the stadium. Chairman Alex Penman stated publicly that they would pull out all the stops to make sure games would go ahead in Kirkcaldy but was privately exploring alternative venues.

One player who had more reason than most to anticipate the looming UEFA Cup draw was new signing Tony Rougier. The Trinidad and Tobago international was starting his first professional contract in football after having recently arrived in Britain. Rougier had grown up with a love of football and had watched as fellow countrymen Dwight Yorke, Russell Latapy, and Jerren Nixon all travelled to the UK to establish successful professional careers. He decided to attempt the same and had initially arrived in the north of England at Bradford City, whose manager Lennie Lawrence had been impressed, but problems obtaining a work permit meant that a deal failed to go through, so he decided to try his luck north of the border. His first stop in Scotland had been Kilmarnock, and although a trial match at Rugby Park had gone well, the potential of securing a deal with the Ayrshire side receded when he was told by the club that they were looking for a player who could score three goals a game. 'I remember my agent saying to them, "Is it Andy Cole you are trying to sign?"' smiles Rougier at the memory.

Kilmarnock's unrealistically high expectations proved fortuitous for Raith, who secured his services after Rougier had impressed in a reserve match against East Fife. Former Rovers player Graham Robertson recalls taking to the pitch with the Trinidadian trialist in his first game at Bayview: 'The pitch wasn't really playable. It was really cold, and the sides were all frozen. I remember him sliding all over the place near the touchline and he had this look on his face that was just, "What is this?" He said to us afterwards, "How can you play on a pitch like that?"

'You immediately knew he had a wee something about him though, and not just as a player. He had that physicality, strength and a good bit of pace about him, and he was a lovely man and a really positive character.'

'He [Rougier] came in on a Monday night in the middle of winter,' reflects Jimmy Nicholl. 'I thought he wouldn't fancy it, but right away I knew we were keen. The pace and strength of the boy was great, so we started working towards getting him a work permit.

'When you bring someone in like that, and you see him play, even in the wee five-a-sides and practice sessions. It was, "Wow." The strength of Tony Rougier, the pace of him and the confidence of him. You couldn't knock him down.'

Rougier had played so well in the trial game that Rovers' opponents had also shown an interest in the young forward. 'It was a freezing cold night at their stadium,' he remembers. 'We played the game, and I was pushing myself to make the most of the opportunity. At half-time in the game, a guy from the other team called me into a room. He said to me, "Here is a contract right now. We will sign you right now. I promise you that your future will be good with East Fife, and I will look after you." It was so weird.' Rougier would later discover that the potential suitor had been former Tottenham and Barcelona player Steve Archibald, but his loyalty was to the club who had invited him to trial, so he rejected the Methil side's advances and signed for Raith.

When asked now whether he had known much about Raith Rovers before arriving, Rougier is honest. 'I had absolutely not a clue,' he laughs. His lack of knowledge didn't deter him from signing on to start his professional career in

Kirkcaldy. Thirty years on, he remains effusive about the manager who handed him his first opportunity. 'Jimmy Nicholl is a class act,' he says. 'He was such a joy to play for and the way he did things, a lot of that I still implement today in my day-to-day work with young kids. Making players comfortable so that they can express themselves in the best way they can.

'Right away, the friendliness of Raith Rovers hit you. The whole culture and attitude towards players was fantastic and they were receptive to a foreigner coming in. I got a warm welcome from Raith that I didn't get anywhere else. Jimmy Nicholl and Martin Harvey made me feel so welcome and I loved that.'

If there is warmth towards his management team and his team-mates, it is reciprocated by those who welcomed him into the Stark's Park dressing room. 'He was a lovely lad,' says Julian Broddle. 'He wasn't crazy talkative at first, but once he got talking, he was a really lovely boy. Then you saw him play, and it was, "Oh my god." When Tony was on my side of the pitch it was fantastic. I knew I could just play it to him, and it was, "On you go mate." You could hardly stop him. It was just pure power and ability.'

'Tony was probably the biggest handful in Scottish football on his day,' says Davie Kirkwood. 'He could run rings round you. He was powerful, quick, everything you wanted in a player. And off the pitch, you couldn't meet a nicer lad, although when it came to snow, he was the worst ever. I remember he stayed in digs just up the street from the club and he would get a taxi from his digs to the front door because he didn't want to walk through the snow!'

The warmth of the welcome and the friendliness Rougier encountered among his team-mates and around the club still brings a smile to his face, but that doesn't mean that his first few months in Fife were not challenging. He was far from home, in a climate that was very different to Trinidad and attempting to become a professional footballer for the first time. Then there were the Scottish accents. 'Thank God football is universal,' he laughs. 'I couldn't understand a word at first!'

If keeping up with the rapid conversation and banter in the dressing room was problematic at first, there was no mistaking the quality in the squad. 'There were some great young players in that team,' continues Rougier. 'Raith Rovers couldn't afford to have the big names in their side, but they were able to take these young players and have them punching above their weight because they believed in what they were doing, and they believed in Jimmy Nicholl.'

When the supporters first saw Rougier play, there was excitement. He had the ability to drive at defenders, creating panic and causing havoc in equal measure. Even when his first touch deserted him, he was able to recover and protect the ball from opposition players with consummate ease. Fans knew that he would be an asset for the upcoming European campaign. There was anticipation among the players as they waited to see who they would face in the UEFA Cup preliminary round draw. 'Everything was just new to us,' says Jason Dair. 'The experience of being in the draw, what tie would we get, how are we going to get to the away ties. It was all new and exciting.'

'I was relatively young and so were a lot of the other boys,' recalls Colin Cameron. 'We knew we were going into a different environment and for the fans we knew it was an opportunity to go to different countries and experience everything that goes along with that. It was just an experience we all wanted to enjoy.'

'Being in Europe was a dream come true for me,' adds Danny Lennon. 'I had watched many European nights on TV as a kid. I remember even my first Celtic game had been a European game against Juventus. European nights were fantastic. We knew it would be a completely different experience of football, but it was like stepping into the spotlight and you wanted to prove that Raith Rovers could compete with the best.'

For the majority of the squad, European football would be a new experience, but even for those who had been there before, there remained an element of the unfamiliar. 'The whole thing about Europe is it is the unknown,' says Davie Kirkwood, who had prior experience of playing in Europe with Rangers and Airdrie. 'When you are playing in Scotland, it is such a small place that you come up against people in the league or cups or pre-season games and you get to know everybody that is in the system. When you go into Europe it is just the unknown. You have no idea of the players you are playing against or their quality.'

Kirkwood had started his own football career just nine miles away from Stark's Park. His early ability had attracted the attention of bigger clubs, but as a 16-year-old schoolboy he opted for a four-year contract with his local club East Fife, quickly forcing his way into the Methil side's first team. 'My 16th birthday was at the start of the season in August,' he recalls. 'I was lucky enough to make my debut for East Fife on my birthday. We had a decent team and some real good players then, Stevie Kirk, Gordon Durie and Gordon Marshall. They helped me along as you had to grow up very quick.'

His talent was unmistakable and at the age of 19, he was signed by Rangers. 'On the Friday I was at college and on the Saturday, I was at Ibrox,' says Kirkwood, as he remembers his move to join the Graeme Souness revolution in Glasgow. 'It was a big change. You went into training and there was Davie Cooper, Ally McCoist, and Ian Durrant. You had to hold your own and you had to fight for everything that you had.'

After a frustrating two-year period at the Ibrox club, where his appearances were limited, he returned to East Fife on loan, before signing for Hearts. However, it was at his next club Airdrie that he truly found his feet in a side that battled their way into the Premier League, a Scottish Cup Final and a place in the Cup Winners' Cup. 'I think we took it in turns to hit people,' laughs Kirkwood, at the memory of featuring in an Airdrie team infamous for their robustness. 'But we had a great side, and we had some great times.'

One of the highlights of his time at Airdrie had been the two-legged Cup Winners' Cup tie against Sparta Prague, and his eventual move to Raith, as a notional replacement for Peter Hetherston who had left for Aberdeen, rewarded him with a return to European competition.

If the players were excited at the prospect of playing in Europe, fans were at fever pitch. There was still a surrealness to the fact that Rovers were even participating in a European tournament and the furthest most had previously travelled to support their team was Stranraer or Dingwall. Few knew what to expect from their first UEFA Cup draw. 'I remember after we qualified for Europe, people started singing about whether they did a chicken supper in Milan,' laughs supporter Steven Wallace. 'But it was kind of tongue in cheek. We knew we were in Europe, but you looked at a lot of teams in that initial draw and there were a lot of teams you hadn't heard of. We had no idea what was going to happen.'

Fans knew that whatever way things worked out, adventure awaited. Prior to the draw, the news came through from UEFA that it would be made in geographical sections. This narrowed the potential opponents for Rovers to Crusaders from Northern Ireland, Dundalk from the Republic of Ireland, Afan Lido from Wales and Gøtu Ítróttarfelag from the Faroe Islands. With the potential of three relatively straightforward and easily accessible trips within the British Isles, to teams that supporters had heard of, Rovers naturally drew the wildcard of Gøtu Ítróttarfelag. 'Of course, we get drawn to a team that you have never heard of before,' laughs Jason Dair. 'We had to have a look up and see where the Faroe Islands were. We didn't know anything about the place, never mind the team and players.'

'It wasn't a name the supporters recognised,' adds Stevie Crawford. 'And it certainly wasn't recognised by us. I think Jason was the only one in our squad who could even pronounce it!'

'We got this team, and it was like, "Who?"' reflects Stephen McAnespie. 'Although, to be fair, Gøtu were probably also thinking, "Who the hell are Raith Rovers?"'

5

Small but Strong

JOHN PETERSEN has many claims to fame. He has represented the Faroe Islands at football and handball, won the Faroese football championship as a player and manager, been the assistant manager of the men's national side and is currently manager of the women's national side. However, it is perhaps his role as the man who got Berti Vogts sacked that may resonate most with Scottish football fans. The date was 7 September 2002, and the location Svangaskarð, Tofta Leikvøllur, or the Toftir Stadium as it is more commonly known. Scotland, under German manager Vogts, were starting their campaign to qualify for the 2004 European Championship in Portugal in an optimistic mood; after just 12 minutes they trailed 2-0 thanks to two goals from Petersen.

Scotland's chaotic defending handed Petersen the chance of a hat-trick, but in a one-on-one with goalkeeper Rab Douglas, the ball bobbled on the turf just as he was about to shoot, and his effort flew just over the bar. Scotland would eventually recover and the game finished 2-2. 'We should have won,' says Petersen, 'but it was a good result and Berti Vogts got sacked. People still talk about that draw with

Scotland, but most Faroese people today remember that I did not score to put us 3-0 ahead more than my two goals! If I had scored that chance I probably would have been sold to Rangers!'

The Faroe Islands is an autonomous territory of Denmark, sitting between Iceland, Norway, and Scotland in the Atlantic Ocean. Made up of 18 major islands and with a population of just under 50,000, roughly equivalent to the size of Kirkcaldy, it is a rugged and rocky place with most of its coastline consisting of cliffs. The scenery has the feel of the Scottish Highlands if they had been picked up and half submerged in the Atlantic Ocean.

The Faroe Islands had been relatively late entrants to international football, admitted as a FIFA member in 1988 and to UEFA two years later. Until then, they had been restricted to playing friendly matches or in minor competitions like the Greenland Cup or the Island Games. In their competitive debut, they announced themselves in dramatic fashion. Playing a home tie in Sweden, as there were no grass pitches available in the Faroe Islands at the time, they defeated Austria 1-0 in a match that became known as 'The miracle of Landskrona', named after the Swedish town it was played in. It was a stunning result that shocked football. 'The whole world knew about our start when we beat Austria 1-0,' says Petersen. 'That shouldn't be possible, but we won. Everybody went crazy. I was in high school at that time and playing in the second division. We all just left school when the national team came back. Everyone went to welcome them, and all the cars were out driving with flags. It was very, very, very big.'

Back in the early 1990s, international football worked to provide both a sense of identity for the Faroe Islands and an opportunity to raise its profile. 'At that time, football was really our window out to the world,' adds Petersen.

The Austria win alerted the world to the arrival of the Faroese national side, but it was a result that was hard to repeat for a group of islands with a small population and a limited number of footballers. The side settled into a familiar pattern of defeat in international matches but, over time, results began to improve. 'We tended not to win against the bigger nations,' says Petersen. 'But we started to have some pretty good results. We won against Malta, Luxembourg, Liechtenstein, San Marino, and got draws against Slovenia, Northern Ireland, and, of course, Scotland.'

If international football provided a platform in those early years, European club competition afforded the same. In 1995, 23-year-old Petersen was the 6ft 1in star striker of reigning Faroese champions Gøtu Ítróttarfelag, having scored 40 goals in 48 appearances for the side, becoming the top scorer in the entire Faroese league.

The team, whose club motto translated as 'Small but Strong', reflected the local area, with the municipality made up of four villages, home to just under 1,000 people. They played their home games at Sarpugerði Stadium, a modest ground with a capacity of 3,000, mostly standing and an artificial surface. Due to the success of the Gøtu team at the time, it was affectionately known by locals as the 'Talent Factory'. Like his team-mates, Petersen was an amateur, with the side drawing its squad largely from the local area. 'Gøtu is not a town,' he explains. 'It is a small village, but football in Gøtu is what unites people. All the kids play football, and everybody is watching football. Football means a lot to that area and still does. At that time, almost all of the players were from the village. Me and the goalkeeper with the bobble hat [Jens Martin Knudsen] came from a village nearby, but all the others were from Gøtu.'

If the village of Gøtu was small, even the Faroe Islands was a place most Rovers players and fans struggled to find on a map. 'We didn't know anything about the place or the football team,' says supporter Kenny Smith. 'Now, you can go on FIFA or the internet and find out about every football team in the world. We just didn't have that type of information back then. It was very much the unknown. It was north, someone told me that there was a lot of daylight and that was about it.'

Fellow supporter Steve Wallace felt equally in the dark. 'In those days, no one really knew where the Faroe Islands were,' he says. 'I remember I went to the wee bookshop on Tolbooth Street in Kirkcaldy and looked at a book to find out where they actually were and to try and find out something about them. When I found the atlas in the bookshop and saw where they were, my immediate reaction was, "How the fuck do you get there?"'

If there was initial confusion in Kirkcaldy when Rovers were paired with Gøtu, it was reciprocated in the Faroe Islands. Rovers were as much an unknown quantity to the Gøtu players as they had been to the Stark's Park squad. 'I have to admit,' says John Petersen, 'I didn't know anything about Raith Rovers. All those interested in Scottish football knew about Rangers and Celtic, but Raith Rovers was a new team for us.'

The lack of knowledge of a small Scottish team from Fife was replicated among his team-mates and a Gøtu official admitted in the run-up to the first leg that most of their initial information had been gleaned from looking at league tables and reading newspaper reports. Gøtu head coach Johan Nielsen underlined the point when he arrived in Scotland to assess his opponents. 'The first chance I had to look at Raith Rovers was when I went to Kirkcaldy High Street and bought a copy of their cup-winning video,' he said.

Although Gøtu had been dominating Faroese football, there was limited expectation going into the UEFA Cup preliminary round. The track record of Faroese teams in the competition at the time was not impressive and UEFA regulations on artificial surfaces meant that the home leg would have to be played away from Gøtu's own ground, instead relocated to Toftir Stadium, the only grass pitch available in the Faroes. 'It was difficult,' reflects Petersen, 'because we never felt that we were playing at home and no Faroese team had had any kind of result in European competition at that stage. Now there are a lot of semi-professionals playing in Faroese football, but at that time, we were all amateurs and the European adventure for the Faroese teams was pretty new.'

Rovers may not have been a familiar name for the GÍ management and players, but there was a realistic recognition that the standard of football in Scotland was far greater than in the Faroes. Few, if any, expected to win the tie.

'Raith Rovers may have not been in the best league when they won the cup,' says Petersen, 'but we still thought they were a much better team than we were.'

Despite the challenge of progressing further in the competition, the Gøtu team were eager to enjoy their European experience. Johan Nielsen had worked wonders with limited resources and could boast several Faroe Islands internationals in his squad. Magni Jarnskor had scored four goals in 16 games for the national side and a trio from the same family, Alvi Justinussen, Simun. P. Justinussen, and Runi Justinussen were also established international players. Gøtu goalkeeper Jens Martin Knudsen was also a regular for the national side and, aged 27, their most-capped player at the time. Knudsen was the best-known member of the Gøtu Ítróttarfelag squad, having risen to fame during the Faroes' famous 1-0 victory over Austria. The distinctive white bobble hat he wore during games attracted the attention of the press and caught the imagination of supporters around Europe.

By the time he was preparing to face Raith in 1995, he had ditched this trademark headwear in an effort to be taken more seriously, with reports at the time that his international manager, Danish coach Allan Simonsen, had heavily encouraged him to do so. 'I wore that hat for protection after being kicked on the head when younger,' explained Knudsen in the build-up to the Raith tie. 'I liked to play with it on. However, a lot of people seem to think it looks silly and that is not how I want potential buyers to see me.'

The goalkeeper, having already spent time in the Icelandic league, was not shy of expressing his desire to play outside of the Faroe Islands again. His ambition was to earn a professional contract in an overseas league, and participation in the UEFA Cup provided the opportunity to capitalise on his reputation and further raise his profile. 'I would not rule anywhere out, but Scotland would certainly be ideal,' he told reporters prior to the first leg in Kirkcaldy. 'At this stage of my career, I really must get away from the Faroes and be playing on Astroturf in particular. Games like this are a great showcase and I will be doing everything I can to promote myself as well as help Gøtu.'

It would be another four years before he realised his ambition to play in Scotland, turning out four times for Ayr

United as a loan player in the later stages of his career, but for the moment his focus was on the challenge ahead of him in the preliminary round of the UEFA Cup. 'Raith have to get the ball past me to score,' said Knudsen. 'So, I should not be short of things to do.'

6

Preparation

WITH ROVERS' preliminary round opponents decided, Jimmy Nicholl began the task of preparing for the club's first ever European tie. His initial reaction to the draw had been one of disappointment that they hadn't landed a more straightforward trip closer to home. 'Obviously, we would have preferred an Irish team,' he said to the assembled press after the draw, 'but you can't always get what you want.'

It was a sentiment echoed by assistant manager Martin Harvey. 'I'm not going to moan about it,' he said. 'Any draw is a good draw in Europe. If I had been standing here at this time last season and someone had told me that one year on Raith Rovers were getting ready for a trip to the Faroe Isles to play in the UEFA Cup, I would have laughed my head off.'

The management team knew that the tie was the most awkward geographically and the least financially beneficial to the club, but it also offered an excellent opportunity to progress. Gøtu's local rivals, Havnar Bóltfelag, had lost 7-1 on aggregate to Alex McLeish's Motherwell the previous season, providing an indication of the quality of Faroese opposition. Nicholl knew that it was important he did not underestimate

Gøtu Ítróttarfelag and recognised the need to assess them in person. He travelled, along with the chairman Alex Penman, to the Faroe Islands to gain a more detailed understanding of the challenge ahead. 'Jimmy Nicholl and myself went over to watch them play in a league match,' recalls Penman. 'We flew to Copenhagen and on to the Faroes, as there weren't any direct flights available. It was worthwhile doing, just to have a look at the opposition and to see the travelling arrangements and accommodation we would need.'

Nicholl returned to Scotland after witnessing Gøtu defeat Tórshavn side HB36 2-0 to move up to fourth in their ten-team league. He was in an upbeat mood at his first press conference afterwards. 'They're halfway through their season,' he told the assembled journalists. 'They have a terrific attitude towards the game, and they were clearly determined to win at the weekend. They work hard and train four times a week. Mind you, maybe that's because there is not a lot else to do over in the Faroe Islands. But while the social life may not be great, their attitude to football is first class.'

Nicholl had witnessed the quality of Gøtu and was privately confident that his team could progress. The Faroese side had several useful players who could be capable of hurting Raith, but he also knew they were a part-time team, and that there would be an opportunity to benefit from superior fitness, particularly towards the latter stages of the match. Among the squad, Nicholl's report on their opponents fuelled optimism that they could progress to the next round. 'We'll win it,' said Shaun Dennis to local newspaper the *Fife Free Press*, adding bullishly, 'We've all seen the standard of their football, and I don't see them posing us any problems at all.'

'We felt that with the players we had then over the two legs we would have a really good chance to qualify and get into the next round,' reflects Colin Cameron. 'No disrespect to Gøtu, but when you had a look at their squad there was nobody that jumped out in terms of their names.'

'I think overall, everybody had in their mind that we should be able to get through the tie,' agrees goalkeeper Scott Thomson. 'At that stage in the competition, we fancied ourselves to keep things rolling and get to the next round.'

The first leg at home was scheduled for 8 August, which was 11 days before the Scottish season officially started. A pre-season trip to Ireland had yielded wins over Derry City, Distillery and Moyola Park, but the final match of the tour against Northern Irish side Glentoran ended in a 3-1 defeat at The Oval in East Belfast. It was a salutary reminder that part-time opponents had the potential to be dangerous. Preparation was completed by an encouraging 2-0 win over English club Oldham Athletic at Stark's Park seven days before their European campaign would start.

As Nicholl prepared his squad for the challenge of the first fixture, supporters faced a rather different task in trying to find a route to the Faroe Islands for the away leg later that month. The club had approached several specialist agencies to charter a plane and could only secure a 46-seater, providing just enough room for the team, officials and press. Fans would have to find their own route north. 'If you went abroad at that stage, it was always just a package holiday,' explains supporter Steve Wallace. 'You couldn't go on the internet and find flights back then; you'd have to go to a travel agent, and they would sort you out. We were basically just young fools who didn't know what to do. Thankfully, there were other people looking into how to get us up to the Faroes.'

Steve, a lifelong fan who also sits on the board of the Raith Supporters Trust, has a room in his house dedicated to his two great passions: music and Raith Rovers. Even through the club's biggest disappointments and countless periods of chronic underperformance, his enthusiasm remains intact. An unusual trait for someone who started life on the opposite side of Fife. 'We lived in Dunfermline,' he explains. 'But my dad was a big Rovers supporter and went to see the team in the 50s. He used to go a lot, but he drifted away a little when he had kids. I think he was part of that generation who experienced the 1980/81 season and when it didn't come off, there was a bit of a feeling that it was never going to happen.'

Despite living in the town of their local rivals, support of the Kirkcaldy club was passed from father to son, and when his family moved back east, the grip of the local team really began to take hold for the young fan. 'We moved to Kirkcaldy in 1984 when I was 11 years old,' explains Steve. 'That was when I thought, "Right, I want to go and see football," and started going to the Rovers on a regular basis. That period was probably as low as we got, being in the bottom three places in the old Second Division, but it was the days of 30p to get in and you'd just go with your mates and watch the team. It was just what we did as part of our routine.'

By the time the European adventure arrived, Wallace had left school and started working. This meant he'd miss the occasional match, but he did his absolute best to manage shifts to get to games. There was never any question about him missing Rovers' first away trip in Europe. 'I just said,

"We are doing this,'" recounts Steve. 'So, [fellow supporter] Niall Russell and I started paying into the Novar Bar's European Club. There was talk of a flight but that was too expensive. It was only £160 for a seat on the ferry, or you could splash out for a cabin for £200, and you had to stay for a week in the Faroes. We signed up for the ferry and went for the cheaper seat option as we didn't have that much money at the time.'

Steve prepared himself for the 25-hour ferry journey and a trip into the unknown. 'The funny thing was that the Faroe Islands sounds exotic,' he recalls. 'I remember going to the Turret to buy myself a new pair of trainers for the trip and telling the woman who sold me them that they were for my holidays. She asked where I was going and when I told her the Faroe Islands, she said, "Oh, it will be really hot there." I was thinking, "Err, I don't think so."'

Also opting for the ferry was Kenny Smith. From the moment Rovers had qualified for Europe, like Steve Wallace, he was certain that he was going to follow the team wherever the journey took them. 'I was 100 per cent going,' Kenny says emphatically. 'I had just bought a house in 1995 and I got the keys the day we played Dunfermline at the end of the season. I would have re-mortgaged that house if I had to. That was how determined I was to follow the team in Europe.'

Kenny, from Kinghorn, laughs as he reflects on his long-standing compulsion to follow Raith. 'I don't know what makes you so addicted to a football club,' he says. 'For me it was a constant in my life from when I was young. Going to Raith Rovers was something I always did. It just hooked me, and I still need my fix every weekend.

'After the Ross County play-off game, the other season, I was reading the programme and it said something like there had been 970-odd league games since we had last been in the Premier League, and I started thinking, "How many of those games have I been at?" I worked out it was probably around 960.'

Kenny admits that he is not sure whether that is an impressive or worrying statistic. Even today, missing a game is only done in the most extreme situations and if completely unavoidable. 'My brother got married in Greece and made me miss a Dunfermline game,' he says. 'The 2-0 with Mark Stewart and Bobby Barr. It was the first derby I'd missed since 1986. What a selfish bastard! That was the opening line of my best man's speech. I said, "I am missing Raith Rovers versus Dunfermline to be at this shite today. I forgive, but I never forget." Everybody was falling about laughing, but I was having a genuine rant about missing the game!'

Like so many others, Kenny's love of his local football club was fostered in an era when it was an unfashionable pastime. 'Today, it is really quite trendy to support Rovers,' he says. 'But it was the exact opposite when I was younger. You were seen as the village idiot if you went to watch Raith Rovers. I used to go to just home games on my own for a couple of seasons, but it all changed when I went to Balwearie High School. I found some other like-minded individuals and we joined the supporters' club. Then it became home and away, and it has never ended.'

Like many young fans in that era, Kenny sold the club's Shoot lottery tickets, a football-themed forerunner of scratchcards, that allowed him free admission on to the supporters' bus to away games, although the actual selling of the tickets was left to his mother on the shop floor of her workplace, Marconi. Those early away trips left an indelible mark and fuelled his passion for the club, even if the journeys weren't always smooth. 'I have always lived in Kinghorn,' explains Kenny. 'I remember once we came back from Arbroath, the supporters' bus just dumped me in Kirkcaldy. It was a midweek game, and I was about 12. I told them that I had no money to get home and it was like, "Tough," so I had to walk home to Kinghorn late at night. My parents went ballistic. I'm surprised they let me go back.'

Having suffered the painful Bobby Wilson era, when the club was relegated on the last day of their centenary season, Frank Connor was a breath of fresh air for Kenny. He had invaded the pitch down at Stranraer along with the rest of the away support when Rovers had clinched promotion on the last day of the season in 1987, and the unlikeliness of that day and how events unfolded means that he still lists it as his favourite ever Raith match, surpassing even the League Cup win in 1994. He could not have anticipated the further transformation under Jimmy Nicholl and the success that would follow. 'I was so into Jimmy Nicholl that I actually wrote him a letter,' Kenny recounts. 'When he arrived he said that his ambition was to see Rovers in the Premier League. That was one of my ambitions as well, so when he was getting touted for Norwich, I wrote him a letter, a full letter, telling him that and asking him to stay. Give him his dues, he wrote me a letter back telling me he was going to stay at the Rovers.'

Nicholl stayed, Rovers soared to even greater heights and a ferry to the Faroe Islands awaited. Steve Wallace and Kenny Smith were not the only fans making plans: another 30 or so fans signed up for the prospect of spending a week on the North Atlantic islands. They would be joined by a similar number taking the flight option organised by Dennis O'Connell, who was a well-known supporter who owned pubs in Glenrothes and Kirkcaldy. He was a regular backer of the club, sponsoring the supporters' club team and organising buses to the League Cup Final in November 1994. It was on the way back from that final he had made the promise of getting fans to any European ties. 'I played for the supporters' club team so knew Dennis pretty well,' says Gavin Quinn. 'He had taken us to the cup final and made the mistake of saying, "I'll start organising trips to Europe then," so it was him who organised the plane to get us up to the Faroes.'

The intrepid fans who had decided to travel were set for an unforgettable adventure, but it was still a fortnight away as there was the small matter of the first leg to negotiate.

7

A Summer Evening

'I DON'T remember so much from the first game,' says former Gøtu Ítróttarfelag striker John Petersen, 'except that we lost 4-0.'

Raith went into their European debut in confident mood and comfortably beat their Faroese opponents on a sun-drenched Kirkcaldy evening. It may have been a historic first match in continental competition, but there was a slightly surreal feel about the whole occasion. UEFA had restricted the attendance to half the capacity of Stark's Park, with just over 5,000 allowed in. The lack of any notable away support, with only around 30 Gøtu fans having travelled, meant that the home supporters filled all four sides of the ground. And, although a midweek evening match, the time of year meant that it was played out in bright sunshine. 'When I was with Rangers and Manchester United it was always dark nights and games under the floodlights in Europe,' reflects Jimmy Nicholl. 'There was a real magic about those ties. In a way there was something unreal about playing a European fixture on a nice, sunny, summer evening.'

Gøtu had reportedly sent spies to watch Rovers in training before the match, but any inside information gleaned from that exercise couldn't prevent a damaging defeat. Nicholl's strategy had been to let his side play their own brand of attacking football and see where it took them. 'There had been examples over the years at Raith Rovers where I was a bit cautious,' he says. 'I would think in some games, "These boys don't deserve to get gubbed," so I maybe over-protected them. I didn't know that much about Gøtu, but I had confidence in our boys. We never had any in-depth meetings about the opposition. I just said, "Do you know your job? Yes. Then go do your job," and away they went.'

'We never really spoke much about them [Gøtu] at all,' reinforces defender Stephen McAnespie. 'We just went out to play our game and that was it. We set up before the game, like we did for every game and it was, "Let's go do this." We knew that as long as we were the attacking force that we were, we would take care of business.'

It was evident from the opening exchanges that Rovers were the stronger team and would dominate the match. 'You often get a sense at the start of a game how things are going to go,' says defender Julian Broddle. 'It was clear from the start that the evening was going to be a good game for us. It didn't take long before we were attacking on a regular basis, and I couldn't see them keeping up with the speed and strength of our team.'

Rovers opened the scoring after 21 minutes through Jason Dair, the young winger bundling the ball into the net after an impressive run and cross from Tony Rougier. 'Being the first goalscorer for Raith Rovers in Europe wasn't really something that I was thinking about at the time,' admits Dair. 'But after a few years I started to think about how big a thing it was. It will always be there. It is not as if somebody is going to take it away from me in the future.

It was a special moment and I still have that picture of me and wee Mickey [Colin Cameron] celebrating. I am very proud of it now.'

'It wasn't the sort of goal that Jason was renowned for,' says former team-mate and friend Stevie Crawford. 'He was usually cutting in and curling one from distance, but I was delighted for him and there is still the picture of him sliding about on his backside celebrating up in Stark's Park.'

The remainder of the first half played out with Rovers dominating, but unable to add to the scoreline. Their opponents may have been amateurs, but at 1-0 they were not being overawed. They were competing well and defending valiantly to keep the scoreline tight. 'For as much as Gøtu were unheard of,' adds Crawford, 'it was a hard-fought game. Maybe the final score makes it seem like an easier game than it was, but it certainly wasn't totally comfortable in that first half.'

'We should have been more than one goal ahead at half-time,' reflects Nicholl. 'It was like a pinball machine out there with the number of chances we had. At one stage, I was worried we wouldn't score again, but we were doing enough damage around the box to think a ricochet or deflection would eventually go in. It took a little time, but I knew if we persevered, the goals would come.'

The second goal arrived just one minute after the restart when Broddle's back-post cross was powered into the net by Rougier. The Trinidadian would later comment that his team-mates nicknamed him Michael Jordan because of how high he'd leapt to get above the ball. A further two goals in three minutes killed the match and handed Rovers a significant advantage to take into the second leg, McAnespie curling a beautiful free kick in, and Colin Cameron finished the scoring with a tap-in. 'I think it was important that we had the first game at home,' says Cameron. 'It gave us the chance to try and get a really positive result and we could get a good sense of how they were and what we needed to do. I think it was only after the game, when we looked back at the game and what had happened in it, that we realised how much control we had. That gave us confidence to take into the second leg.'

Having scored in European competition in such style remains an achievement that Stephen McAnespie takes pride in. 'Goals like that certainly don't happen every day,' he reflects. 'We'd mess about in training with free kicks, and I always wanted to have a go during games, but when it comes off like that it is a wee bit special. Scoring a goal in Europe was amazing.'

Rovers had stepped on to the European stage and performed well. The evening had gone as well as they could have expected. 'The lads played brilliantly in the first leg,' says Julian Broddle. 'It was the perfect start to Raith in Europe. I had a look last night through the little trophy cabinet I have at home and discovered I got [named] man of the match. I had forgotten that, but there is a plaque in there with the date on it and man of the match. I am not sure if there was more than one sponsor, but I'm still claiming it!'

The press reports after the game were glowing. 'Rovers storm to Euro Glory' was the headline emblazoned in the *Fife Free Press*, with chief reporter John Greechan stating in his match report, 'Rovers blasted Faroese fall guys Gøtu Ítróttarfelag to pieces in a stunning display of pace and power at Stark's Park on Tuesday night.' The consensus was that Rovers had taken a major step towards the next round and the tabloid headlines included the usual round of puns – 'It's Rover and out' and 'Almost Dair' being the most memorable.

For the fans, it had been a surreal but memorable night. It may not have delivered a famous name or the big-game atmosphere that they had anticipated when Raith first qualified for Europe, but the result meant that, barring a catastrophic collapse in the away leg, there would be at least one more European tie to experience. 'After that game I had the realisation that we would probably go through,' says Steve Wallace. 'I had expected a tougher game, but it was all fairly straightforward. We got the goals at good times and never really looked in any sort of trouble. It felt like, "This European lark is a dawdle." I didn't think that even the Rovers could lose a four-goal lead!'

Steve's confidence was shared by most of the players, even if publicly the message was that there would be no complacency ahead of the second leg. There was satisfaction in the way that they had performed and dominated their opponents, particularly in the latter stages. They knew they had another 90 minutes to play in unfamiliar surroundings, but the big advantage was a welcome safety net. 'I think after that game there was confidence,' says Stevie Crawford. 'I was pleased that we were going over there with a four-goal lead. Not that we were going to go there and hump them, but it was more a belief that we should have enough to get through. You sort of knew that we had enough in the tank that they weren't going to come back from 4-0 down.'

Speaking to the press after the match, Jimmy Nicholl expressed satisfaction with his team.

'I've got to be happy with the result,' he said. 'We were never in danger of losing, but their keeper pulled off some good saves. For the first time in Europe, scoring four and keeping a clean sheet really is a great achievement. To even suggest something might go wrong when we go to the Faroes in a fortnight is too crazy to consider. We have given ourselves a great chance of reaching the first round, but I'm not looking too far forward into the future.'

Nicholl went on to address press speculation around the young players in his squad. Interest had grown in the exceptional crop of talented youngsters that Rovers had in their side and there was talk of clubs being interested in Stevie Crawford, Jason Dair, Colin Cameron, and Stephen McAnespie. Rivals were rumoured to be lining up bids in order to prise the young stars away from Kirkcaldy. It was a theme the manager tackled head-on in his comments after the Gøtu match. 'There has been a lot of speculation about these lads,' said Nicholl. 'If they get an early move, it means they are doing it for us on the park, but we don't want to lose anybody while we're still in Europe.'

Nicholl was aware his young stars were attracting attention so proceeded to warn them about the importance of maintaining their high levels of performance, while simultaneously dangling the carrot of what may lie ahead if they remained at Raith. 'These boys have to be doing it here before they can think about doing it anywhere else,' he said. 'Four good games and they could be away by the end of August. Four bad games and nobody wants to know you. Playing against amateurs in front of 5,000 fans at Stark's Park obviously isn't Milan in the San Siro, but it is what the game could lead to that matters. It is not just the chance to play against one of the big clubs in the next round, but for these younger players maybe join one of them sometime.'

Across in the Faroese camp, Jens Martin Knudsen also had his mind on a potential transfer. 'I want to move away,' said the goalkeeper after the first leg. 'But it's very hard when you play with a defence like I do every day. It's almost impossible not to give away three or four goals under that pressure. I was a busy man, and I didn't think before the game that I would be that busy. We didn't even manage a shot on goal and Raith Rovers were deserved winners. They are definitely in the next round, but I think it will be a very different game back in the Faroes.'

If the evening had been a success on the park, it was also deemed a success off it. The support had been in good spirits throughout and at one point serenaded their visitors with a rendition of 'You only sing when you're fishing'. After the match, Rovers' general manager Billy McPhee praised the reaction of the fans, 'We said before that the way the supporters conducted themselves would reflect on us and this is exactly the response we were hoping for. It was a great night, and the fans really played their part. UEFA were happy with our entire setup, and they loved our fans. They couldn't believe the way they applauded the Faroese side at the end of the game. We've been given good marks as a result and that's a real bonus for ourselves and Scottish football. The club are over the moon about it all.'

'The fans were great that night,' recalls goalkeeper Scott Thomson. 'It was a great crowd for our first European start, with people hanging out of the windows over on Pratt Street. I think we had that wee bit of an edge because of that. It was a great experience and fantastic night.'

If there was a reminder needed of how well the evening had gone for Rovers, it came in the news from Scotland's other representative in the UEFA Cup. Motherwell had been defeated 3-1 at home by Finnish side MyPa 47 in their first leg and were roundly booed off the park by their own support.

8

In-Between Days

THERE ARE few players in the history of Raith Rovers who can claim to have scored the winner in a cup final against Dunfermline, but Graham Robertson is one. It may have been 30 years ago, but if there is any danger of the former striker forgetting that moment, then the picture on his wall of his younger self turning away to celebrate after the goal acts as a perpetual reminder. 'It is definitely one of my fondest memories from playing at Raith,' says Robertson. 'At the time, the Fife Cup Final was more or less a first-team game and there was a good crowd in the stadium. We had a relatively young side out and Dunfermline had their first team out. I was fortunate enough to get clean through and not only slot the ball past Ian Westwater but put it through his legs as well!'

The Fife Cup Final was played seven days after Rovers' 4-0 UEFA Cup win over Gøtu Ítróttarfelag. Their team for the final was a blend of young YTS players like Robertson and first-teamers such as Stephen McAnespie, Davie Kirkwood and Ronnie Coyle trying to recover from injury or add crucial game time before the second leg of their UEFA Cup tie. Defender Coyle, who had been carrying a knock through the pre-season, captained the side but had to go off injured after half an hour. He would later require a minor operation to clear up an issue with his ankle, a setback that would rule him out of a potential trip to the Faroes.

Robertson's goal secured the victory and ensured the Fife Cup would be added to the Scottish League Cup and the First Division trophy in the Stark's Park boardroom. 'I always remember the photoshoot afterwards for the start of the season,' he recalls. 'We were all laughing, because we had all these trophies in front of us. We had the league trophy, the League Cup trophy, the Fife Cup. We also won the Reserve League East that season. It was like you were playing for Rangers or Celtic or something. There was a real buzz about the whole place.'

Robertson was 19 at the time and finding his way in the game. He was part of a talented batch of YTS apprentices at Stark's Park that included Gordon Forrest, Brian Potter, Ian McMillan, Craig McKinley and Mark Buist. Most were Fife-based and had played against each other in local leagues, so there was already a sense of camaraderie among the young group. Robertson's move to Raith Rovers arose from a chance conversation between his brother Dave and Jimmy Nicholl. 'Jimmy came down and took a training session with my older brother's team,' he explains. 'My brother was quite talented with his left foot, but he couldn't even kick a ball with his right foot. Jimmy was speaking to him after the game saying to him, "If only you could kick the ball with both feet, you'd be an amazing player," and Dave replied, "Well, you should see my wee brother play because he can do both." Derek Smith, the Raith youth coach at the time, was listening and told Jimmy that it was true as I was at Dundee United, and he had seen me play a few times. Jimmy Nic just said, "Get him down," and I went down to Stark's Park on a Tuesday night.'

The young frontman was immediately blown away by the difference in atmosphere between Rovers and Dundee United. At United, the young striker felt like one of hundreds of young prospects and that it was simply a numbers game. In Kirkcaldy it felt much more personal, with Nicholl co-ordinating the training session and calling everyone by their name. Robertson was aware that several younger players had already broken into the first team at 17 or 18 years old, providing the reassurance that a pathway to success was possible. Living in Glenrothes, it felt like an easy decision. 'They were my local team,' he says. 'They had just been promoted. It just felt like a no-brainer to go with Raith.'

Robertson signed in 1993 just as the team made their debut in the Premier League. As the club did not have a huge squad, the young apprentices trained with the first team. 'Dave Narey was at the club in my first few years, and people like Ian Redford and Gordon Dalziel,' recounts Robertson. 'There was a whole year where Dave Narey would be my partner when we were doing the warm-up in training. He would just shout, "Robbo, you come with me." I also played up front with Daz [Dalziel] quite a few times in reserve games and you got to learn from someone who had played the game for years. What an amazing experience. I still look back on that now and have to pinch myself.'

Being at a club in the top tier also provided the opportunity to play in the Premier Reserve League. The fixtures were on a Saturday and the reverse of the first-team match; if Rovers were playing Hearts at Stark's Park, the reserve sides would meet at the same time at Tynecastle. This handed Robertson and other young players at the club the chance to play at the best grounds and against some of the best players in the country making their way back from injury.

Apprentices would also be offered the opportunity to attend games with the first-team squad. They would travel, help carry in the kit and be allowed to sit on the bench with the rest of the players, acting as emergency cover if someone took ill or got injured in the warm-up. 'The manager was very good,' says Robertson. 'He rotated who got to go so that everybody had that experience. It was usually seen as a reward. If you were training well and doing well in the reserves, then you got to go with the first team and that was a real incentive to keep you interested and keep your progression going.'

Jimmy Nicholl and his assistant Martin Harvey worked hard to include the younger players in the day-to-day activities at Stark's Park, making them an integral part of what was happening at the club. 'We used to have our golf days,' recounts Nicholl. 'I would do the draws and pull the names out of a hat to mix the players up, but I would always make sure that Harv and I had two of the young lads with us to get them used to being in our company. I would say, "Now the last two out will be with me and Harv and we will be first off the tee," but I always had these two names hidden in my hand that were always the young kids. So, it would be a case of, "Gordon Forrest and Graham Robertson, you are with me and Harv." I used to rotate the names to give all the kids a shot.

'I didn't want them walking around with us and not speaking. So, on the first tee, I would say to them, "Right Gordy [Gordon Forrest], see if I miss a putt from three foot, you turn round and say, "Gaffer, you're fucking useless," and if it is a good putt then shout and cheer. It got them comfortable talking and being around us.

'I also used to love taking on the kids at *Countdown*. I would sit in the tearoom, Channel 4 on, waiting for the conundrum. The kids would pop their head in and ask what I was doing. I said, "I'm waiting on the conundrum. No one will beat me at the conundrum. I tell you what, if anybody beats me at the conundrum, I will do your chores the next day and you can get away home early." They were there every day from then on trying to beat me at the conundrum. The old *Countdown* clock would start ticking down and I would just go, "Dominance," and they'd all groan.'

With a mischievous grin, Nicholl adds, 'They never ever once beat me at the conundrum.'

Nicholl's strategy of inclusion made the young players feel like they were part of the club and as important as anyone else in the squad. Everyone was valued, regardless of their position, age, or status. 'The young boys weren't shy because they weren't treated any different to the senior players,' says Shaun Dennis. 'They were treated the same and that gave them confidence.'

'You never felt inferior for being a younger player when you were around him [Nicholl],' agrees Graham Robertson. 'In fact, most of the time you left a conversation with Jimmy Nic, you were walking like you were ten feet tall after it. He was just that motivating and inspiring.'

If there is one slight regret for Robertson, it is that being at Raith during the club's most successful spell in its history meant that breaking into the first team was almost impossible. 'We played 18 games in the Reserve League East that season and I scored 22 goals,' he says. 'There would probably be no other time in Raith's history where you had an 18-year-old banging in 22 goals for the reserves and he wouldn't get a chance of a game for the first team.'

He adds ruefully, 'It was a tough gig. I was banging in goals, but the only challenge was that the first team were winning the league and winning the Coca-Cola [League] Cup and I had great players like Stevie Crawford, Ally Graham, Gordon Dalziel, Mickey Cameron and Jason Dair all ahead of me in the pecking order! So, I can't really complain too much.'

Between the Gøtu Ítróttarfelag legs, Rovers also played a friendly against Manchester City, securing a 2-2 draw with goals from Danny Lennon and substitute Gordon Forrest. Forrest was another young player from the same YTS ranks as Robertson. He was from Dunfermline and had originally signed with the East End Park club, but the attraction of what Jimmy Nicholl was building proved too strong for the young midfielder. 'I went down the Raith Rovers route because of Jimmy Nic and Martin Harvey,' he explains. 'They told me what they were trying to do at Raith Rovers and sold the club to me. To go straight from school into a club like that and experience two to three years of an apprenticeship in football, I don't think I could have asked for a better place to be.'

Forrest is currently coaching in China, but back in 1995 he was a 17-year-old apprentice with Rovers. Like fellow trainee Graham Robertson, he has strong memories of the inclusive environment fostered around the club. 'On a matchday we were always involved,' explains Forrest. 'Whether it was getting the kit out or doing the boots, we were in and around the dressing room. They used to get a few young boys in at half-time to listen to the team talk. You felt the feelgood factor, and you were supporting from the stands, then jumping in on the celebrations afterwards. That was the experience you got as a young kid at Raith Rovers.

'I was Jock McStay's and Gordon Dalziel's boot boy. These guys were superb and the two of them looked after me tremendously. I remember being in the paper and having a picture of me and Daz, because he gave me £10 for every goal he scored because I was shining his boots!'

It is unlikely that Forrest's boot-cleaning skills were contributing to the veteran striker's prolific run of form in front of goal, but for the young apprentice, the publicity and extra income were welcome. Forrest would make his competitive debut later that season against Celtic at Stark's Park in front of 9,000 spectators, a moment he still recalls with pride, even if the game was lost 3-1. 'To get that opportunity was exciting,' he says. 'It was a shock to even be in the squad and I got a bit of a fright, but when Jimmy Nic called me when I was warming up to come off the bench, it was one of those special moments. Celtic had Jorge Cadete, Pierre van Hoijdonk and John Collins and there I was coming on in midfield with Danny Lennon and Colin Cameron!'

Nicholl had no fear in handing youth an opportunity if they approached their football with the right attitude. 'I have always said that it is not just about ability in football,' he says. 'You have to have something in your temperament and make-up. Wee Gordy Forrest had that. He had brilliant ability. There was nothing to him physically at that point, but he wasn't getting brushed off the ball all the time because he was tenacious and determined. If he hadn't been, he wouldn't have been picked.'

Forrest's goal against Manchester City in the friendly before the second leg against Gøtu was also a special moment for the young midfielder. 'I scored against Man City, and it was brilliant,' he says. 'The first-team boys were brilliant with me after the goal, and it just made you relax. I know now from working with young players in squads how influential older players can be. You need older players to work like that with you and it was a great place to be. When you walked into Stark's Park there was just so much energy and enthusiasm. That is so important in a football club, and it meant that you would run through a brick wall for Jimmy and Harv.'

'Harv' was Jimmy Nicholl's assistant Martin Harvey, a fellow Northern Irishman who had also played for Sunderland and his national side. He had shifted to coaching after injury had forced his premature retirement from playing at the age of 30, and as assistant to Northern Ireland manager Billy Bingham at the 1982 and 1986 World Cups, Nicholl had witnessed first-hand his temperament, attributes, and coaching ability. He had no hesitation in appointing him as his assistant when he joined Raith and together, they made the perfect management team. 'Harv was great for me, and I still miss him,' says Nicholl of his former colleague and friend, who passed away in 2019. 'There was probably a lot went on in those days that I didn't know about that Harv sorted out for me. It is a bit like me and Michael [O'Neill] now at Northern Ireland. You just have to keep things away from the manager's door, without disrespecting him. That is what Harv did for me.'

'Harv took the pressure off Jimmy,' agrees Shaun Dennis. 'He let him go and do his own thing. Harv started the coaching side and he used to put on great sessions. Harv would start the sessions and then Jimmy would come and finish them off. They worked really well together.'

Martin Harvey worked closely with the young apprentices at Raith, nurturing and guiding them as they tried to establish themselves at the club. All still speak fondly of their mentor. 'Martin was one of the best I have come across,' says Gordon Forrest. 'He was fantastic with the young players. He was very supportive, but tough as well. He taught us a lot of life lessons. When you look back on it, you learned so much, about discipline, about working hard, wanting to do well, looking after each other, and teamwork.'

'He really instilled a sense of values in us as people and as individuals,' agrees Graham Robertson. 'I always remember he used to say, "If a job is worth doing, then it is worth doing right." We used to have to sweep the terraces, help with the laundry and do it all. We were the first ones there in the morning and the last ones to leave at night doing jobs and cleaning the place. Martin Harvey would come round and inspect things and run his finger along something and go, "There's a bit of dust there," but it instilled a work ethic in all of us.'

Harvey made sure that every young apprentice at the club took their responsibilities seriously, whether that was training, playing, cleaning the dressing rooms, the boots, the stands or, at times, even his own car. 'I was doing a job in my house at the weekend,' laughs Robertson, 'and I had Martin Harvey's voice in my head going, "If a job is worth doing, then it is worth doing right." I saw Potts [Brian Potter] recently when I was down at Stark's Park doing the Raith TV stuff and he was the goalkeeping coach at Hamilton. We were having a bit of banter, then he came out after the game and said, "I have just been sweeping the dressing room and cleaning the place. I couldn't leave it because I had Martin Harvey in my head saying, 'You need to tidy up. You need to clean the place!'" Any dressing room we went to, we had to leave it spotless. You see these posts on social media now as if it is some big, impressive thing, to do that but we were doing that 30 years ago. That was down to Martin Harvey.'

Under the watchful guidance of Harvey, Robertson and Forrest were flourishing and with both having scored in the games between the Gøtu legs, Jimmy Nicholl had no hesitation in including them, along with fellow apprentice Craig McKinlay, in the squad to make the journey north to the Faroe Islands.

9

Crooked Jack, Gull Beer
and a Tambourine

AS THE small group of supporters boarded the bus outside Stark's Bar on the Sunday morning, the air was bristling with anticipation. Having signed up for the ferry trip, this was the beginning of a journey that would end in the Faroe Islands watching Raith Rovers playing their first away match in European competition. The excitement was curtailed slightly by the knowledge that they would not reach their destination until the following day. The bus was an ill-assorted tribe of young, old, male, female, familiar faces and those who had never been seen before all bonded by the journey they were about to undertake. 'It was just this strange, dysfunctional band of Rovers supporters,' says Steve Wallace at the memory of his fellow football groundbreakers. 'All excited at going to a new place they hadn't been before.'

Dropped off in Aberdeen with a few hours to the ferry departure, the supporters looked for a variety of ways to kill time. Some went straight to the nearest pub, others to get something to eat, and some to find an open off-licence to stock up for the ferry. Jonathan Tippetts-Aylmer headed to Union Street to sort out his entertainment for the week. 'They said we had three hours until the ferry left,' he says. 'I popped up to HMV and decided to buy a new cassette for my Walkman. I bought *Doolittle* by the Pixies as a friend had told me it was brilliant, and I also bought *The Acid House* by Irvine Welsh. That was basically my music and my entertainment for the entire week. There was so little to do over there, I listened to that album hundreds of times and read *The Acid House* twice!'

'At that age,' says fellow supporter Kenny Smith, 'we were young, and not really worried about culture or sightseeing, it was all about going to see the Rovers in Europe. I think it helped that we had won the first leg 4-0, so you had that sense of, "Surely, we are not going to get beat," and it was kind of like a party atmosphere.'

The ferry departed Aberdeen at 5pm, and the fun began. A group of supporters had gathered on the top deck of the ferry as it set sail. The sun was shining, the mood was high and as they sipped their drink of choice, it had the feel of a Mediterranean cruise. It didn't last. They were barely ten minutes outside of the Granite City when the cloud rolled in, the temperature dropped, the rain started, and the ferry began to rock. They cut their losses and headed for the refuge of the bar.

The next 25 hours were the most surreal experience for every fan who was fortunate enough to be on the trip, as the ferry turned into a night-long party. The ship was relatively empty apart from a few people who worked in oil and gas and a handful of Faroese families returning after an early Christmas shopping visit to Aberdeen, but the supporters ensured the atmosphere in the bar crackled late into the evening. 'We got on the ferry, and it was just 24 hours of mayhem,' laughs Jonathan Tippetts-Aylmer. 'I remember just looking at the portholes and they were under the water and then they were above the water. It was terrifying. I remember sailing past an oil rig with the flame coming out at the top. I'm sure there were whales. That might be a false memory, but I'm sure we saw whales at one point.

'There was a guy that came with us, nobody had ever seen before at a game, and no one has ever seen him since. He was this tall guy, and he was famous because he brought a tambourine with him. We were having a sing-song in the bar, and he went into his bag and brought out a tambourine. We just looked at him and thought, "Who the hell brings a tambourine on an away trip?"'

The fan had also brought a bodhrán (a frame drum used mainly in Irish music), and along with the piano in the corner of the bar, they became the focus of a slightly chaotic evening. They would not be the only musical accompaniment. Steve Wallace had brought his *Singing the Blues* cassette; an eclectic collection of Geordie Munro and other Rovers songs recorded by Kirkcaldy band Crooked Jack. It was not long before he had persuaded the barman to put it on and it played on a loop for the rest of the evening. 'My main memories of that ferry are Gull beer, Crooked Jack and a tambourine,' Steve laughs. 'It was just a great night out on a ferry. I don't think we'd gone into it expecting it to be that. You thought it would probably be long and boring, but it was just a great night of shenanigans.'

Steve had paid extra for reclining seats, but on discovering they were little better than a normal seat, he slept in the bar. Kenny Smith had splashed out on a cabin with friends, but after an evening of revelry, he discovered that the large heavy doors on the ferry posed a problem for someone who had consumed several Gull beers. 'We had a cabin with four of us in there,' recounts Kenny. 'I stumbled into bed but had been drinking all night so was quickly up to go to the toilet. I went out into the corridor on this ferry and into the toilet. After I was done, I couldn't open the door to get out. I was still a bit drunk, and I think it was one of those ferry push, turn, twist jobs. I was banging on the door shouting, "Help, I'm stuck!" but no one came because it was obviously the middle of the night. I thought, "I'm just going to have to sleep here."'

After a few minutes, Kenny tried the door again and it opened first time. Safely back in his cabin, one of his roommates asked where he'd been. 'I told him I'd been locked in the toilet and had been banging on the door,' he says. 'He looked at me with a straight face and said, "Oh, was it you that was shouting?" I was absolutely raging. The funny thing is the next morning, we all woke up and this guy's bunk is empty, and he is nowhere to be seen. Eventually he comes back, and we ask him where he has been. He says, "I went to the toilet in the middle of the night, and I got stuck. I couldn't open the door, so I slept in the toilet." I just thought, "What goes around, comes around pal!"'

The next morning, the slightly less energetic band of supporters sat out the remaining hours of the trip until they arrived in the Faroe Islands. Accommodation was to be provided at a local youth hostel in the capital Tórshavn, but a group of older fans on the trip decided to pass on the hostel experience and booked themselves into a hotel in the centre of town. For the rest of the intrepid travellers, it was on to a bus and up the hill to their home for the next five days, as the return ferry was not scheduled until the following Friday. 'The youth hostel,' laughs Kenny. 'Can we even call it a youth hostel? It was just a games hall with these wooden partitions up and camping beds. It was like *Stalag 13*.'

Tórshavn Youth Hostel turned out to be a sports hall on the edge of town that was converted in the summer months to provide accommodation for any traveller who found their way to the Faroe Islands. Over the next week, the Rovers supporters would share it with bird watchers, independent travellers and a group of Danish schoolchildren. Tórshavn was also relatively small, with no pubs as alcohol had been prohibited until the early 90s, so options for entertainment were in short supply. With limited cash and a few days to pass before the game, every day most supporters would walk into town, kill a few hours, then walk back to the youth hostel. 'I was just living on cheese slices and bread and butter most days,' says Jonathan Tippetts-Aylmer.

'I had taken a lot of pasta sauce food sachets,' says Steve Wallace. 'I had no idea what the food was going to be like, and someone had told me that it was really expensive. We didn't have a lot of money to do stuff, so the first couple of days there was a lot of wandering around and hanging about. After the first few days, someone managed to find a brewery, so we were at least able to go and get a crate of beer for the day of the game.'

If the ferry travellers were busy passing time in Tórshavn, those travelling by plane were back home preparing for their own trip north. Among their number was John Greer. A familiar and friendly face around Stark's Park, Greer is someone who understands the importance of history to a football club. As chair of the club's former players' association, member of the Hall of Fame committee and host of Reminiscing Raith, a superb initiative that brings together former players and fans, no one has done more to celebrate the proud history of Raith Rovers in recent years. Surprisingly, for someone so steeped in club history, his own first match remains a blur. 'I am not one of these guys who can tell you when he got taken to his first Rovers game or who it was against or what the score was,' John says. 'It doesn't work like that for me. I got taken along when I was around three and the football was totally incidental. You went along because your grandad went.'

Greer was born and brought up in Kirkcaldy and his grandad, Henry Norville, was known around the Lang Toun for two things, being an insurance agent and being a big Rovers man. He had been born in 1907 and had witnessed all the great teams and players of the past, from the team that finished third in Scotland in 1922 to the side that set the British goalscoring record in the 1937/38 season. He had taken John along to Stark's Park as an infant in order to imbue him with the same passion he had for the Kirkcaldy side. 'For the first few years I didn't take much notice of the football,' admits John. 'I would kick paper cups about and stuff, but then my grandad would put me up on the wall. At one game the linesman came over and said, "You need to get that boy's legs back over the wall as he could get hit with the ball."'

Slowly, John started to pay attention to the games unfolding before him, and by the mid-60s he was hooked. It was the era of Ian Porterfield, Bobby Reid, Alex Rae, and Gordon Wallace. The latter became one of John's first heroes in a blue shirt. 'My grandad passed away,' he continues. 'Then I started to go with pals, joined the supporters' club as everybody did back in the day, and sold my tickets to get to away games. I always remember that if you went over 80 miles then you stopped for your tea and the supporters' club gave you 80p for a fish supper.'

There were memorable away trips to Dumfries, Berwick, Brechin, and Stranraer, and not just because of the free fish tea. Even when John moved away from Fife for work, he continued to support Rovers, regularly travelling up for games from his home in Yorkshire and doing whatever he could to raise money for the club. 'I sponsored my first player Keith Wright,' he says. 'And the Rovers sold him! I then sponsored my second player who was Colin Harris and the Rovers sold him too! When I lived down in Yorkshire, I had 30 people at Shipley Golf Club, who had barely heard of Raith Rovers, but every week they would pay their money into the Rovers Super Ten. I remember going round and I'd give them their wee plastic card which gave them discounts around Kirkcaldy. They'd be like, "What am I going to do with this? I live 250 miles away!"'

On a Saturday, John would drive from Shipley to York to get the train at half seven in the morning, sometimes bumping into a fellow Rover making his own pilgrimage from his home in Sheffield. He would go to great lengths to attend matches and keep up with what was happening at Stark's Park. 'I discovered that if I phoned Stark's Park at ten to six on a Thursday night, then Frank Connor would be in the office waiting on the team coming in for training,' he recounts. 'So, I would phone up and be on the phone to him for 45 minutes. He would be telling me all about the team and what he was trying to do. I remember him saying, "I want Ken Eadie at the Rovers. I'm trying to get the board to agree to it. If we get Gordon Dalziel and Ken Eadie playing together up front, we are going to the Premier League." He was such an enthusiast. It was wonderful.'

Despite the distance, John's passion for the club did not dim and he did everything he could to follow the team. 'My wife Alison was due to have our first baby around the time we had our Scottish Cup run in 1986,' he says. 'She had been kept in hospital in the run-up to the baby being born and I'd gone in to visit. At five to eight, I'd said, "I'm going to have to go now Alison, as the Rovers are playing Peterhead at Arbroath and if I go now, I'll catch the second half live on the radio."'

A few weeks later, when his wife told them that they were going to induce their baby on the Friday, he replied that they couldn't do that as Rovers were playing St Mirren in the Scottish Cup quarter-final on Saturday. The inducement was postponed to the Monday so he made the match. The birth of John's first child would prove to be the only joyous occasion that week as Rovers lost 2-0 and exited the cup.

John had booked up on the flight to the Faroe Islands organised by Dennis O'Connell. There would be just under 30 people travelling, including a few journalists and photographers. There was excitement as they gathered on the morning of the game outside the Town House in Kirkcaldy. 'On the first trip to the Faroes, I felt like a footballing pioneer,' reflects John. 'It was like that old thing when you were going on a trip with the school and they say to you before you go, "Remember, today you are an ambassador for the school." We were ambassadors for the club, and it was just magical. You just thought, "This is a brave new world we are going into. The Rovers in Europe."'

If there was excitement at what lay ahead, it was tempered slightly when they arrived at Aberdeen Airport and saw the plane that would take them there. 'When we got to Aberdeen, we checked in and we headed to get on the plane,' recalls Gavin Quinn, who had also chosen the flight option. 'I always remember walking along this big walkway and seeing all the big planes, and we got to the very end and there is this wee green plane with propellors. That was ours.'

'It was like a Ford Transit with wings,' laughs John Greer.

The rudimentary nature of their transport did not dampen the mood and the atmosphere was boisterous as they got ready for departure. As the plane was about to take-off, supporter Phil Nicholson shouted to his fellow passengers, 'Right boys, Rovers first time in Europe, get your scarves out the windaes!' The Shorts of Belfast plane took off from Aberdeen, but just 20 minutes later it was back on the ground in Wick for refuelling.

'I ended up on the supporters' plane,' recalls football journalist Scott Davie. 'I have never had to go on such a small plane on a European trip, and I certainly have never had to stop over in Wick for refuelling! That was bizarre. When we got to the Faroes, you were flying through that wee narrow gap between the mountains and suddenly the airstrip appears out of nowhere. It was completely unforgettable.

'We weren't staying in Tórshavn; we were staying up near Toftir. You had the bus, the ferry and the bus again to get there and we were staying in the fishermen's mission instead of being pampered in a luxury hotel. It just made it all the better really. You were there with Rovers fans and we had a great time.'

There would be one final surreal moment at the end of the journey as the first 'local' the supporters encountered on arrival at their destination turned out to be anything but local. 'We are getting off the bus,' remembers John Greer. 'This boy comes walking over towards us and says in a Fife accent, "Are you boys here to see the Rovers?" We were, "Aye, are you?" and he replied, "Am I fuck. I support the Rangers." It turned out he was from Buckhaven and had lived there for six years working in the local fish factory. I'm sure he must have been on the run from somebody and hiding out.'

Their new-found friend turned out to be a useful contact when he helped them source some pre-match refreshments. 'We asked him if there was a bar anywhere and he told us that there wasn't but there was a beer shop two miles away,' continues John. 'There was no bus and the only taxi had just taken the journalists to the ground, so he flagged down a big Saab that was coming along the road and says, "I work with this boy, he'll take you." We got a kitty together and some of the guys went to get the beer. They came back with a crate of Gull lager and something which was kind of a malty flavour. It was like a cross between beer and Horlicks. That was our pre-match drinks.'

Back in Tórshavn, the ferry crowd boarded their bus to take them on the long and winding drive up to Toftir. 'On the bus trip up the ground, there was an English guy,' recalls Jonathan Tippetts-Aylmer. 'He ran a sweep on the bus, but he didn't understand the concept of the local money, because he charged something like 50 Kroner for a ticket, which I think he thought was 50p. He just didn't realise and neither did we at first. We all bought one thinking it was 50p and then later someone worked out it was a fiver. Whoever had the right score must have made an absolute fortune!'

As the bus arrived at the ground, those who had taken the ferry were greeted by those who had flown, and stories of their respective journeys shared. It was hard to know whether the unorthodox flight or the 25-hour ferry had been the better option. The two groups combined totalled fewer than 60 supporters. It was a small support, but each and every one of them felt incredibly lucky to be there.

10

Typical Rovers

AT TIMES it can feel that at Raith Rovers, calamity is never more than two steps away. This is perhaps best summed up by the story of the 1923 side who took up the offer of a handful of friendly matches on the Canary Islands, only to end up making headlines worldwide when they became, as far as we know, the only football team ever to have been shipwrecked. The return to Europe in 1995 may not have been as calamitous as that ill-fated trip, but it was far from smooth. The initial flight booked by the club had to be cancelled when it was discovered that the pilot didn't hold the necessary licence to land a plane at Vágar Airport in the Faroes. 'I hadn't known if it was true or not,' says Jason Dair, 'or it was just to put the frighteners up us, but Jimmy [Nicholl] told us beforehand that there were only six pilots who could fly the plane and land it in the airport because of the mountains either side.'

The unique geography of the Faroes meant that it required extra skill to negotiate the terrain and bring the plane down and land on the relatively short runway. The club were forced to reschedule at short notice to specialists Faroes Travel, meaning a later than anticipated arrival.

If Rovers thought their problems were over, they were mistaken. Their rescheduled flight from Edinburgh Airport was delayed by fog in the Faroes, not leaving until after midnight, meaning that they would fail to meet the UEFA requirement that teams should be in the country 24 hours before their match. 'That is typical Rovers, isn't it?' says Scott Davie, who as a journalist had covered numerous European trips with Dundee United and Aberdeen. 'To this day you have got to be in the country 24 hours ahead, so it turned into the perfect newspaper story and the perfect summing up of Raith Rovers down the years.'

It may have made good newspaper copy, but for the manager it had been a tense delay. 'We had been assured that as long as we got in by midnight, we would be OK,' recalls Jimmy Nicholl. 'When I heard about the fog and extra delay, I felt physically sick. Fog was the last thing you wanted with those mountains! I was terrified about UEFA's reaction and started convincing myself that we would be thrown out of the cup with the tie awarded to Gøtu.

'In desperation, I called Craig Brown, who put us in touch with Andy Roxburgh. He was very, very helpful and saved the day for us. Andy said they were well aware of the difficulties playing in the islands and told us just to be sure and get there. In the end everything was sorted out with the person at UEFA who deals with late arrivals.' The squad would eventually touch down in the Faroes at 2am and not check into their hotel until after 3am. It was far from ideal preparation for the players and would mean that their first sight of Toftir Stadium would be when they arrived for the game later that day.

The delay was an inconvenience, but by that stage many of the squad were just happy to be safely on the ground after the experience of landing at Vágar. *Fife Free Press* reporter John Greechan would later describe the landing as one that made even the scariest ride at the Links Market seem tame. 'We were coming down,' recounts goalkeeper Scott Thomson, 'and the pilot said, "Can you get your seatbelts on." It was pitch black and we couldn't see lights or anything, so we thought, "We must be coming in to land, and will glide down like you usually do." Then it was boom, you hit the ground. The seats in front of us actually folded over because we had hit the ground so hard. Julian Broddle was sitting next to me, and he was going, "Please God, please God! Please God!"'

'The flight dropped down and big Ally Graham let out the loudest scream I have ever heard,' laughs Robbie Raeside. 'He will deny it, but I am telling you now, he screamed. He is a great guy and I love him to bits, but all I remember about that landing is big Ally screaming.'

With the plane on the ground there was cheering and clapping. As the commotion died down, Nicholl stood up at the front of the plane and shouted, 'If you think that was bad boys, wait until you see the take-off when we go back!'

Finally at their hotel, the squad rested up as best they could. The kick-off was scheduled for 6pm and a bus would take them across to Toftir Stadium. The four-goal lead meant that there was a relaxed atmosphere among the players, with much of the jeopardy removed from the tie. 'The fact that we got such a good result in the first tie,' says Colin Cameron, 'I think we were able to enjoy the second game a wee bit more and we were able to enjoy it and take it all in.

'The thing that stuck out for me was how light it was. You had your blackout curtains in the hotel, but it was almost daylight. I opened the curtains at the hotel and there was a sheep right there at the window. The hotel had grass on some parts of the roof and the sheep was right there grazing at my window.'

'I roomed with Tony Rougier on that trip,' recalls Graham Robertson. 'I just remember being on the bus with him to go to the game. When we set off, it was just a lot of hills and a lot of sheep. I was sat next to Tony, and he was looking at me as if to go, "Where on earth is this, boys?" His face was a picture.'

The supporters had gathered at Toftir Stadium in weather reminiscent of a miserable day in Burntisland. The stadium, opened in 1980, was perched at the top of a mountain, with its footprint chiselled out of the rock. A small, white, pavilion-like stand flanked one side of the pitch with the rest of the stadium made up of rudimentary wooden benches, reminiscent of Clydebank's old Kilbowie Stadium. 'When we first qualified,' reflects Gavin Quinn, 'we were looking to go to Barcelona or Real Madrid or somewhere. We didn't think we would be going to the Faroe Islands at the top of a hill where it was raining, windy, and blowing a gale.'

'It was the coldest place ever,' agrees former defender Shaun Dennis. 'And we were playing in the middle of a rock!'

Toftir was not only used as a football stadium, but also functioned as a training centre with accommodation attached. This provided the makeshift press box for journalists. 'The press box that we had for the game,' laughs Scott Davie, 'I was there with John Greechan and Danny Stewart from DC Thomson, and our press box was actually a bedroom where the windows looked out on to the pitch!

There was a double bed that we had to move out of the way to watch the game. It was the most unique experience of watching a football match, because we then had to move the bed back again at the final whistle.'

The trip was a surreal experience for Scott in more ways than one. Although covering the game as a journalist, he was from Kirkcaldy and a Rovers supporter. 'My dad had been going to watch Rovers since just after the Second World War,' he says. 'So, he took me to Raith Rovers when I was too young to know any better. I can even remember being at a game at Stark's Park when they played Third Lanark.'

Scott spent most of his journalism career working in Dundee, but by the time Raith won the League Cup and ventured into Europe, he was based in Aberdeen. His personal connection to the Kirkcaldy club meant that he was perfectly placed to report on their UEFA Cup exploits. 'I did some newspaper stuff on Raith when they were going quite well,' he adds. 'People were aware of my Kirkcaldy connections and knew I could get some stories. They were quite happy to let me cover their games, so I covered all of the European ties.'

Reflecting back on his career now, the Faroes trip stands out as one of his highlights. 'Over my time for the BBC and newspapers, I reckon I have done trips to 40 different countries covering European football,' says Scott. 'I had been to many countries including communist countries during the communist era, but I have never been on a more surreal trip than the Faroe Islands with Raith Rovers.

'The Rovers trips as a whole stand out for me because of the complete disbelief that Raith Rovers actually got around to playing European football. I had grown up with a chip on my shoulder about Dunfermline, as in my era, they had been playing regularly in European football and had a European history. So, you had that chip on your shoulder, and you never thought you would see Raith Rovers playing European football. It was a wonderful experience.'

That evening at Toftir Stadium would be one that no one connected with Raith Rovers would forget. 'It was just a fantastic football experience,' says supporter Steve Wallace. 'If you want a different place to go and watch football, then Toftir Stadium has got to be up there as a place to go and experience something totally different. It was a bit rickety and a bit ramshackle, and it felt like Arbroath on steroids.'

Many in the squad felt that the rustic nature of the surroundings suited the Kirkcaldy club. 'Going to Gøtu and travelling the road to get to the stadium and just the wee unique stadium,' says Stevie Crawford. 'It felt like it was in the middle of nowhere and it wasn't your big flashy stadium or anything like that. It wasn't an Ibrox, a Parkhead, or a Pittodrie. It was a weird feeling to try and take that in with the importance of the game. I think our grounding helped us. Mickey [Colin Cameron] had played his football through Kirkcaldy way, Shaun Dennis through Leven and Methil, Sinky [Davie Sinclair] through Valleyfield and me and Jason [Dair] played in Oakley, and we hadn't forgotten where we were from.'

The players were thankful that so many fans had made the trip to somewhere so remote to cheer them on. For one, there was a very personal show of support. 'The bus got to the stadium, and we are getting off and there are some Rovers supporters waiting for us,' explains Robbie Raeside. 'Among them is my best mate from school, Neil Smith. I still go to Scotland games with him to this day. He didn't even tell me he was going, but he is standing there with a

Rovers top on, in the pissing rain with a bottle of beer in his hand. He told me that he had a mate from Kirkcaldy at university who was a Rovers fan who said he was going, so he was like, "So am I!" It had taken them three or four days to get there!'

'We had our fans, and those guys were amazing,' says Stephen McAnespie. 'Travelling all over the place which was brilliant. The fans are there and want to enjoy it. They want to enjoy the build-up and the atmosphere and all the surroundings. We just wanted to get in and get out, just get the result and get the job done for them.'

All Rovers now had to do was not lose 5-0.

11

Singing in the Rain

'THAT WAS a horrible game,' says goalkeeper Scott Thomson on the second leg at Toftir Stadium. 'It was gloomy, rainy and kind of bleak. We didn't play well at all, but we did enough to get through.'

The 2-2 draw with Gøtu Ítróttarfelag was played out in miserable conditions with incessant rain and was, at least from a Rovers perspective, a forgettable 90 minutes. The away side had opened the scoring through Danny Lennon after 31 minutes. Supporter John Greer had taken his sister-in-law's video camera to document the trip and the game but somehow managed to miss Lennon's goal. When he checked the footage later, the only thing captured was the midfielder running away in celebration. With Raith five goals ahead and with an away goal, the tie was effectively over. The match played out with a flurry of goals in the closing stages: Pauli Jarnskor equalised for Gøtu on 78 minutes, Stevie Crawford restored Rovers' advantage three minutes later, only for Magni Jarnskor to level the game on 87 minutes. The game finished 2-2, and Rovers progressed 6-2 on aggregate.

Perhaps the most notable moment on the pitch aside from the goals was an astonishing miss from Tony Rougier just after half-time when he managed to scoop an effort from two yards out up and over the bar. One newspaper report would later describe it as 'a contender for miss of the century'. Rougier makes no excuses for his misfire but feels that the less-than-ideal circumstances around the game contributed to the overall performance. 'You could feel there was a certain nervousness there amongst the players in that game,' he reflects. 'With the environment and everything, it was something that was new to the club. We also hardly got any sleep when we eventually got into our hotel, so towards the end of the match I think we were beginning to feel the pace.'

For Gøtu Ítróttarfelag, to have drawn the second leg was a pleasing result. After the first match in Kirkcaldy, they had no expectations of progressing, but they were satisfied with their performance and goals in the second leg. 'You just go in as if it was the first match,' says former Gøtu striker John Petersen, reflecting on how his side had approached the game. 'We knew that it would take something very special, three or four red cards to the opponents for us to get through maybe, so we went in to just get a result in that match. A draw maybe or a victory.

'We levelled at the end and that was a big deal. We knew that we would not go through, but it was a good result for Gøtu and for Faroese football to get a draw. Some people said that it was only a small team from Scotland, but still, everything was better than the Faroe Islands at that time.'

The Faroese side had competed well throughout the match, never giving up and putting in robust challenges to unsettle their opponents. 'I remember the referee was Welsh,' says Ally Graham. 'He was tremendous. The Gøtu boys were trying to foul us and intimidate us. They were holding jerseys and pulling us back, but the referee was great. He said to me, "You just keep playing. You have got this guy. He is fouling you all the time, but don't worry about that. I will deal with that." He was brilliant.'

The arduous trip across and late arrival at their hotel on the morning of the game certainly hadn't helped, but the manager was disappointed with the result and performance and vented his frustration to the press after the match. 'Jimmy Nicholl was absolutely raging after the game,' recalls Scott Davie. 'They were absolutely terrible, there was no getting away from that and he didn't miss them after it. He savaged them for the poor performance that they put in, but it has to be said that it was in pretty awful conditions up there.'

Reflecting on the performance now, midfielder Colin Cameron is philosophical. 'We were able to keep them at arm's length,' he says. 'There was never any point in the game that we were under real pressure.'

The scorer of the first goal, Danny Lennon, agrees, focusing on the path the team was on rather than the level of performance on the night. 'To score that night in the UEFA Cup was fantastic,' he reflects. 'Regardless of whether it was in the preliminary round or the big rounds, it was a personal achievement and one for the club. We may not have been at our best, but every tackle and every goal we had that night was important and drew us closer to something more significant.'

That night was memorable for two younger members of the squad, Gordon Forrest and Robbie Raeside, with both handed the opportunity to take to the pitch in a UEFA Cup tie. Forrest had been brought on to replace Alex Taylor after 77 minutes. 'There was obviously a nervousness about it, as a young player,' reflects Forrest. 'But I look back now and realise how comfortable I was in that environment. I am not saying it was easy, but I had so many guys around me like Stevie Crawford, Colin Cameron, Sinky, a Valleyfield boy, who were just great with you. They smothered you, they protected you, they wanted you to do well, which was important and made it easy for you to be involved.

'The crazy thing is I went on to play in Iceland later in my career. And I had two Faroe Island internationalists in my team. The goalkeeper with the bobble hat was our goalkeeper, so it was a place I could relate to, because I had been there and played on the top of that mountain.'

Robbie Raeside would also get the chance to feature when he replaced fellow centre-half Shaun Dennis with five minutes left. 'I was just delighted to get on the pitch and say I played in the UEFA Cup,' he says. 'I was just like a wee boy in the sweetie shop getting a wee taster of something.'

Among the supporters who had travelled the evening was more memorable for the location, conditions and sense of occasion, rather than anything that happened on the pitch. The whole match had a surreal quality as the rain poured down, a brass band played, and fans entertained themselves with a chorus of 'Singing in the Rain'. At one point, high on the hill above the stadium two horsemen arrived to observe what was happening in the ground. They resembled a couple of extras out of *Game of Thrones*, if it had existed at the time. Anyone who wandered for a look down the cliff at the opposite end of the ground was treated to the sight of a man mowing the lawn on his roof. Not something you see every day at a football stadium.

With no covering available and rain continuing to fall throughout the 90 minutes, most were soaked by full time.

The electronic scoreboard, which had shown the away side as 'Raith Rowers' at the start of the evening, began to feel more and more relevant as the rain continued to plummet. John Greer and Gavin Quinn had both brought flags for the match, which had been laid out over the wooden seats. 'Our big flag was soaked,' says John. 'People would be coming across and saying, "John, the flag is saturated, what are we going to do?" We managed to get it back to the seaman's mission where we were staying after the match, and thankfully they had a drying room. We just threw it in there. It took about 16 of us to fold it back up and put it back in the holdall the next morning, but it survived.'

Quinn's flag was not so lucky. 'One of my mates was Graeme Dick. He's a painter and decorator, but he is a great artist,' he recounts. 'I got him to paint a flag for me – The Swalligator. When I was up at Euro 92 in Sweden, some Glasgow boys gave me the nickname of Big Chief Swalligator, so that was the inspiration for the flag. We both came up with the design and it had the Rovers badge on it and everything.' What Quinn didn't know at the time was that his friend had mistakenly used poster paints, so the minute it started to rain, the paint started to wash away. By full time, all that was left with a blank white sheet. It would be left at the ground.

Other supporters left Toftir with personal mementoes of their trip. 'At half-time I saw a guy with a Gøtu top,' says Jonathan Tippetts-Aylmer. 'He pointed at me, and I pointed at him, and it was, "Let's swap tops." So, we went into the Portakabin toilet as it was pretty cold, and swapped tops. I still have that GI top somewhere in the house.' Fellow fan Kenny Smith was less enamoured with his exchange. 'My main memory of that game is that I lost my scarf that I had since I was a child,' he bemoans. 'A kid wanted to swap, and I was just being nice. I traded my scarf for this horrible yellow Gøtu Ítróttarfelag hat.'

For fans at home, there had been a virtual blackout of the match, with it impossible to find updates of what was happening. Well-known Raith fan Jim McIntosh summed up the frustration of those who had not travelled in an angry letter to the *Daily Record*, 'I was furious with the lack of coverage. I listened to Radio Scotland for the Motherwell game expecting to hear what was going on with our boys in the Faroes. But they didn't give us a mention. All they talked about was Rangers. It was ten o'clock before I found out we had drawn 2-2 and that was off Ceefax.'

The important fact, despite the lack of updates, was that Rovers had won the tie and were now in the hat for the first round proper, a feat that eluded all the other teams from Britain and Ireland that night. Welsh side Bangor had lost 5-0 to Widzew Łódź of Poland, their compatriots Afan Lido had gone out 2-1 to Latvians RAF Jelgava, Crusaders of Belfast had crashed out 6-1 to Danish club Silkeborg and Shelbourne from the League of Ireland had lost 6-0 to ÍA of Iceland. Scotland's other representatives in the competition, Motherwell, had recovered from their first-leg defeat to win 2-0 away in Finland, but their opponents still advanced on away goals. 'Motherwell played MyPa 47 at the same time and got beat,' says Rovers supporter Graeme Meldrum. 'I remember thinking, "Great. We are not the worst Scottish team in Europe this season." It was always in the back of my mind, that we could go into Europe and be stinking. But we'd gotten further than Motherwell, so it felt like a free hit for the rest of the competition!'

There were other notable departures from the competition that night. Galatasaray of Turkey, who were managed by Graeme Souness, were knocked out 4-2 on aggregate by Sparta Prague and Red Star Belgrade, who had won the European Cup four years earlier, crashed out to Swiss side Neuchâtel Xamax.

As the players and fans departed Toftir Stadium to begin the long journey home, there was relief that they had successfully navigated their first European tie. Young players Colin Cameron and Stevie Crawford would both return to the Faroe Islands later in their careers as Scottish internationals, Cameron for a 1-1 draw in 1995 and Crawford for that match in 2002 when former Gøtu Ítróttarfelag striker John Petersen scored twice to secure a 2-2 draw. There just seemed to be something about Raith players, Toftir Stadium and draws.

On the journey home, the squad discovered that taking off from the Faroe Islands was as challenging as landing. 'The flight back. Oh my god,' recalls Stephen McAnespie. 'The runway was only the length of Stark's Park, but he had to get the plane up and over this mountain. We couldn't get off the ground at first. They said we were too heavy. We were barrelling down the runway, and he slammed the brakes on. We looked at the pilot because we could see him and he was like, "Oh, we have to turn around and go all the way back."'

Julian Broddle, whose fear of flying persists to this day, had a simple strategy. 'Have several drinks and try not to think about that mountain too much,' laughs the former defender. The next group to depart were the supporters who had arrived by plane. They stayed the night in the local seamen's mission after the game, where their hosts laid on a sumptuous banquet of food, before departing for Scotland the following morning. That just left the 30 brave souls who travelled by ferry. The return ferry was not until Friday, so it was a bus back to Tórshavn Youth Hostel and the challenge of what to do for the next three days. 'Tórshavn came alive the day after the game,' laughs Steve Wallace. 'The cinema opened!'

The following night a group of fans headed into town to see a little-known film called *Braveheart*. The world premiere of the Mel Gibson blockbuster was held in Stirling a month later, so how it had reached Tórshavn first remains a mystery, but it did provide a small group of supporters with the unusual claim to fame of being the first Scots to have seen the iconic movie. The last night of the trip coincided with the opening of the local nightclub, and after an evening of experiencing the Faroese equivalent of Jackie O's, a few supporters 'borrowed' a horse from someone's front garden and walked it a distance along the road before realising that it probably wasn't the smartest idea they had ever had. No harm came to the horse, it was simply let go and as there were no reports of equine-related incidents the following morning, we have to presume that it simply returned home after its impromptu stroll with a group of inebriated but ultimately harmless Fifers.

The final surreal act of the week-long stay was a post-midnight game of five-a-side with a Danish rock band. The group, who had originally been called Disneyland After Dark but were forced to resort to calling themselves DAD when the Disney Corporation threatened to sue, were at the end of a northern European tour for their new album. Hazy memory means that it's unclear whether they had a gig in Tórshavn or were just there to unwind, but they did provide the opposition in an impromptu late-night kickabout. 'Niall

Russell and I were dreading the ferry trip back,' recalls Kenny Smith. 'So, we planned on going without sleep for two days and had decided to do an all-nighter. We ended up going out on the pitch next to the youth hostel with these guys at two in the morning and having a game of football because it was still light. The next morning, I was a dead man walking getting on to that ferry.'

For the fans who made the trip to the Faroe Islands, it remains something special. It is a place that they might never have experienced were it not for the randomness of a UEFA Cup draw. 'I think of the whole European experience, the Faroes was probably my favourite trip,' says Kenny. 'I think it was because it was our first ever trip, we were there for a week and it was so surreal. Having that week there, it just let you savour it. It was a wonderful time.'

'I'm just excited to be able to say that I was one of a gang of maybe 50 or 60 that went to Raith Rovers' first ever away game in Europe,' says Jonathan Tippetts-Aylmer. 'It's hard to explain and it doesn't impress any of my friends, but it is something I still feel a bit of pride in.'

The name Raith Rovers still means something to John Petersen, who played in both legs for Gøtu. 'If I hear the name Raith Rovers, I have to step back 30 years,' he laughs. 'But I still follow them because we played them. I don't know any player that plays for Raith Rovers now, but when I look at [football website] LiveScore, I always look out for them and think, "How is it going?"'

Petersen played with Gøtu for another year, before going semi-professional in 1996 with Tórshavn side B36. He would go on to have an impressive career in Iceland and Denmark before moving into coaching. He feels grateful for the opportunity football provided. 'I just feel that I have been very lucky to experience playing in all the European countries,' he reflects. 'Playing against Spain, Germany, France, Holland and a lot of big football stars. All the big nations and the big names. The Faroe Islands is so small, so I am very pleased about everything that I have got through football.'

If Petersen progressed on to bigger and better things, then what of Gøtu Ítróttarfelag? Today Gøtu Ítróttarfelag is a name that no longer exists in Faroese football, having merged in 2008 with neighbouring side LÍF Leirvík to form a new club in Víkingur Gøta. 'We still play as GÍ old boys on some special occasions, festivals and the like,' says Petersen. 'So, some of the locals still want to keep it alive. For me, GÍ was the start and that will always be something that I remember. It is something special.'

With their Faroese opponents defeated, the thoughts of everyone turned to who they would face in the next round. The list of potential opponents included Leeds United, AS Monaco, Brøndby, Lillestrøm, Sparta Prague, FC Freiburg, and Icelandic side ÍA. As the draw was about to be made at UEFA HQ in Switzerland, those who had taken the ferry to the Faroe Islands were still onboard with another 20 hours of sailing time in front of them. One of their number was sent to the top of the ship with a radio to find a signal as the rest waited below with thoughts of the more glamorous destination ahead. When he returned to impart the news of their next opponents, there was a momentary silence. 'Very good,' said one of the expectant supporters, assuming that it was a joke. 'Tell us where we are really going.' When it was made clear that there was no joke, there was a stunned silence, before the same exasperated voice piped up, 'That's even further north than we've just been!'

Rovers had drawn ÍA.

12

Skagamenn

BRYNJÓLFUR ÞÓR Guðmundsson was born in Reykjavík, the capital of Iceland, but when he was just four years old his family made the decision to move across the bay to Akranes. The relocation became the catalyst for his 40-year love affair with local side ÍA – Íþróttabandalag Akraness to give their full name. 'They used to be a saying before I was born that said Akranes had three things to offer,' jokes Brynjólfur, speaking from his current home in Reykjavík. 'Beautiful women, lots of potatoes and good football. I hope they still have the beautiful women because the other two things went away.'

Much like Raith Rovers, the ÍA of today is perhaps a paler imitation of their 1990s side, an era when they monopolised Icelandic football, dominated opponents and won five championships in a row, a feat that has never been repeated. Today, they are a club striving to recapture former glories. A cursory glance at the towns of Akranes and Kirkcaldy reveals some shared traits. They are both hard-working, industrial towns sitting across the water from a more fashionable and cosmopolitan capital city. Akranes sits around 30 miles from Reykjavík, in the shadow of the

Akrafjall mountain. The local economy centres around fishing, a cement plant and an aluminium smelting plant. 'Akranes is a very hard-working town,' explains Brynjólfur. 'A hard town and, maybe in some respects, a very unforgiving town. You had to show you could handle things. You learned how to stand on your own and fight for everything. That aspect had a great impact on ÍA being the best club in Iceland for 50 years.'

Football has always been at the heart of the town. The team, referred to by locals as either ÍA or *Skagamenn*, derived from the name for those living in the Akranes area, has been a constant source of pride and conversation. 'It is such a big part of the town spirit and life of the locals,' continues Guðmundsson. 'Whenever you met someone, you talked football with them. I was so surprised when my big sister started dating a guy who had no interest in football. He was born in Akranes, he was raised in Akranes, but he had no interest in the team. I think he was the first person I had ever met in Akranes who didn't care about football!'

Most players were drawn from families in the town, which deepened the connection between community and club. All players lived, worked and played in Akranes. Like many other countryside clubs in Iceland, they became a huge expression of the town outwards. When the club did well, it was embraced and celebrated. Much of ÍA's early success was down to the vision of Ríkharður Jónsson, a legendary figure in both ÍA and Icelandic football. When Jónsson first started out in the late 1940s, kick and run dominated, a style imported by the Scottish and English coaches who had arrived to teach Icelanders the beautiful game. Jónsson changed all that. He travelled to Germany and brought back a more continental style of play to ÍA.

Installed as player-manager in 1951, the transformation was immediate, securing the national title in his first season in charge, the first team outside of Reykjavík to win the Icelandic championship.

The remarkable thing was that at the time Jónsson was just 21 years of age. 'Being a coach that young,' says Brynjólfur, 'he had to be very mentally strong, but everyone I know who knew Ríkharður Jónsson said that he was a person that commanded respect without trying. A very honest man, a very firm man, someone who will give you your chance, but he will expect you to do your best.'

When Raith were paired with ÍA, the spirit of Ríkharður Jónsson's side in the 1950s had been rekindled and ÍA were once again dominating Icelandic football, having just won their third championship in a row. Many of the players who were winning championships in the 1990s had dads or grandads who had won it in the 50s.

The quality of the ÍA squad meant that expectations were high. The club and its supporters demanded not just success, but success with a certain flair. At the heart of the squad were three unique talents – Siggi Jónsson and twin brothers Arnar and Bjarki Gunnlaugsson. Jónsson was the most well-known of the trio, having established a successful career in England with Sheffield Wednesday and Arsenal. He was from an Akranes football family and had shone from an early age. 'I spoke to someone recently who had watched Siggi Jónsson play when he was 12 or 13 years old,' says Brynjólfur. 'He told me it was just like watching an artist. He could do anything with a ball. When he first came into the ÍA team, he was the youngest player in Icelandic history to play league football. He was just 15. He just had so much talent and technique.

'He first played for ÍA in 1982 and in 1983, when he was 16 years old, he played for all four Iceland national teams. He played for the under-17s, he was playing for the under-19s, the under-21s and he was playing for the full first team. This would never happen today, but he was just such an amazing talent.'

The ability of Jónsson was soon attracting the interest of suitors across Europe and despite having the opportunity to make the move to Germany or Spain, he chose England to further his career. Icelanders have had a lengthy infatuation with English football, and the attraction of playing in the top tier with Sheffield Wednesday proved too strong to resist. He later signed for Arsenal, but a series of injuries wrecked his spell in London, and he made just ten appearances in a Gunners shirt.

He initially announced his retirement in 1991, but the following year returned to football and his hometown club, re-signing for ÍA. 'When he went out to England, he was a very technical young player,' explains Brynjólfur. 'But then when he came back, this young guy who flew around the pitch and did such wonderful things, was a giant of a man and was all muscle and was a very different player. Very gifted, but also a guy you wouldn't want to come anywhere close to, because he was really hard.' This strength earned him the nickname of 'The Icelandic Beast'.

Alongside Jónsson in the ÍA squad were Arnar and Bjarki Gunnlaugsson. The phenomenally talented twins had demonstrated their potential from a very early age and were fiercely driven. 'They were incredibly motivated and competitive,' explains Brynjólfur. 'They were competitive against everybody else, but when they were playing each other, it was almost like going to war. There is a story about them when they were 12 years old playing badminton in the sports hall in Akranes, things got so heated that somebody called over the announcing system over the entire sports hall, "Arnar and Bjarki. Will you please calm down!"'

The siblings quickly earned a place in the ÍA first team, and their outstanding performances earned both a transfer to Dutch side Feyenoord, aged just 20. The move to the Netherlands was a huge opportunity at such a young age but lasted only two years. 'They had been the very best wherever they had played,' says Brynjólfur. 'Then they go out to Feyenoord, and they are mostly playing in the reserves or youth teams. They were unhappy, so they returned to Akranes. They later said that this was the biggest mistake of their career. They were impatient and should have stayed on and played through it.'

Feyenoord's loss was ÍA's gain, and the twins bolstered their squad for the second half of the league season and their 1995 UEFA Cup campaign. On the way to becoming Icelandic champions that year, Arnar scored 15 goals in the seven games after his return, becoming the top scorer in the league despite having played less than half of the season.

If Raith Rovers were dipping their toe in European competition for the first time, ÍA were European veterans: as one of Iceland's top sides they had played in Europe almost constantly from 1976 to 1989. Playing in Europe was one thing, winning an entirely different matter. They had won only one tie in their first 20 years of European competition, but by 1995 things had started to change. In the two years prior to facing Raith they had progressed through two-legged ties against Partizani Tirana from Albania and Bangor City of Wales, and while Rovers were overcoming Gøtu Ítróttarfelag, ÍA had comfortably defeated Shelbourne 6-0 on aggregate.

Confidence had been further boosted by a historic home leg win over Feyenoord at the Akranesvöllur a few years earlier. 'We played Feyenoord in 1993,' recalls Brynjólfur. 'They had won the first six games of the Dutch season and then they came to Iceland and lost 1-0. At the time, it was one of the greatest wins in Icelandic football history. We ended up losing 3-0 over in the Netherlands, but it was still a stunning result.'

The win at home against such illustrious opposition fostered a belief that they could compete with anyone and having been drawn against a relatively unknown Scottish side in Raith, there was confidence that they could progress further in the UEFA Cup than ever before. 'When we met Raith Rovers, we had started winning in Europe,' says Brynjólfur. 'We had beaten Feyenoord and just beaten Shelbourne comfortably so when we heard we were going to be playing Raith Rovers people were very optimistic. They were obviously a good team, but we were, "Hey, we beat Feyenoord at home. We have a good chance here."'

With the Icelandic championship secured, the *Skagamenn* turned their attention to overcoming their Scottish opponents in the first round of the UEFA Cup. At their last league game, coach Logi Ólafsson was absent having already flown out to Scotland to watch Rovers in action, with several key players rested for their trip to Kirkcaldy. With their scouting done and confidence high, the ÍA squad boarded their flight to Scotland in expectant mood.

13

Express Yourself

JIMMY NICHOLL had watched the first-round draw on Ceefax and was pleased to have drawn ÍA. He knew they would be no pushover, but also was aware that they were the opponents who offered the best chance of progression. Club captain Shaun Dennis shared his view. 'We didn't want to get a big team and get beaten,' he says. 'Of course, it would give the club the extra money, but so too will a prolonged run in the competition. We couldn't have hand-picked a better tie.'

ÍA were more of a known proposition than Gøtu Ítróttarfelag. They had recently played Aberdeen in European competition and had Icelandic international players in their side. 'I remember seeing their 6-0 result against Shelbourne in the previous round,' recalls Nicholl. 'Shelbourne weren't shabby as they were paying a lot of money to players at that stage, so I knew Akranes would have quality players who could cause us problems.'

Before their Icelandic opponents arrived for the first leg at Stark's Park, Rovers had to play three difficult matches against the Old Firm. The Premier League had handed them the toughest possible start to their campaign – at home to Celtic and then away to Rangers. Both were lost, the first a narrow 1-0 defeat to Celtic from a late Pierre van Hooijdonk goal and the second a more bruising 4-0 away loss to a Brian Laudrup-inspired Rangers. Mindful of the important European tie to come, the manager did not give his players too hard a time after the heavy defeat at Ibrox. 'I wasn't going to destroy them in the dressing room after the game,' says Nicholl. 'Not when they had a big match coming up and they'd already been destroyed on the park!'

ÍA manager Logi Ólafsson had chosen the Rangers game to watch Rovers, and was diplomatic when speaking to the Scottish press afterwards. 'You only have to look at the margins by which they win the championship in Scotland to realise that Rangers are a different class to the rest of the teams,' he said. 'They have a lot of good players, and in Brian Laudrup and Paul Gascoigne two of the best in Europe, so it is no wonder that Raith Rovers lost. I saw enough to confirm the opinion I had formed from watching videos of them that Raith deserve our respect.'

The third match against the Old Firm was a controversial 2-1 loss after extra time to Celtic in the League Cup at Parkhead. It was notable for a truly magnificent Tony Rougier free kick and a notorious incident as the match drifted towards penalties, when Rovers put the ball out to allow treatment to one of the Celtic players who was down injured and the hosts failed to return the ball in the usual sporting manner. 'We pushed them that night,' recalls Stevie Crawford. 'Then there was an incident in that game where we put the ball out for a throw-in, and they never gave us it back and it led to a goal. That was frustrating.'

Rougier's glorious free kick had earned him the man of the match award. The Trinidadian admits that he seemed to save his best performances for against the two Glasgow giants. 'I still have in my glass case the man of the match awards I got for Raith and most of them are for games against Celtic and Rangers!' he laughs. 'I was always excited to play Celtic and Rangers.'

As the ÍA match neared, there were injury worries over striker Ally Graham, defender Ronnie Coyle and midfielder Jim McInally. The latter had been suffering from a virus and had lost half a stone, so was extremely doubtful to feature. Nicholl used McInally's illness to raise the possibility of playing himself in midfield for the European tie, a prospect that dominated the headlines for the days before the game. Whether he was truly considering playing or it was simply a tactic to distract the media, it helped take the focus of his players prior to the match. In the end, Davie Kirkwood fulfilled McInally's role.

One player determined to feature was Shaun Dennis. He had been suffering from back trouble and was told that he may need an operation, but there was no way that he was going to miss out on a rare European night. 'I had a scan on the base of my spine last week,' said Dennis in the build-up to the game. 'The specialist told me that the next time the disc is damaged I'll have to have an operation. I was in a bit of pain after the cup tie against Celtic but was OK at Ibrox on Saturday. I've been told I won't make the problem any worse by playing on, so that's what I intend to do. A good result against Akranes will be the best painkiller.'

Dennis was not the type of player to let a little pain distract him. The uncompromising defender had been with the club since the days of Frank Connor. He had made his debut in 1988 in a pre-season friendly against a Graeme Souness-led Rangers side, packed with English internationals. 'I was going to Tenerife,' recounts Dennis. 'I had a holiday booked. Wee Frank said to me, "If you cancel your holiday to Tenerife, I will give you a game against Rangers." So, I sold the holiday to my pal and played against Rangers on the Saturday.'

Early performances cemented his place in the first team and quickly established him as a fan favourite with his ability to win balls in his trademark unforgiving manner, a skill he'd learned from older team-mates. 'I was playing with Bobby Glennie, Cammy Fraser and Brasher [Alex Brash],' he says. 'Those three would put their head where you wouldn't park your car! I just learned from them. They used to say to me, "Don't try and nick the ball, just take everything." You would come up against strikers that were fast in those days, but I was quite happy to be three yards behind a striker because it meant I always had the option of the slide tackle!

'When I first came into the team Frank Connor used to tell me that I could only take two touches. Any more, and I would be taken off. He used to say to me, "Ball. Man. Advertising boards. I don't care what order you take them in!"'

It was an approach to football that he passed on to others. 'I remember meeting Shaun for the first time,' recounts fellow centre-half Robbie Raeside. 'I was just a young lad, and we were playing East Stirling away in the reserves. I made a challenge in the game and the boy goes down injured. I went over to apologise. Shaun quickly took me aside and said, "Listen, if you kick someone, don't you dare go over and apologise. Go over and pick him up by the oxter hair and then he'll be really screaming!'"

Dennis was unbending, but he could also play. His ability earned him a call-up to the Scotland under-21 side managed by Craig Brown, the only part-time player among a squad of talented youngsters from Aberdeen, Dundee United and the Old Firm. 'I was working in Seafield at the time,' he explains. 'You would go through to training with the under-21s and all the other boys like Eoin Jess and Scott Booth, Alex Cleland, Ray McKinnon would be turning up in brand new cars and I was arriving in this battered old Escort. They would ask me if I'd been training that week and I'd tell them, "No, I have been down the pit!"'

'It was great to get away to different countries and you got paid for it. I got three caps. I think for being the best hamper carrier they had ever had because that is mostly what I did.'

Throughout Dennis's Rovers career, there would be rumours of a move away from Stark's Park, with Celtic, the team the young defender supported, frequently mentioned. There were also several trials down south. 'I went to Barnsley, I went to Swindon, and I went to Southampton,' he remembers. 'Jimmy and Chris Nicholl had played together in the Northern Ireland squad, so he sent me down to Southampton over Christmas and new year when I was suspended. That was when Alan Shearer was bursting on to the scene, and I played a practice game against him.

'He battered me! He scored against Man United the following week, so he obviously got a bit of confidence knocking me about! Southampton told Jimmy I was a bit soft and wouldn't make it, but that was based on playing against Shearer who went on to batter everybody.' Despite the speculation, Dennis remained at Rovers and became the beating heart of their defence.

Dennis would not be the only player taking to the field in the UEFA Cup while experiencing discomfort. Across in the ÍA camp, veteran midfielder Siggi Jónsson was also struggling. 'I get stiffness after games,' explained Jónsson. 'I imagine I'll be very sore after playing Raith, but it will be worth it if we can get a good result. This will be a much harder game than we get in Iceland, but we are hopeful our chances will still be alive for the return leg.'

ÍA held a full training session on the pitch at Stark's Park the night before the game. Around 100 of their supporters had travelled for the match and would be there to support their team the following evening. Back home in Iceland, excitement was building. 'It was being shown live on TV by the national broadcaster and that was almost unheard of,' recalls Akranes fan Brynjólfur Þór Guðmundsson. 'At that point, not many Icelanders flew abroad to see their team play and the story that I heard was that some supporters of Akranes who couldn't make it to Scotland collected the money and paid for the match to be broadcast!'

The anticipation and expectation among both sets of fans was high. 'There was a much bigger build-up in the media for the Akranes game,' reflects supporter Steve Wallace. 'The more you got to know about them then you definitely got the sense they were going to be better than Gøtu. They had brothers who had played for Feyenoord. We had no one in our side who had been at anyone like Feyenoord!'

'The atmosphere was definitely a step up from Gøtu,' agrees fellow fan Graeme Meldrum. 'The cameras were there to do proper coverage and it did feel as if something was building. It wasn't a case of, "We are going to beat these guys and go to the next round," it was more like the initial nervousness of being in Europe had gone and we were just enjoying it. Akranes were champions of Iceland, so you thought that these guys are going to be half decent, and so it transpired.'

The ground was virtually sold out, but with UEFA again imposing a reduced capacity, there wasn't the packed feel of the previous league game against Celtic. The arbitrary crowd restriction may have removed spectators, but it did not remove the atmosphere; the stadium was pulsating with expectation. 'It was brilliant to see all the Rovers fans in there,' says goalkeeper Scott Thomson. 'Those games in Europe we had that aspect of the whole ground being ours. We had fans on all sides, and that was a great incentive for the team.'

There was a slight delay to proceedings as ÍA officials questioned the height of the goalposts at one end of the ground. Stark's Park was infamous for the slope from the Beveridge Park end down towards where home supporters gathered, and it must have given the Icelanders a sense that the goalposts were non-regulation. A pair of ladders and a tape measure were quickly found to quash the objection.

The Rovers team took on a familiar shape at the back with Scott Thomson in goal behind a defensive line of Stephen McAnespie, Shaun Dennis, Davie Sinclair and Julian Broddle. Colin Cameron, Davie Kirkwood and Danny Lennon formed the core of the team, with an attacking line-up of Stevie Crawford and two wingers in the shape of Tony Rougier and Barry Wilson. There would be no place in the starting line-up for Ally Graham, Jason Dair or Ronnie Coyle, but they would be available from the bench along with the manager himself and substitute goalkeeper Les Fridge. There was no place in the squad for midfielder Alex Taylor, who had featured in the Faroe Islands. 'You are disappointed of course,' reflects Taylor. 'But I didn't take it personally. It was a fair enough decision.'

It was a brave selection that hinted at a strategy of taking the game to ÍA. Nicholl's message to his team immediately before the game was upbeat. 'Jimmy was great at helping us relax,' says Tony Rougier. 'He would say, "What do we have to lose? We already have the success of getting here and now it is just the trimmings around it. The horn blowing and the trumpets." His message to us was just go and enjoy it. Go out there and express yourself.'

14

A Special Night

IF MANY in the Raith side were unaware of the Gunnlaugsson brothers' talent before the start of the first leg against ÍA at Stark's Park on 12 September, it didn't take long for them to appreciate their ability once the game had kicked off. They caused the Rovers defence problems straight from the first whistle with their quick, skilful, one-touch triangle play. 'The Gunnlaugsson twins were a real handful,' reflects Jimmy Nicholl. 'Arnar Gunnlaugsson, the twin with the long hair and great left foot, was especially good. Sinky [Davie Sinclair] and Shaun [Dennis] had their work cut out that evening.'

The Raith supporters watching immediately grew concerned as they witnessed the speed and movement of the ÍA side in those opening exchanges. 'When you saw their pace and skill,' recalls Graeme Meldrum, 'it felt like, "These guys are going to score here."'

ÍA were a dynamic team and their attacking intent straight from the kick-off caught Raith by surprise. The home side needed something to settle them down and it arrived on 13 minutes when Danny Lennon opened the scoring. Stevie Crawford picked up the ball deep and laid it off to Stephen McAnespie on the edge of the box; the young right-back rolled a pass invitingly on to Lennon's right foot, and he thumped in a low drive to the bottom corner of the net. It had taken a slight deflection on its way to goal, but it gave Rovers a crucial lead.

The goal appeared to calm Rovers' nerves and they began to create chances in an attempt to extend their lead. A Shaun Dennis header was tipped over the bar, then Barry Wilson struck a vicious 25-yard drive which stung the hands of the goalkeeper and fell to Tony Rougier, but his attempt to shoot was blocked. It would be the last contribution of the Trinidadian as after half an hour he was forced off with injury, to be replaced by Jason Dair. The game was incredibly open with no caution on display with both sides consistently attacking their opponents and trying to score. 'It was like a boxing match,' recalls Stevie Crawford. 'We were really tested that night. They put a lot of pressure on our boys at the back.'

The star siblings continued to cause the Raith defence problems, but they began to adapt to deny them the room they needed. 'You just have to give yourself a bit more space when you come up against guys that quick,' explains Julian Broddle. 'Give yourself more space and try and close them down. Hopefully you have the space to slide in and make a challenge or they will pass away from you to somebody else rather than try and take you on.'

'I've played against Brian Laudrup,' says Davie Sinclair. 'But that boy [Bjarki Gunnlaugsson] had much quicker feet and was trickier in tight situations. You couldn't afford to get too close. Even when you think you had got to him, he'd do something to get away.'

Rovers were also doing their fair share of attacking and on 34 minutes there were claims for a penalty. Substitute

Jason Dair showed tremendous skill to skip past three ÍA defender, inside the box and when he was halted by Siggi Jónsson, the ball appeared to strike the arm of Palmi Haraldsson. Despite howls from the crowd and appeals from the Raith players, the referee waved away the claim. A minute later Dair was involved again, almost claiming a wonder goal with an audacious chipped shot on the volley, but the ball skimmed agonisingly over the bar.

Jimmy Nicholl had every reason to be pleased with how the game was progressing, but with his mind drifting to his half-time team talk, ÍA broke forward and scored. Ólafur Þórðarson, their lorry-driving skipper, pressurised Dennis and when the ball broke off the defender and moved perfectly into his path, the striker gratefully rolled it past Scott Thomson. The equaliser shocked Rovers and silenced the crowd.

It was a frustrating goal to concede at a frustrating time. 'When they scored that night, you were immediately thinking, "This is not good,"' reflects journalist Scott Davie. 'You thought that Rovers might have to go over to Iceland and nick a goal and that would be difficult. You don't know what the conditions will be like when you go over there or what the pitch will be like, and they hadn't played well over in the Faroe Islands. If you haven't played well in the away leg in the Faroe Islands, then what was it going to be like in Iceland?'

The players understood the significance of conceding an away goal. It was something that they had talked about in the run up to the game. Jimmy Nicholl had played in Europe numerous times throughout his career and understood the psychological impact conceding an away goal can have on a team. 'We had spoken about trying to keep a clean sheet and what to do if we did concede,' says Stevie Crawford. 'They score and what do you do? We were conscious of that and our inexperience of being able to handle the emotions of that. I don't think we would have prepared for that had Jimmy not had all his experience in Europe.'

Half-time arrived and Rovers needed to get in, recharge and regroup. 'Losing that goal on the stroke of half-time was a real kick in the teeth,' says Nicholl. 'We were sitting in the dressing room and all we could hear was the Akranes players shouting as they were full of themselves after scoring. I had to keep the boys' heads up by reminding them that there was still a long way to go. I told the players not to worry because if they got stuck in it could still finish 3-1 or 4-1. I wanted them to go out and battle and show our supporters that we weren't going to get down about the situation.'

At the restart, ÍA were buoyed by their equaliser and looked like they had found an extra two yards of pace. On 58 minutes, there was a heart-stopping moment for the Rovers support when Arnar Gunnlaugsson sprinted clear down the left and crossed for Bjarki to stroke the ball into the net. To the huge relief for everyone of a Raith persuasion, the linesman raised his flag to indicate that Bjarki had been offside. It was an extremely tight call, but the game remained level.

On the hour mark, Nicholl decided to make a change in an attempt to shift the momentum of the match, with Ally Graham replacing Stevie Crawford up front. 'In the end I had to change the way we were playing,' explains Nicholl. 'It wasn't as effective as I'd hoped and putting big Ally Graham on thankfully worked. The great thing about Ally is that not only did he make it hard for opposing defenders, but he also eased the pressure on ours too and gave the wingers the option of just hanging balls up for him to flick on.'

Graham made an immediate impact, putting the ÍA defence under pressure and presenting them with a different challenge. Rovers started to put the visitors on the back foot. The two teams continued to go at each other fearlessly, but the physicality of Graham started to turn the tie in the favour of the home side. 'Sending Ally on made the difference,' reflects Nicholl. 'We had to mix it up. It wasn't pretty but it was effective.'

Rovers re-established a lead after 66 minutes when Lennon popped up on the edge of the box to blast home a low drive which nestled just inside the right post. The atmosphere in Stark's Park immediately energised and, with darkness having fallen, it began to feel like a proper European night. Rovers were pushing forward at every opportunity in search of a bigger lead to take to Iceland, but their opponents almost levelled after 77 minutes when Bjarki Gunnlaugsson ran in on goal unchallenged and faced a one-on-one with Scott Thomson. The goalkeeper stood his ground brilliantly and managed to block the shot, deflecting the ball to safety. It was a crucial save and two minutes later Rovers added the third goal that they desperately craved.

Barry Wilson is someone who had been familiar with Stark's Park from a young age. His father, Bobby, had managed Raith in the early 1980s and as a boy he had gone along to support the team. His own move to Kirkcaldy came after a fortuitous pairing of his team Ross County with Rovers in the first round of the 1994 League Cup. 'We won the match easily,' recounts Nicholl. 'But Barry tore us apart down the wing. If County had any players capable of taking advantage of his services, we could very well have been beaten. I decided right away to sign him because I liked his direct style.'

Wilson's pace and directness impressed Nicholl and had also attracted the interest of Southampton and Hearts earlier in his career. Neither club had been willing to take a chance on the young winger, so he was delighted to make the move to Kirkcaldy. He moved in with family in Leven and began travelling in to training with Shaun Dennis and Stephen McAnespie. It wouldn't be long before Nicholl handed him his first start for the club in a league game against Dunfermline. 'I had scored two goals after about 15 minutes,' recalls Wilson. 'I thought, "Here we go," but we got battered 5-2! I remember after the game Jimmy was slaughtering the players but said, "Everyone except Willo." That was what he used to call me. I was buzzing. That eased me in and made me think I could handle it.'

Wilson immediately settled in to the squad and the unique atmosphere in Kirkcaldy. 'There was quite a young dressing room,' he explains. 'Mickey [Colin Cameron] was the same age as me, and we were a year or so older than Jason [Dair] or Stevie [Crawford]. Stevie Mac [McAnespie] and wee Danny [Lennon] were probably the same age as me as well. Then you had the more senior ones like Coylie [Ronnie Coyle], Daz [Gordon Dalziel] and Ally Graham. It was pretty wild, and it was pretty mad, but it was a lot of fun.'

His team-mates instantly recognised that Wilson was an asset to the squad. 'Barry came in and fitted in right away,' recalls Stevie Crawford. 'He was brilliant in the dressing room and just clicked with the boys right away. A great boy and a great player. Barry was a wide player and had goals in him. He was absolutely rapid and always willing to run in behind and stretch the game.'

It was this ability to stretch that game that directly contributed to Rovers' third goal against ÍA. Having made an attacking run, Colin Cameron slipped him in to run past the opposing defender. Wilson showed composure and raised the ball over the advancing goalkeeper and into the net. The Stark's Park crowd erupted, knowing that the goal added that little extra bit of breathing space that could prove crucial in the second leg.

If Wilson's goal was memorable, his celebration was less so. He had injured his wrist in the weeks before the match and mindful of exacerbating the injury, he did a slightly awkward roll. 'Every time Barry came to Stark's Park as assistant with Inverness,' says supporter John Greer, 'I would say to him, "Barry, come and show me where you did your roly-poly."'

'The celebration was dreadful to be fair,' admits Wilson.

After the goal, Graham grabbed the winger and encouraged him to walk quickly back to the centre circle just in case the linesman had been tempted to flag for offside, but there was never any danger of that as he had timed his run perfectly. Wilson reflects back on that night with a smile. 'Is mine still the last UEFA Cup goal at Stark's?' he asks knowingly. 'I think it might be.'

Even at the time, the addition of a third goal felt significant. There was relief among the players that they had weathered the storm and managed to come away with a two-goal lead against difficult opponents. 'Thinking back on it now,' reflects Cameron, 'that was the biggest tie that we had in the whole competition. Barry's goal gave us that extra cushion going into the second leg. We knew that even if we conceded in Iceland we wouldn't panic as we would still be ahead in the tie.'

'I think we probably just edged it,' Crawford says of the game. 'But it was a tough, tough match. I think the fans appreciated that we were up against good players that night and thought, "This could go the wrong way here." In the second half we were shooting up towards the Beveridge Park end with the Rovers fans there and I think subconsciously that let us know that they were right behind us and helped us over the line. The fans really played their part that night.'

The atmosphere throughout the match had been fantastic. 'That was one of the best atmospheres I ever tasted at Stark's Park,' recalls Danny Lennon. 'The crowd was electric.'

'It was just brilliant,' agrees supporter Steve Wallace. 'Everything in the second 45 minutes just started to feel brilliant. We got the goals and a good lead which was absolutely fantastic. It felt like a proper cup tie, and we even got decent highlights on the TV that night. It felt like proper European football. It was one of those special nights at Stark's Park.'

For Jimmy Nicholl, there remains a lingering frustration that he underestimated the strength of ÍA. 'The twins seemed to have an understanding,' he reflects. 'Not knowing their threat was my downfall. The runs that the long-haired one was making, in between the full-backs, little darting runs caught us out. We were fortunate to win 3-1 and I knew that it wasn't game over.'

The match had been an enthralling spectacle. Reporter Gordon Simpson labelled it a 'tense sweaty affair', and the newspapers played on the Icelandic theme when crafting their headlines. 'Lucky geysers' wrote the *Daily Record*, following it up with 'Ice One Dan' in reference to midfielder Lennon's brace. 'Ice 'n easy for Danny' wrote *The Star*, continuing the theme. 'Raithing Certs' said *The Sun*, but anyone involved with Rovers knew that progressing from the tie was anything but a foregone conclusion.

The away goal scored by ÍA loomed large and was on the minds of players and fans alike. 'We need to score over there just to kill the tie off,' said captain Shaun Dennis after the game. 'They were very nippy up front, and their number nine was outstanding. I actually think the result flattered us tonight because it wasn't a good performance. We'll need to stay tight over there and probably put one in to make sure.'

If the squad and support were happy with the two-goal win, the opposite was true in the ÍA camp. There had been high expectations going into the fixture and to leave Scotland defeated was a blow. 'I was distraught after the first game,' recalls supporter Brynjólfur Þór Guðmundsson. 'I thought we should never have lost 3-1. We had a chance to even it up to 2-2, but then Raith Rovers finished it with the third goal. That was such a shock for us.'

Ólafur Þórðarson, the ÍA captain and Icelandic international midfielder, expressed his frustration: 'I was disappointed with the result because although they were much better than us for the first 20 minutes, we came into the game after that. Raith Rovers are very difficult to play against. They are strong physically and never stop running, but we can win 2-0 at home, which would be enough to take us through.'

It was a theme picked up on by team-mate and tormentor Arnar Gunnlaugsson. 'I was impressed with the standards set by Raith,' he said. 'Our mistakes allowed them in when we had the game under control. It's only half-time and we have a good record at home. Our away goal will prove important and I'm confident we can score twice in the return.'

There would be an interesting postscript to the trip to Kirkcaldy for ÍA. 'There was a story that emerged just the year before last when a guy published a history of football in Akranes,' explains Brynjólfur Þór Guðmundsson. 'It was that when the chairman of ÍA was paying the hotel bills in Scotland, he got the phone records of our coach at the time, Logi Ólafsson, and realised he had been on the phone all the time to the chairman of the Icelandic Football Association. They were telling him that they were going to hire him as the next national team manager. In this book, the Akranes chairman at the time said, "I should have just fired him on the spot!"'

Ólafsson was announced as the next Icelandic national team manager a day or two after the loss to Raith but stated his intention to finish the season with ÍA. He stressed that his mind would be completely on his club 'well into the winter', the implication being that he expected his team to advance to the next round.

'We still believed,' says Brynjólfur.

15

Welcome to Iceland

THE DAY before the second leg in Iceland, Rovers supporter Graeme Meldrum had gone to Carlton Bakery in Kirkcaldy. The following morning, with his two sausage rolls and two fudge doughnuts safely stored in his bag, along with some cans of beer and a warm jumper, he was all set for ÍA away. As a student, Graeme had decided not to travel to the Faroe Islands to save money for future rounds in the UEFA Cup, but there was no way that he was missing out on the trip to Iceland.

Graeme had been introduced to Rovers by his father Stuart, with family stories that as a toddler he would cry as his dad and older brother Derek left to go to a game on Saturday. His father had gone to watch Rovers through the 50s with his own father, so was keen to introduce his two sons to the pleasure of following the club. Graeme's early memories of standing on the terracing at Stark's Park are extremely fond ones, under the shed listening wide-eyed to the swearing and shouting. 'There was a game in the 1980s,' says Graeme, 'when Donald Urquhart hit a shot into the crowd, and it knocked me flying. There was a big ball patch on my jacket, and I wouldn't let my mum wash it for weeks.'

His dad fostered in him a love for both Raith and football as a whole. 'My dad was a great one for taking us to all sorts of football,' recalls Graeme. 'Midweeks in the 80s, he would take us up to Dundee United saying, "You'll never see European football with the Rovers son, so we're going to see United." Then in the 1990s he took us to the Skol [League] Cup Final between Hibernian and Dunfermline. "You'll never see a Fife team in a cup final, son."'

Graeme smiles at the thought of how wrong his father would be proved by Jimmy Nicholl's side. The memories they shared together of watching that glorious period in the club's history remains incredibly special, more so since his father passed away. After his loss, Graeme had initially questioned whether he could continue to attend games. 'I said to my wife that I couldn't go back after my dad died,' he recounts. 'Within three days I had Eric Drysdale on the phone telling me I had won the Rovers lottery. He said, "We want to do the presentation before the game on Saturday, are you coming?" I don't believe in that sort of thing, but if there was ever a sign to say, "Just go back," that was it. So, that was me, back at the Rovers. Absolutely ridiculous.'

Graeme now lives in Ayr, but being exiled in the south-west of Scotland has not dampened his enthusiasm for Rovers. He is proud that his connection to his hometown club remains as strong as ever. 'My dad was a Rovers fan, my grandad was a Rovers fan, and my great, great grandfather was a Rovers supporter,' he says proudly. 'There is a bit of legacy there. It just connects you. When you walk into Stark's Park you just get that feeling of, "I belong here."'

One supporter also making the trip to Iceland, but who could not claim to be from a long-established Rovers family, was Glaswegian Jim Clark. His route to Stark's Park took a slightly more circuitous path. 'I was born within 200 yards of Celtic Park,' says Jim. 'My grandmother's house was where the Emirates stadium now sits. I went to school at St Michaels, right next door to the football stadium. It would have been easy for me just to fall into being a mad Celtic fan from the East End of Glasgow.'

For the first part of his life that was the path that Jim was on. It would take a chance meeting with Ronnie Coyle to alter his course. 'I met Ronnie on my first day at university in 1981,' he recalls. 'We were both working-class boys a little bit out of our depth at university among all these middle-class types. I looked at him and thought I kind of recognised him and he asked me if I would help him out as he was going to miss the first week of classes as he was away with football. He said, "Don't tell anybody, I don't want anyone to know who I am or this Celtic connection, I just want to be a student." That was the beginning of our friendship.'

The two students would go on to become close friends, with Jim following Coyle's career from that day on as the defender moved from Celtic to Middlesbrough, then on to Rochdale. It was there that Coyle's former coach at Celtic, Frank Connor, found him, offering him a move back north to join Raith Rovers. 'Frank came in for him at the perfect time,' explains Jim. 'Ronnie wanted to come back up the road and get married. That was the first time in his career he went part-time. It was a big, big move for him. He was happy at Rochdale, but Frank was his mentor and once he came up to Stark's Park, he discovered that there were a lot of boys in the dressing room that he really got on with.

'I think part of Ronnie's role at first was to help develop a young Shaun Dennis. Frank thought that Ronnie and Shaun could work together. The experienced head and the big raw laddie who had all the talent but might throw it away. I think Frank half thought that's what Ronnie had done, and he was determined that it wouldn't happen with Shaun.'

Coyle would go on to become a stalwart of the team as Rovers progressed through the divisions. Throughout that period, Jim travelled up to Kirkcaldy to watch his friend play. In doing so, his affection for Rovers grew and it was not long before he took the decision to give up his Celtic season ticket. 'I know they say in football that you should never change your club,' says Jim. 'I kind of get that, but in the end, it was an easy decision to make. When you were at Rovers games on a Saturday, you felt really comfortable. You enjoyed it, you had a laugh and you felt that winning wasn't everything. At Celtic, winning was everything and if you didn't win it was dreadful. I loved Ronnie's company and then you met people like Jock [McStay] and Peter [Hetherston]. Coming up to Stark's Park, arriving at half one and going into the 200 Club for a few pints, it was just great fun.

'The night after Rovers won the league against Dumbarton and took over Kirkcaldy was one of the greatest nights of my life. I had travelled up with the players and was ready to just go home after it. Peter Hetherston grabbed me and said, "You're with us the night," and I started to go round the town with the players. We were in the Penny Farthing, and somebody was speaking to the players, looked at me and said, "Who is he?" Quick as a flash Peter said, "That's Jim. He signed in the close-season, done his knee in and hasn't been able to play. He's just one of the boys." I was thinner back then so could just about pass for a football player who was down on his luck, but that just summed up what that group of guys was like.' Three years on, he was preparing to board a plane for what would prove to be one of the most unforgettable away trips in Rovers' history.

Dennis O'Connell had again organised a charter flight to take supporters up to Iceland for the day. The plan was to depart Glasgow Airport early in the morning, bus supporters to the game in Akranes and then fly back that night. Around 150 fans had signed up for the flight, along with a few journalists looking for a way to get to the match, including Richard Gordon and Chic Young for the BBC.

There was excitement as the fans began their journey in the early hours of the morning. 'As the bus pulled out of Kirkcaldy bus station,' recalls Graeme Meldrum, 'you could just hear the sound of beer cans being opened. The only things we knew about Iceland was it was cold; Björk is from there and beer is expensive. So, when a lot of the guys got to duty free in Glasgow Airport, they stocked up for the trip. Then it was just 24 hours of having a laugh, being with your pals, drinking and Rovers.'

'We had met up at Pinkertons in Glenrothes beforehand,' says fellow supporter Gavin Quinn. 'We had a few drinks and then got on a minibus to Glasgow. We got to Glasgow Airport and Dennis [O'Connell] was, "Oh, shit, I've forgot my passport!" He's the organiser of the whole trip and he's the one who forgets his passport!'

A quick call back to his pub in Glenrothes led to a fax of his passport being sent through to the airline, meaning that O'Connell could join the flight. 'I think his passport was brought over to Glasgow and came up on a cargo plane later in the day so that he could make it home,' laughs fellow traveller John Greer.

The fans boarded their early morning Icelandair flight, with most stopping at the plane steps to capture a photograph of the start of their adventure. Excitement levels were high, despite the early hour. 'The whole plane was buzzing with excitement,' says Graeme Meldrum. 'You are on a flight heading to Iceland and you are sitting next to someone you stood next to when the Rovers were getting beat by the likes of Stenhousemuir and Stranraer. It was just surreal.'

The surrealness of the trip continued on arrival at Keflavík Airport. Fans were put on to buses for the short journey into Reykjavík. Before being dropped off in the capital, they were treated to a slightly bizarre tour. First stop was Perlan, a cluster of hot water tanks situated at the top of the Öskjuhlíð hill. It seemed closed, but there was at least an observation deck offering a panoramic view over Reykjavík. Next up was Laugardalslaug, a public thermal baths and swimming pool complex. The bemused supporters were led into a concrete stand that would not have looked out of place at a Scottish lower-league ground to be greeted by the sight of some elderly residents of Reykjavík in the middle of their morning swim. If they were confused, it was matched by the swimmers at the sight of over 100 football fans from Fife observing their morning exercise routine. One elderly gentleman decided to entertain the crowd with a series of impromptu star jumps, resulting in a chorus of laughter and cheers. The tour over, fans were dropped in the centre of the capital for a few hours to entertain themselves before the journey out to Akranes. 'It was like a school trip,' says John Greer. 'We were left to our own devices, and everybody just scattered everywhere in different directions. There were guys who came back at the end who had been to some restaurant and been served shark.'

'It was idiots abroad,' laughs Graeme Meldrum. 'I don't mean that in a disrespectful sense. It was just not really understanding where we were, where we were going, or what we were going into. We found what we thought were goalposts in the centre of Reykjavík. I was sent away to a sports shop to get a football and all I could find was a handball. So, we ended up playing 15-a-side in Reykjavík high street with a handball against what we thought were goalposts. It was only later that I discovered that it was actually some historic sculpture.'

Several supporters had attempted to have a look around the town but were soon forced indoors to shelter from the biting cold. Others immediately found a pub, put up a large Rovers flag in the window and took it over. It was not long before local TV news turned up to interview the Scottish visitors. Their free time in Reykjavík over, the fans boarded the bus for the long, scenic drive around the fjord towards Akranes.

It was not just the supporters who embraced the circular trip around the fjord. 'We were driving on the team bus through Iceland,' says Robbie Raeside. 'It was before mobile phones and Barry Wilson had this camera, and he is taking pictures through the windows as we drive past places. Big Shaun was like, "Barry, what are you doing?" Barry says, "I am taking pictures. I might never get back to Iceland again." It was like we were tourists.'

On arrival, the travelling fans were greeted by Akranesvöllur, a small, compact stadium, located adjacent to the bay. On one side was a small, functional stand and opposite was a large grass bank accommodating most of the home supporters. The sight of the Akranes faithful standing on a grass slope, with some sitting on blankets having brought picnics, made many visitors question exactly why the Stark's Park capacity had been cut for the home leg.

The Rovers fans were in high spirits. 'When we arrived at the ground on the bus, the excitement was amazing,' recalls John Greer. 'I'm not a big drinker, but I'd had a couple of beers and I remember screaming and shouting, because I was so pumped up for it.'

'I remember we were all getting our photographs taken with our arms round the police and there was a guy who had taken in a full bottle of Grouse Whisky,' adds Kenny Smith. 'He was standing next to the police with this bottle of whisky in his hand and they weren't even bothered. They just seemed to be embracing it.'

It had already been a fantastic trip. Now there was the small matter of Rovers holding on to their two-goal lead.

16

Two Sweepers

THE RAITH squad had arrived in Iceland in confident mood, determined to enjoy the trip, although their preparations had been disrupted by injury concerns. Tony Rougier was struggling with a knee problem, Stephen McAnespie was nursing a calf injury and Ally Graham had been carried off in a win over Partick Thistle. There had also been doubt over Julian Broddle, who the club had initially thought was suspended after picking up two bookings in the previous round. It turned out that the Welsh referee in the Faroe Island had not officially registered his second booking, so the defender was free to play.

ÍA had warmed up for the game by thrashing IPV 5-1 in their final league match. Ominously, all five goals had come from the Gunnlaugsson brothers, with Arnar netting a hat-trick. For a side that needed goals to force their way back into the tie, it was the perfect preparation. Jimmy Nicholl was acutely aware of their threat and already formulating a defensive plan to stop them, even if his outward demeanour suggested otherwise. 'Nicholl was very relaxed and cracking jokes with everybody and talking things up,' recalls journalist Scott Davie, who travelled across on the same flight as the team. 'The pre-match stuff was typical Jimmy, "Yes, we are going to go for the away goal, have a go and make sure we score. We can hit them on the counter-attack." It was all absolutely positive stuff about what they were going to do.'

The Rovers squad knew that this would be a more difficult challenge than they had faced in the previous round against Gøtu Ítróttarfelag. They only had a two-goal lead to take into the second match and had conceded an away goal. 'To have lost a goal at home,' says Danny Lennon, 'we knew that we still had a hell of a lot of work to do over in Akranes and this was going to be a real test of our character.'

'We were in a good place,' says Barry Wilson. 'But we knew also that they were a good side. We knew that we would have to be at it when we went up there. It wasn't like the last round where we were 4-0 up, this was going to be tough. Although at that point we probably didn't realise how tough.'

Wilson would be taken aside before the match and informed that he would not be starting. It was a disappointment having played such a crucial role in the first leg, but when the young winger saw the formation that Nicholl intended to play, he understood. Thirty years later, Nicholl borrows a pen and attempts to explain the system on a hotel napkin. 'Years ago,' he starts as he draws the setup, 'Terry Venables had the Christmas tree. My Christmas tree was just a wee bit lop-sided.'

Although he had expressed to the press his side's intention to attack, his sole focus was on stopping the threat of the Gunnlaugsson siblings. He had seen how they had tormented his defence in the first leg and his priority was to curtail their threat. 'We went with a flat back four and two sweepers behind,' explains Nicholl. 'I hadn't told anyone, and we never worked on the formation. I sat with Martin Harvey the night before and said, "Thinking back to the last game, both Gunnlaugsson twins were darting between our centre-backs and full-backs, causing us problems. If we deny them that space, we could stop them."

'Arnar Gunnlaugsson was making darting runs. So, I set it up so that it would make it difficult to play the ball into his feet and even if they did and he turns the defender, then he sees the sweeper behind. He has nowhere to go. That was my idea. I just wanted to nullify the spaces and give them nowhere to go.'

It can best be described as a 6-3-1, but it was the inclusion of the two sweepers behind the back four that made it unusual. 'We normally played with two attacking full-backs with me and Jules going down the outside,' says Stephen McAnespie. 'We worked on that during the week, but I ended up playing centre-back with Sinky [Sinclair] with Shaun [Dennis] and Ronnie [Coyle] playing sweeper behind us. We just ended up man-marking the two brothers and that was it. The thinking was that if they don't touch the ball then we are good.'

'I know it was a weird formation,' says Julian Broddle. 'But for me, I thought at first, "The more defenders the better!" I thought it would make my life a bit easier. That's not quite how it worked out though.'

Nicholl's assistant Martin Harvey was unconvinced. 'I showed it to Harv,' says Nicholl, 'and he said to me, "There is no way we are going to be able to get out with that formation, Jimmy." I told him we would trust the one up top to hold the ball up for us. We hadn't worked on it and in the end, I was over-cautious. Stevie Crawford was just up there on his own and there was just waves of attack.'

'It was a system that not even [José] Mourinho has tried yet,' laughs Shaun Dennis. 'It was like *Keystone Cops* in the 18-yard box. We were all bumping into each other. We never got out of our own half. Every time we got the ball up, they just came straight back with it.'

When asked today whether he would repeat the formation, he laughs. 'No, no never,' Nicholl replies. 'At the very least I would go 5-3-2!'

A crowd of 4,000 had turned up and in the dazzling afternoon sun, the Dutch referee signalled the start of the match which would feel like one of the longest in history by the time the final whistle came. 'It turned into the siege of Akranes,' says Scott Davie. The immediate impact of Nicholl's defensive formation was apparent, even through the lens of an alcoholic haze for some. 'It took us a while to work out what we were actually doing,' recalls supporter Graeme Meldrum. 'There seemed to be no focal point up front. There seemed to be six at the back with two sweepers. It was very bizarre.'

ÍA came out with the clear intention of immediately getting back into the tie and their attacking intent was helped by the defensive formation of their opponents. As early as the fifth minute, Alexander Högnason fired a 20-yard shot over the top. A minute later, Ólafur Þórðarson was presented with a chance by Bjarki Gunnlaugsson and only a late challenge by Shaun Dennis blocked the shot before it reached Scott Thomson. On 12 minutes, Arnar Gunnlaugsson was left in the perfect position to meet a cross after Bjarki Gunnlaugsson had skipped past three men in midfield. Luckily for Rovers, he flashed his header wide. It had been a torrid start to the match for the away side. 'Jimmy had told us how it was going to be before the game,' says Thomson. 'He said, "We are going to take care of these two twins." Yes, they were the threat, but then that forgot about the other nine players in their team!'

ÍA were dominating possession and Rovers were struggling to get forward or even hold on to possession when they did get the ball in advanced areas. Stevie Crawford, playing in theory as the lone striker, effectively became the first line of defence. 'That night Jimmy said to me, "Try and hold up as many balls as you can, win as many free kicks as you can and just run with it. And if you run out of legs, I'll make the change,"' he recalls. 'If we had got a chance to go forward in that first half, then it may have given us a wee breather, but we just didn't.'

ÍA continued to threaten the Rovers goal. Bjarki Gunnlaugsson hit a wonderful deep cross from the right which found Haraldur Ingólfsson steaming into the danger area unmarked, but the midfielder poked the ball wide on the volley from 15 yards. Thomson was then almost caught out by a short Broddle throw-in and had to race to kick clear as Arnar Gunnlaugsson pressed. Minutes later, Ólafur Adolfsson worked his way into a good position inside the box but could only manage a tame header into the arms of Thomson.

As half-time approached, Rovers had a rare opportunity to go forward and Stephen McAnespie came close with a superb free kick from 30 yards that was only inches over the bar. It would turn out to be the away side's only shot at goal the entire game. The ÍA response was immediate, with perhaps the most glaring miss of the match. Siggi Jónsson found space and blasted in a shot-come-cross which full-back Högnason somehow managed to touch wide of Thomson's left post from only two yards out. It was an astonishing miss and a huge relief. There was one last chance of the half when Palmi Haraldsson let fly with a cracking 20-yard strike which deflected off Davie Kirkwood and drifted wide. It had been a battering, but the Rovers goal remained intact, and they reached the half level.

Scott Davie was reporting on the game for several newspapers, and although he wasn't operating out of a hotel bedroom as he had been at Toftir Stadium, the setup was far from ideal. 'I had about four newspapers to do,' recalls Davie. 'In those days, there were no mobile phones, so you had to organise through BT International a phone line installed in the press box. They didn't actually have a press box in Akranes, just a clubhouse in one corner. The phones were installed in the clubhouse, but you couldn't see the pitch from it. So, you had to go out, watch the game and then run back into the clubhouse at half-time to use the phone.'

Despite the imbalance in possession, the mood among the Rovers support remained upbeat. ÍA had not scored, the two-goal lead was intact, and the party atmosphere continued, fuelled by the numerous bottles of duty free that were being passed around the away end. 'At half-time I think we thought, "We are doing all right here," recalls Jonathan Tippetts-Aylmer. 'I went round to mingle with the Akranes fans and there was a car with the boot open. I think that was the merchandise stall, so I bought an Akranes hat as a souvenir.'

Among the players there was little sense of panic or fear. 'It was a tough afternoon,' says Scott Thomson. 'We knew that right from the start of the game. They had a lot of pressure in the first half, but I didn't think they troubled us too much. I didn't have loads to do. There were a lot of corners and a lot of things into the box, but they didn't threaten us, and we still had a great chance.'

In the Rovers dressing room, things were calm. It had been a bruising half, but they were still halfway to achieving what they had come for. 'We were in a good situation,' reflects Jimmy Nicholl. 'I thought we had done well resisting their shots. My message was, "OK, get a clean sheet in the second half and we are there."'

17

Don't Panic

RAITH'S RESISTANCE lasted just six minutes into the second half: Haraldur Ingólfsson floated a corner into the box where it found an unmarked Alexander Högnason, who headed the ball back towards the far post where, lurking menacingly, was Arnar Gunnlaugsson. The striker dived towards the ball and forced it into the net from two yards; ÍA were right back in the tie.

The party-like mood among the Raith support had continued through half-time and into the early stages of the second half. They had been halfway through a chorus of 'We all dream of a team of Ronnie Coyles' when ÍA scored. Conceding a goal stopped the song in its tracks. Now, the situation felt perilous. 'It had been backs to the wall for the whole first half,' says supporter Gavin Quinn. 'Jimmy Nicholl with his ten defenders. I had never seen anything like that before. When they got their goal, we started to panic a wee bit.'

The fans had gone eerily silent after the goal, but those who had travelled quickly realised that they now needed to get behind their team like never before. 'Conceding that goal almost flicked a switch from having a party to sobriety,' says Steve Wallace, who was watching anxiously from the away stand. 'From then on in, it was just constant support and encouragement.' The shift in the support did not go unnoticed on the pitch. 'The noise the supporters were making changed,' recalls midfielder Colin Cameron. 'At the start, they were more on cloud nine probably thinking, "This is going to be like the last round. We are going to be able to enjoy ourselves," but when Akranes scored the fans really rallied and got behind us and were giving us that extra wee bit of support that we needed.'

If the goal had shocked the supporters, it had also unsettled the management team. Across on the sidelines, Jimmy Nicholl contemplated his next move. 'When you lose a goal five minutes after half-time it becomes very difficult,' he says. 'I was left wondering whether to change the system, but we couldn't do any more defensively, so all I could say to the players was, "Don't panic!"' The manager knew that it would be hard for his players to shift from such a defensive approach to an attacking one, and at 1-0 his side were still ahead in the tie. Rovers resumed the tactics that had brought them this far and tried to see out the final third of the match. 'At that point we couldn't change our mindset,' agrees defender Stephen McAnespie. 'We couldn't flick a switch. We had already set out our stall on how we were going to play.'

On the hour mark, Scott Thomson dropped an Ingólfsson corner, but McAnespie stepped in to clear. Two minutes later, McAnespie attempted a pass inside his own area but inadvertently pushed the ball into the path of Bjarki Gunnlaugsson who should have done better, but the forward shot over the bar from 20 yards. Ingólfsson then hit a hard, left-footed shot which whistled dangerously past the post. The pressure from the home side was becoming relentless.

ÍA seemed to have a shoot on sight mentality, and it felt like a second goal was inevitable. 'We even had Stevie Crawford back defending,' says Davie Kirkwood. 'You wouldn't have seen that if we were playing in Scotland, but we were in Europe, and it was what we had to do. It was all hands to the pump and defend, defend, defend.'

'After they scored, it was just like the Alamo,' agrees Scott Thomson. 'If we couldn't get out of our own half in the first half, we couldn't get out of our own box in the second half. It was awful. You just go into protection mode. For me it was, "Protect your goal. Protect your goal," and you do your damnedest to do that.'

If the fans in the Akranesvöllur were suffering, those back home who had not travelled were sharing their anguish as they listened to the match on the radio. Richard Gordon and Rovers player Alex Taylor were commentating on the match for the BBC. Taylor, who was injured, had been volunteered for the role. 'I just got told I was doing it,' explains Taylor. 'So, I watched the game sitting next to Richard Gordon for Radio Scotland. He was a lovely guy and he said, "Just say what you think, add your opinion." I'm not sure it would have made any sense what I said, especially in those last 20 minutes!'

As Taylor struggled to find the words to describe the one-sided match that was unfolding in front of him, sitting at home listening nervously was Shaughan McGuigan. Shaughan may now be a recognisable face as a regular on the BBC's highly successful *A View From the Terrace*, but in 1995 he was still at high school in Kirkcaldy. He had first become a Rovers fan in the mid-1980s. His grandad, a Celtic and

Rovers fan, had initially introduced him to both clubs, but it had been his local club that had captured his heart. He started supporting Rovers in Frank Connor's first season, 1986/87, when they were promoted out of the bottom tier and had no idea of the successful period they were about to enter. 'I think when you are young and you pick your team, or maybe the team picks you, I don't know,' says Shaughan. 'And your team are in the bottom tier of Scottish football then there are things that you know are probably never going to happen or you presume they are never going to happen. Never in a million years did I think they could win a trophy or get into Europe.'

As someone who was, in his own words, obsessed with European football, he never thought that Raith would have any chance of participating in a European competition, so when they qualified for the UEFA Cup his intention was to experience at least one away game. 'Looking back, when we won the cup final against Celtic,' says Shaughan, 'I was celebrating two things. I was celebrating the here and now of we'd just beaten Celtic, and won a cup, but also the fact of what was to come and that was to go and watch Raith Rovers in Europe. I was absolutely desperate to go to an away game because in my mind it felt like the ultimate. Imagine going to a Raith Rovers away game in Europe?'

Aged 17 with a paper round as his sole source of income, Shaughan knew that when European football arrived the following season, he would only have one opportunity to travel. His financial constraints resulted in a game of jeopardy with high stakes. As each round arrived, he had to decide whether or not to travel or wait for the prospect of Rovers advancing further. The preliminary round against Gøtu Ítróttarfelag had felt relatively risk-free. 'I looked at the preliminary round and saw who was involved,' he explains. 'I must admit I fancied our chances to get into the first round proper. When Gøtu came out, I was maybe a bit brazen, but I thought we would dispense with them fairly comfortably. When they came to Stark's Park and we won 4-0, it felt like we were a couple of levels above them.'

ÍA had presented a trickier decision, but Shaughan again decided to gamble on Rovers winning the tie. 'I looked at the other Icelandic teams that had been in Europe,' he continues. 'I kind of thought we would be OK and thought we would get through. I was comparing other results against Icelandic teams over the years, without knowing anything about Akranes.'

With a nervous laugh, he adds, 'As soon as the home leg started, I thought I might be in a wee bit of bother.'

Along with every other Rovers supporter, he had been taken aback by the quality of ÍA in the first match and started to question his decision not to travel. That fear increased as he listened to the radio commentary of the second leg on Radio Scotland. Even without pictures, the one-sided nature of the match was obvious and after ÍA took the lead, it became almost unbearable. 'I knew that if we went out, I would never get to see Rovers away in Europe,' says Shaughan. 'I was gutted because I thought it was a foregone conclusion that we would concede a second goal the way it was coming across on the radio. You could hear the Icelandic fans getting more and more boisterous. It sounded like we were getting pumped.

'I am always a bit of a chicken when it comes to big games. When Scotland were 1-0 up in France and it got to 83 minutes, I just switched it off. The Rovers game in Akranes came under that sort of category. I was, "Right, I'm switching this off and coming back in 25 minutes when the game is finished."'

McGuigan switched off his radio, went downstairs, waited for the final whistle and prepared himself for the pain of missing out on seeing his team play in Europe. He was not the only one suffering from a distance. 'I missed the return leg because I was injured,' says striker Ally Graham. 'I did my ankle ligaments at Partick Thistle and was done. I tried to recover, but I didn't make it so they decided that there was no point travelling, because I wouldn't even be on the bench or anything. I stayed at home and listened to it on the radio. It was nerve-wracking because you knew if they scored another we would be out. And you knew you were going to get a big gun next, so there was everything to lose.'

After 76 minutes, ÍA brought on Dejan Stojić, a 25-year-old Serbian centre-forward. He made an immediate impact, rising four minutes later to meet a deep cross by Högnason, but his header was cleared from danger by Stephen McAnespie. Scott Thomson then had a terrific one-handed diving save from a Þórðarson low drive, with McAnespie again clearing the danger. The pressure was becoming relentless and a second goal for the home side felt inevitable. 'They had our number,' says Graeme Meldrum. 'You knew that there was no way we were going to score. It felt like it was just waiting on them getting a second goal. I remember at one point the ball came in beside us and nobody was for throwing it back. The feeling was, "Well, if we keep it, then they can't play."'

If the game was proving a challenge for those watching, for the players on the pitch it was equally bruising. 'Shots were bouncing off us,' says Shaun Dennis. 'Then bouncing off another centre-half and going for corner after corner.'

'It was hard to maintain your focus because it was just constant wave after wave after wave of attack,' says Colin Cameron. 'Because we were all so compact and tight, we were just clearing it to the halfway line, and it was coming straight back. You know how players have got this GPS system nowadays, there would have just been a massive heat map from 18 yards to 30 yards out. Just all red from where we played in that second half. Distances would have been not very big, but there would be a hell of a lot of acceleration and deceleration!

'The game was more mentally draining than physical. Although you weren't covering big distances, you had to be switched on every single second. If you switched off, they would have caused us problems. It happened a few times, because it was impossible to go through a game without that, but once they did breach the back line, thankfully Thommo was on his game, and he managed to keep them at bay.'

Scott Thomson was having the game of his life in goal. 'Thommo was on fire,' says Stephen McAnespie. 'He was good every game, but that day he absolutely had a blinder. It was like he grew an extra set of arms, and he made saves that I have never seen anyone save.'

The goalkeeper reflects on his performance that night with both humility and pride. 'As a goalie, it is your job,' says Thomson. 'Once you make a couple of saves under pressure and you are dealing with stuff, then your confidence grows. I never felt like we were going to get beat. If I am being honest, that was one of my best games at Raith and one of the games that is up there in terms of my career.'

His defining moment of the game came after 82 minutes. ÍA were awarded a free kick just outside the box, and when Siggi Jónsson fired the ball towards goal it looked inevitable that the net would bulge. Thomson made a magnificent stop and was immediately surrounded by his team-mates in congratulations. It felt as good as a goal. 'If that goes in, then it is all over,' reflects Scott Davie. 'For Scott Thomson, that one has to go down with the penalty save in the cup final as the two most important saves he ever made for the club. The way he stood up that day was incredible.'

The final few minutes of the game ticked by, with the away supporters whistling frantically for the referee to bring it to a conclusion. 'I was just shot to bits,' says fan Kenny Smith. 'To this day it was one of the most backs-to-the-wall, nervous performances I have ever seen. I remember having a drink of this guy's whisky. Just anything to get me through those final few minutes.' The final whistle, when it came, was euphoric.

Football statistics today would tell you that it was a battering. Rovers had one shot on goal, no shots on target, hardly any attacks and minimal possession. If expected goals had existed, theirs would have been virtually zero, with the ÍA equivalent off the scale.

It had indeed been a siege. Yet, the only important statistic that mattered was the scoreline.

'It was weird,' says Stevie Crawford. 'We had lost a game of football, but it was absolute relief, immediate relief right away. Then it quickly turned into pride that you had actually got through. You go back to the previous season and the character shown in the Dunfermline and Hamilton games. That character came into us that Akranes game. We hadn't played free-flowing football, but we had dug in and got through.'

Back in Kirkcaldy, a despondent Shaughan McGuigan turned his radio back on expecting to hear that Rovers had been knocked out and that his one chance of following his side in Europe had evaporated. 'I switched the radio back on and the commentator was going daft,' he says. 'It was something about Scott Thomson running towards the Raith fans. I could not believe that they had actually done it.'

Thirty years later, for those who watched that game unfold in that glorious Icelandic sunshine, that sense of disbelief still remains.

18

The Airport

'I WENT back to watch the second game yesterday just to see all the chances we had,' says ÍA supporter Brynjólfur Þór Guðmundsson. 'It is still incomprehensible how we did not win.'

The defeat, and the manner in which it had arrived, was a huge blow for ÍA, who had clearly been the better side at the Akranesvöllur. 'When I look over all the games that ÍA has played in European competition,' reflects Brynjólfur, 'there are three games that I have been most disappointed by. One is when I was 11 years old back in 1986 and we lost 9-0 against Sporting Lisbon. The other two are those games against Raith Rovers.'

The fortunes of ÍA after defeat to Raith fluctuated. They retained their league championship for the fifth time in 1996, but by then the rest of Iceland was starting to grow weary of their dominance. They then began to struggle, going through three coaches in five years, the last of which was Ivan Golac who had won the Scottish Cup with Dundee United. Some of the players would later describe him as the worst coach they ever had, and midway through the season he was fired. By the end of 2000, ÍA was bankrupt, and a deal had to be struck between the bank and the town to keep the club going. 'Had we got through and met Bayern Munich our finances may have been very different,' muses Brynjólfur.

Bjarki Gunnlaugsson would go on to play for clubs in Germany, Norway, and England, but struggled with injuries in the late 90s and never really recovered the form of his early career. Arnar would move to play in French football before signing with Bolton Wanderers. He would also feature for Leicester City, Stoke City and Dundee United briefly before returning home to Iceland to see out his career. He progressed into coaching and is currently the manager of the Icelandic national side. To date, he hasn't drawn on the experience of that sunny afternoon in 1995 and replicated Jimmy Nicholl's two-sweeper approach in any Iceland fixtures.

Thirty years on, the hurt of the exit to Raith may have faded for Brynjólfur Þór Guðmundsson, but the name of the Kirkcaldy club still conjures up disappointment. 'I think you are the first Raith Rovers supporter I have ever spoken to,' he says during our Sunday morning Zoom call. 'And when I hear that team name, it doesn't fill me with joy. Let's just say that.

'This is your European adventure, right? Your one time in Europe? I love it when a team goes and has an adventure, goes far in a cup or makes it into Europe. I just wish you hadn't done it against us! Your European adventure is the biggest disappointment in ÍA's European history.'

If there remains sadness from an Icelandic perspective, back in 1995, there was elation for Rovers' players and supporters in Iceland. 'It was straight on the beer,' laughs midfielder Davie Kirkwood.

With the players back on the team bus, the party began. 'The duty free was bought on the way over,' says Robbie Raeside. 'It was bottles of vodka and everything, but it never got touched before the game. Nothing was opened. See when we got through the tie and got back on the bus, everything was getting opened. We knew we had a game at the weekend, but the celebration was brilliant. It was a major session, even from the ground to the airport.'

Raeside adds, 'I am not sure if we won on the Saturday after, that's something to research. 'Unsurprisingly, Rovers lost 3-0 to Aberdeen, but a party was the least they deserved for their heroic efforts. After the match, fans were also keen to get back to the airport to celebrate, but for one group the party would have to wait. 'We were on the bus with the supporters back to the airport,' explains journalist Scott Davie. 'There is usually a separate bus or minibus for the press, but what they had done is just put us on the same bus as the fans. The unlucky ones who were on the bus with us, instead of being able to get back to the airport and celebrate, they had to sit about for an hour until we had interviewed players and filed our copy. When we got on the bus, we got absolute dog's abuse!'

Jonathan Tippetts-Aylmer was one of the unlucky fans. 'When Chic Young came on the bus, he got absolute pelters,' says Jonathan. 'It wasn't that we wanted to kill the guy or anything, we just wanted to get back and celebrate.'

Once back at the airport, the party started right back up again. On arrival, the team were clapped into the terminal building by supporters and that night at Keflavík Airport went on to become a magical moment in the history of Raith Rovers Football Club. It may not be noted in any official record like the winning of a cup or the securing of a promotion, but for every single person associated with the club who was there, it is thought of just as fondly. 'The airport was just magical,' says John Greer. 'That was the greatest moment to be a Rovers supporter.'

The players and fans waited in the departure lounge together, elated from what had just been achieved. They chatted, laughed and drank together, knowing that they had just taken a step towards something significant. 'When you talk about the togetherness at the club back then, that night at the airport summed it up perfectly,' reflects Steve Wallace. 'The fans, the players, all together. You wouldn't get that with other clubs. The players were as high as anything. We were as high as anything. We were there together, and it was a special, special moment.'

'I remember chatting to Scott Thomson and Stephen McAnespie at the airport,' recalls Jonathan Tippetts-Aylmer with a smile. 'That was a highlight. I am quite a shy guy by nature, so for me to speak to these guys was fantastic. If I'd have seen them in a pub in Kirkcaldy, I wouldn't have gone near them, so to get a chance to speak to them in that moment was amazing. In my head I was already thinking, "I'm going to have these memories for ever." Now I'm bringing those memories back 30 years later and it's still fantastic.'

If it was a special time for the supporters, it was equally special for the players and management. 'When we were at the airport with the Rovers supporters, it was great,' says Jimmy Nicholl. 'Meeting and mixing with the supporters was really special. These are the moments you remember. The moments you cherish.'

There was appreciation that fans had travelled to support the team. 'Those guys were what it was all about,' says Davie

Kirkwood. 'It is not about the players. It is about the club and the supporters. The players are obviously the ones that get the club through to the next round, but the supporters' experience is just as important. It was their first time in Europe. We looked at the fans who travelled with us and we knew that they would love to have been in our shoes. So, to share that with them at the airport was a great experience.'

'I always believe that the fans are the most important people at the football club,' agrees Danny Lennon. 'Managers, coaches, players, they pass through football clubs and some you have a better experience than others, some you create fantastic memories at, but, let me tell you, all the great memories I have of all the clubs I have been at, the fans are always at the forefront of them.

'At Raith Rovers, our fans travelled far and wide, loving every moment of those games, but it wasn't just the big games and the big nights. Those guys turned up every week and there was a true connection. We shared that destiny. They believed in us, and it felt like more than just football. There was a great love for the club. I remember coming back to the airport and we went up the stairs and bang, all the Raith fans were there, and it turned into a great night.'

Supporters bought players drinks and players bought supporters drinks. There was no sense of them and us, or anyone being more important than anyone else. Everyone involved with the club just wanted to share the moment, knowing that they had achieved something special. 'It felt like we had all succeeded together,' agrees Stephen McAnespie. 'It was such a feeling of family and camaraderie.'

The mood was one of euphoria. Barry Wilson entertained fans with impressions of Jimmy Nicholl and an unforgettable rendition of 'Scatman', a slightly ridiculous dance song popular in the charts at the time. 'John Greer still calls me "The Scatman" to this day,' laughs Wilson. 'We were blasting that song out in the airport and I kind of did it in jest. It was just mad scenes. We didn't even need alcohol to be honest, it was just great banter and crazy stuff. I think fans saw the hard work, they saw the enjoyment, what it meant to us as well.'

'You are aware of the supporters and what it means to them,' says Stevie Crawford. 'To have followed the team all the way to Iceland, you knew what it meant. We were focused on the game, but once the game was won, Jimmy found a great balance of allowing us to go to supporters or for them to come and speak to us at the airport so that the fans can enjoy it with us. That creates great memories for everyone.'

'I don't think you would see that nowadays,' reflects supporter Gavin Quinn. 'Just fans and players mingling together. We all got on really well too and that all stemmed from Jimmy. He was just an easy-going, lovely guy. He loved meeting the fans and he wanted the fans and the club to have that close relationship and that is exactly what happened with that party at the airport.'

Reflecting back now on the ÍA tie, there remains relief that the club managed to progress against such a talented side. 'I think we were fortunate,' says Jason Dair. 'We played well in the first leg but in the second leg they had the upper hand and I think we were a wee bit fortunate to get through, but we got through and that was all that mattered.'

'I think it is easy to focus on the fairytale, that team and that night in Munich,' says Stevie Crawford, 'but if you look at the previous round against Akranes, we could easily have lost in that second leg and Munich would never have happened. It was a sliding doors moment, but you look at the characters we had on the park at the time. That fight and determination. It showed that day.'

'I remember speaking to Siggi [Jónsson] about the two games during our time at Tannadice together,' says Davie Sinclair. 'He told me that they came over to Stark's Park expecting to beat us, because they thought they had more quality in their side. He said that they had destroyed us in the second leg and were gutted when we, and not they, progressed into the next round. I just told him we'd played them at their own game, defended well and Thommo had pulled off some of the best saves you'll ever see.'

The magnitude of the achievement was reinforced when supporters looked at some of the names who exited the UEFA Cup that night: AS Monaco, Standard Liege, Fenerbahçe, Inter Milan and Manchester United. Rovers had gone further in the tournament than Manchester United; it was almost laughable. 'It was just, "How are we in the hat for the next round and Man United aren't?"' laughs Graeme Meldrum. 'I just thought, "What is happening here?"'

It had been a magical trip for supporters and a night that summed up everything that is great about being a fan of a club like Raith Rovers. The togetherness, the sense of community, belonging and the feeling that you are all in it together. The stars had aligned to see Rovers through that day, when they could have easily been knocked out by more experienced and, possibly, more talented opponents. Yet they weren't. They'd succeeded and progressed and now the potential for something even more exciting awaited. All that was left to do was head home. 'We got back to Glasgow, and I got back in the car and drove back to Crieff,' says John

Greer. 'The strangest thing was I got back to my house at 3am, exactly 24 hours after I'd left the morning before. It was the whole 24 hours complete. I woke up the following day with no voice. We'd sung, we'd shouted, we'd gotten emotional, and it was just the most amazing time.'

'I think it was one of the best days being a Rover,' says Steve Wallace. 'You had been to the game, got through a really difficult tie that the bookies probably said we weren't going to get through and everyone was just there at the airport together. So much was condensed into this one day. Does that day beat the cup final? I don't know, but it runs it close. At that point, it felt like we were invincible.'

19

They Don't Come Much Bigger

THE JOURNEY that Rovers were on had delivered some incredible moments for players and supporters but hidden among the euphoria of every football story can be moments that don't follow the conventional narrative of elation and excitement. For individual players there can be frustration, disappointment and even extreme lows. That night at the airport in Iceland is rightly remembered as an incredibly special moment for the club, but for one player it marked the end of his Raith Rovers story.

Stephen McAnespie was settled at the club. He was in terrific form and playing the best football of his career. 'I don't remember thinking, "I want a move, or I want to go to a big team,"' he recalls, speaking from his home in New Orleans. 'We were a big team in my mind. It was like Christmas every day for us. I was just interested in doing my best for the Rovers. It was all about who we would be playing in the Premier League on the Saturday and who we were going to get in the next round in Europe.

'There was a bit of naivety about it all. Of course, when you go on runs like that and the team is doing well, then players are going to gather interest. There was obviously talk about me, but there was talk about a lot of the players. Jimmy did a great job of telling us, "Block it out. Don't even think about it." We weren't bothered about what was coming down the line later.'

After the elation of the ÍA game, McAnespie was with the rest of the squad enjoying a well-earned beer and the company of the supporters at Keflavík Airport. The pleasure of the moment was shattered when he was taken away from the group and told that he had been sold. 'I got pulled aside at the airport and told basically, "We have accepted an offer for you,"' he recounts.

It is a moment that still holds a measure of pain. Rumours had been circulating around the press on the trip that McAnespie was about to be sold to Bolton Wanderers and in the club's defence, they may have just been trying to avoid the player learning of the move in the newspapers the following day, but the timing couldn't have been worse. 'For it to happen the way it did, I was so disappointed,' says McAnespie. 'I was there with my team-mates, and we were trying to celebrate and have a good time with the fans, and they are taking me aside to tell me that I'm sold. They should have waited until the next day. To pull me aside right in the middle of everyone to say that they have accepted an offer. That was a bad time.'

The immediate emotion for the young defender was hurt. He had just helped his team reach the second round of the UEFA Cup and now it felt like he had been discarded. 'Honestly, I went into the bathroom in the airport, and I cried,' says a candid McAnespie. 'It felt like the team wanted rid of me. That was how it felt in that moment. We have just gone through probably one of the biggest moments in the club's history and suddenly I'm not wanted. I mean hindsight is different now, in context, that is not how it was, but in that moment that was how it felt. It was pretty hurtful.'

McAnespie felt blindsided, but quickly realised he had to find an agent who could represent his interests. He headed into the Stark's Park office the following morning to discuss the move.

Bolton had offered £900,000 for the right-back. A figure of that magnitude would have smashed the record fee received by Raith, who therefore were keen to sell. Reflecting back on it now, McAnespie believes that pressure was applied on him to sign for the English side, with some sleight of hand in relation to what other potential offers were available to him. 'This is the cloak and dagger side of it,' says McAnespie. 'At the time there were other options on the table that I never knew about. I only found that out later. For the club the monetary values were not as much, but with hindsight, those options would probably have been better for me.

'I went down to Bolton and spoke to them. I wasn't totally happy about it, but I came back and was kind of strong-armed into it. I was told, "Do the best for the club, blah, blah, blah." Being a young player and naive, I wanted to do the best for the club and that was how it transpired.'

If the circumstances were less than ideal, McAnespie is now grateful for the opportunity that the move presented him. 'I signed on Friday and played in the Premier League on Saturday,' he says. 'From that perspective, I will never be mad at it. It was amazing and it was a positive thing in the end. You go from playing in Scotland and playing against Akranes and in the Faroes, to playing against world-class players. I was coming up against [Dennis] Bergkamp and

[David] Ginola, and these guys were just off the chart. It was a massive jump, and a jolt to your system, but it was a pretty amazing experience.

'I got to play in the Premier League in England. I mean, how many players can say that? No one can ever take that away.'

The one postscript of his move to Bolton was that it would reunite him with the ÍA forward he had been tormented by in Iceland, when Arnar Gunnlaugsson later joined the Trotters. 'I ended up playing with Arni,' smiles McAnespie. 'He actually ended up buying my house in Manchester. We spoke about the games, but not to any great length. I think I ribbed him about it a couple of times at training.'

To this day, not completing the UEFA Cup journey with Raith remains a regret for McAnespie. 'It was like I had done all the hard work and suddenly I am not there,' he reflects. 'Of course, I watched the next round on TV. Like everyone else, I was a fan, but I just wished I was playing. I just wished I was there.'

For the remaining members of the squad, the loss of McAnespie was unexpected, but they understood the financial reality of playing for a club like Raith. 'The club got a bit of money for him,' says Colin Cameron. 'So, it was good business from the club's point of view. It was understandable that he got a move. He was different class for us when he came in and he just got better as each game progressed. We would have loved to have kept him, but that is football. People move and new people come in. It is part and parcel of the game. You have got to embrace it and just move on.'

Attention soon switched to the pressing matter of who Raith would draw in the next round. Jimmy Nicholl had always dreamed of landing his former side Manchester United and taking his team back to Old Trafford, but with the English giants having failed to progress through the first round, that possibility was removed. His desire was still to draw a big name and deliver an occasion that the whole town of Kirkcaldy would remember for years to come. 'Having come that far, I didn't want to see us go out to a team from Azerbaijan,' he laughs now. 'I wanted more than anything to put these players on the highest level they've ever played. If we go out, I wanted to go out in the big time.'

Most of the players and supporters shared his desire. 'You had been through it by that stage,' says fan Steve Wallace. 'You had been through two home games, two away trips and had invested a lot financially and emotionally, and you just wanted it to come to some sort of crescendo. You looked at some of the teams that were available and there was talk of Leeds or whoever, but when you think of the big teams in Europe, Real Madrid, Barcelona, AC Milan and Bayern Munich are the big four. You wanted the biggest team in the hat.'

If there was one dissenting voice in the camp, it was striker Ally Graham. 'All the boys were buzzing and talking about getting a really big name,' he recalls. 'But I fancied one of those mad Greek or Turkish mobs, like a Famagusta or an Olympiakos. You know the ones where you go to their stadium, and it is all flares, and they are all wanting your blood and trying to intimidate you. I fancied that. I would like to have given a wee bit of intimidation back and seen where it took us.'

Graham's optimism is admirable, but looking at the quality of the sides that were left in the competition there was realism that this may be where the UEFA Cup journey ended for Rovers. 'There was hardly anybody in that last 32 where you would have thought, "Maybe we can give them a game,"' says Shaughan McGuigan. 'It was like 32 juggernauts from some of the best leagues all across Europe.'

The squad gathered expectantly on the Friday morning waiting to find out the next destination in this fantastic adventure. 'It was almost like the Scottish Cup when you are a smaller team,' reflects Scott Thomson. 'You get through three rounds and the big guys come in and you are waiting to get one of them. It was like that. We were the small fish, and it was waiting on which big guy we were going to get. We knew we were going to get a big tie and it just so happened that we pulled out one of the biggest.'

The screen on Ceefax flicked over to reveal Bayern Munich v Raith Rovers.

There were immediate cheers in the Stark's Park tearoom. 'You wouldn't have put Raith Rovers and Bayern Munich in the same sentence,' laughs Danny Lennon. 'It just didn't go. It was like chalk and cheese.'

'We had finally got the big boys,' says Julian Broddle. 'They don't come much bigger. You knew just about every player that played for them. You knew their history. You knew that we were going to Germany and playing in this historic stadium that had been used for the World Cup and the Olympics. Wow.'

Stevie Crawford now reflects on the magnitude of the draw and is thankful that what lay in wait wasn't known in that final half an hour in Iceland. 'I think if we knew what was ahead in the future,' he says, 'we might have lost that game. If we knew it was Bayern Munich then you might be in the mindset of thinking, "We could miss out on something that we might never experience again in our life."

Thankfully we didn't, so we could live in the moment and our focus was still there to get us through to what awaited.'

What awaited was one of the most famous names in world football.

The delight of the players in being paired with Bayern Munich was matched by the supporters. This was exactly the sort of tie that many had anticipated when they first qualified for Europe. 'When we got Bayern Munich, it was wonderful,' says John Greer, with emotion in his voice. 'Absolutely wonderful. That was like all the dreams come true. I turned on *Reporting Scotland* that night and there was Steve Wallace! We always joked with Stevie that he must have walked for two hours along the high street looking for reporters.'

'I worked at Tesco in the Mercat at the time,' recounts Steve Wallace. 'I was on back shift when the draw was made, and this was the days of landlines. There were three landlines into Tesco and at one point all three lines were taken up with people phoning me to tell me that they were interviewing folk in the high street. I nipped out to see what was going on and then I thought, "I need to go and speak to these people." When I watched it back that night, I cringed!'

Bayern Munich were not only one of the most famous names in the competition, but they were also arguably the most lucrative. Up until then the European run had not generated any significant income for Rovers, largely due to the travel costs to the Faroe Islands and Iceland and UEFA regulations restricting attendances. Chairman Alex Penman later revealed that the club generated more revenue from the sell-out league match with Celtic than they did from their first two UEFA Cup ties combined. Being paired with a German club offered the prospect of selling TV rights and advertising to one of Europe's biggest markets. 'I was at the UEFA draw when we got Bayern,' recounted Penman. 'The television companies were keen to sign clubs like ours up if you got a plum draw. You'd give them the coverage rights and every country had a tariff – Germany £500k, Spain £400k and England £350k.'

Bayern Munich had been drawn first in the tie, meaning that they would be at home in the first leg. Penman made the decision to reverse the fixtures to maximise the television income.

'I spoke to [Bayern general manager] Uli Hoeneß,' said Penman. 'He was happy to swap the games round so we were at home first. It gave us two prime-time kick-offs live on TV.'

The final decision was where the home match would be played. 'I remember being in the boardroom when the Bayern draw was made,' says Jimmy Nicholl. 'My first thought was, "Could we play the game at Stark's Park?" I wanted that to happen. I wanted Bayern to come to play on our sloping pitch, with 9,500 supporters closely packed into the ground.

'They [UEFA] had reduced our crowd for the Akranes game though. So I thought they will reduce our crowd again for the Bayern Munich game, so there will be a financial hit, but at least it would be on the TV. Then UEFA turned around and said Stark's Park was not suitable. That was a disappointment. I just think being at home, familiar with the pitch, familiar with the surroundings and Bayern Munich walking in and thinking, "What the hell?" would have been fantastic.'

Nicholl did at least have a say in where the game would be played, opting for Hibernian's Easter Road, largely because it was also a pitch with a slope at the time. Moving the tie away from Stark's Park was perhaps unsurprising, as the suitability of the stadium had been debated in both of the previous rounds, but it was still disappointing and one aspect of the UEFA Cup journey that players and fans regret to this day. A full Stark's Park welcoming the German giants would have been a truly magnificent thing.

'The atmosphere at Stark's Park would have been absolutely amazing,' says Kirkcaldy-born Colin Cameron. 'It was a blow, I think so. I was gutted about that at the time to be honest with you. That is probably the only thing I have a wee regret about around the whole European experience. That we never got to play the home leg at Stark's Park. That was a disappointment for me, being a local guy as well, I would have loved to have experienced that atmosphere. All these wee things might have just given us a better result in the first tie, but we'll never know.'

'Can you imagine them in the old away dressing room and the showers not working?' laughs Davie Kirkwood. 'Bayern would have thought, "What the hell have we come to here?" and with the crowd right on top of them and playing a pitch that we knew and that they didn't know. You never know.'

Whether the tie would have unfolded differently had it been played in Kirkcaldy is one that many players and supporters have ruminated on in the 30 years that have passed since, but the financial realities of the time are well understood. 'Ultimately it was a financial thing,' says Scott Thomson. 'The club made a lot of money from the gate receipts and the live television, so financially it was a no-brainer.'

'We probably would have given them a better game at Stark's Park,' says Danny Lennon. 'But then again for the opportunity to play Bayern Munich, you would have played them in a public park.'

The reversal of the ties at least ensured that Rovers would go into the first match at Easter Road competitive in the tie, rather than risk the prospect of a meaningless home fixture after a damaging away defeat. It also helpfully afforded supporters another pay packet to pay for their trip to the return leg in Germany.

20

The Superstars Are Coming

IF RAITH Rovers felt lucky to have drawn Bayern Munich, in Germany the feeling was mutual. With ambitions of winning the entire tournament, Bayern's focus was on progressing through each round as effortlessly as possible and most associated with the German club felt Rovers offered them the best chance to do so. Bayern midfielder Thomas Strunz, in an unguarded moment, captured the mood. 'Oh man, what luck,' he said. 'Getting Raith Rovers is the best draw we could have had!'

The tone from senior members of the Bayern camp was more measured, but privately their confidence would have reflected Strunz's comments. 'This is not a bad draw for us,' said former German international Karl-Heinz Rummenigge, by this point a vice-president at Bayern. 'I think we can get through to the third round, but Scottish teams have proved difficult for FC Bayern in the past, so we need to be careful.'

The Bayern squad was littered with internationals, with a price tag that even Rangers and Celtic could only dream about, never mind Raith Rovers. Goalkeeper Oliver Kahn had cost £2.4m, Austrian international Andreas Herzog

£2m, Thomas Strunz £2m, Oliver Kreuzer £1.8m, Mehmet Scholl £1.8m, Christian Ziege £1.5m and Dietmar Hamann £1.2m. Yet all these transfer fees were surpassed by the signings of Thomas Helmer and Ciriaco Sforza, weighing in at £3.5m and £3.7m respectively. Oh, and there was the not insignificant strike partnership of German international Jürgen Klinsmann and French international Jean-Pierre Papin. It was a stellar line-up that read like a Who's Who in football and one that the Rovers players were acutely aware of as the matches neared.

The transfer fees paid to assemble the Bayern squad was in stark contrast to what it had taken to build the Raith team, most of whom had come through the youth system or been picked up for free. Their most extravagant purchase, £120,000 for striker Ally Graham, was a fee roughly equivalent to Oliver Kahn's left arm. 'Bayern Munich,' says Graham. 'Just the name itself scares people. The superstars were coming. You were in awe of these guys and getting them was a dream come true, but let's be honest, you know in your heart of hearts that you are not going to get through the tie. They were a level above.'

Graham's assessment of Raith's chances was reflected by most of his team-mates. 'We knew as soon as the draw was made that it would be the biggest shock in world football if we came out on top against Bayern,' reflects Colin Cameron.

'We knew we wouldn't let ourselves down or embarrass ourselves,' says Julian Broddle. 'But we also knew that we had just got the biggest boys in the competition, so we had to make the most of it. Did we believe we could actually do it? I think deep down we probably knew that this is where our story ends.'

The scale of the task created a nervousness for some, but Raith had not achieved what they had achieved over the previous few years without believing in their own ability. This had been a trait instilled into them by their manager. No one underestimated the challenges playing such an illustrious opponent would bring, but at the same time there was nothing to fear. No one expected them to advance, so they had nothing to lose. 'You looked at their team and at first have a wee panic about the gulf in class in terms of the internationals they had at that stage,' says Jason Dair. 'There was a sense of thinking, "Hopefully we can do ourselves justice." But there was not a fear. There was never a fear with us. You were just looking forward to it.'

Among the fanbase, Gavin Quinn, Rovers' most optimistic fan, was confident. 'I thought we would beat Bayern as well,' he laughs. 'As a football fan, I just expect to win every game. That is how I am. I just thought we'll go on and beat Bayern Munich, one of the best and biggest teams in Europe, and maybe win the UEFA Cup.'

It was not a confidence shared by most of his fellow supporters. 'I think if I am being really honest, then damage limitation was in my head,' admits Steve Wallace. 'Klinsmann was one of the best players in the world at that time. Jean-Pierre Papin, Markus Babbel, Oliver Kahn. All these players were phenomenal and had great careers. All of a sudden, our wee Rovers are playing against this team.'

'I thought there was no chance at all,' laughs Jonathan Tippetts-Aylmer. 'We were a good team, but this was still Bayern Munich!'

Regardless of whether you felt there was a good chance, a slight chance or no chance at all, all at Raith were determined to make the most of the two matches and savour every moment. The excitement built towards the first leg, with supporters, relatives and friends looking for tickets. The North, South and Main Stands at Easter Road were set aside for the Raith support, with the East Stand sold to people in Edinburgh who wanted to take in the game. News that the opening encounter would be broadcast live on Sky Sports heightened the excitement.

Preparations were put in place by the management team of Jimmy Nicholl and Martin Harvey, but there was often a thread of humour throughout their analysis of their opponents. 'Jimmy sat us all down and told us that we needed to watch some clips of Bayern Munich,' says defender Robbie Raeside. 'He then went through the Bayern Munich team and slaughtered them all. He was like, "Ziege. He's all left foot, Show him on to his right. Honestly hopeless. Scholl. Cannae run. Honestly, he cannae run. Get him turned, he's murder. Klinsmann. Doesn't fancy it. Sinky, just give him one early doors." He slaughtered every single one of them and all of us young ones are sitting there thinking, "Aye, nae bother," but I remember big Ally Graham just looking at Coylie and laughing.'

'We watched a couple of videos of their strikers,' smiles Ally Graham. 'They were the two up and coming young guys in the Bayern team. I watched the video and was like, "My god, look at the pace and skill of these guys. Poor old Julian Broddle or Alex Taylor going to have to mark those guys!" Unreal.

'I bumped into big [former Bayern striker and Scotland international] Alan McInally at one point. He was doing the dossier on us all for Bayern. I remember taking my old man for a pint down to Cricklewood and Alan came in and he has the folder with all the players in it and he was telling us what he wrote about us. He was very good with my old man, because he was saying to my dad, "Look at the stats I have got on your boy. He'll terrorise them. He'll terrorise them." It was a great laugh.'

None of the players wanted to get injured in training and miss out on one of the biggest occasions in the club's history, and it was a challenge to remain focused on the Premier League games in the run-up to the first leg. Bayern Munich sought every advantage in the tie and offered the home side money to change balls for the game, preferring to use Adidas balls, but Rovers refused. They would strike another minor moral victory over their opponents by booking their preferred accommodation, the Dalmahoy Hotel just outside Edinburgh. 'The Germans wanted Dalmahoy,' says Jimmy Nicholl. 'I remember speaking to the hotel manager when we were there and he told me that Bayern had tried to get the Dalmahoy, but we got in there before them.'

With their Premier League games out of the way, the squad decanted to the Dalmahoy for their final preparations. As the players relaxed and enjoyed their surroundings, Bayern arrived at Edinburgh Airport. 'We were told that Bayern Munich were landing late afternoon,' recounts journalist Scott Davie. 'There was a press conference later, but I was sent down to the airport to see if we could get a player to speak to help preview the game. You were basically doorstepping them. When they came out, the first thing that struck you was that everyone was huge. I was thinking, "Bloody hell, wee Mickey and the rest will be going up against these guys!" You were standing there looking at magnificent specimens of football players, all six foot plus.

'Jürgen Klinsmann comes past, and we shout, "Jürgen, can we have a word?" He replies, "Yes, I have to put my stuff on the bus first, but I will come back in a minute." We were just thinking that they all say that, but a couple of minutes later, sure enough, he comes off the bus and says, "What can I do for you boys?" He was one of the biggest players in the world and he couldn't have been more complimentary about Rovers. Absolutely first class. A complete professional.'

Bayern Munich, at that time, were a club in a relative state of turmoil. Their participation in the UEFA Cup had initially been a disappointment as it was a result of not having won the previous season's Bundesliga. Under coach Otto Rehhagel, there had been significant unrest in the squad as many of their stars weren't playing regularly, with Jean-Pierre Papin, Alain Sutter, Mehmet Scholl, Marcel Witeczek and Dieter Frey all having submitted transfer requests. A damaging loss to rivals Borussia Dortmund on the weekend prior to coming to Scotland had compounded the problem. After the match a no-holds barred team 90-minute meeting was held and the air cleared. Uli Hoeneß spoke after the meeting: 'There has been much aggression within our club,' he said, 'which I hope can now be directed at Raith Rovers.'

The disruption in the Bayern camp was in stark contrast to the relaxed and joyful mood of their opponents. The biggest game of their careers may have been days away, but the traditional Rovers approach to life continued. Shaun Dennis and Danny Lennon found a screwdriver and proceeded to swap the brass numbers on the room doors in the upmarket hotel, causing confusion when others tried to return to their rooms. 'It was carnage,' says Jimmy Nicholl with a shake of his head. Nicholl had planned on showing the squad a video of Bayern's weekend match with Dortmund on the Monday evening but was told in no uncertain terms by his players that they had to watch Wimbledon play West Ham on Sky Sports instead as there was a £2 a head, first goalscorer sweep running. An earlier slot for the Bayern video was found.

There was cautious optimism among the players as they spoke to the press pre-match. 'I believe we can beat Bayern,' said captain Dennis. 'The good thing about German sides is that they will let you have the ball, and we will be doing our best to get a result that everyone can be proud of.'

'I've seen Klinsmann play in England and he looks a handful,' said Davie Sinclair, before jokingly adding, 'Maybe if I put Klinsmann in a stranglehold in the tunnel before the game, it will scare him off.'

'There are lots of individual things I'll be telling the players,' explained Jimmy Nicholl. 'But the most important thing I can tell them is once they cross that white line and get out on the pitch forget all about reputations. Forget about the players they are up against, the history of Bayern Munich and the status of the club. Our players must remember that they are there on merit. At the moment we are the talk of Scottish football, but by 8pm tomorrow night we'll be the talk of Europe if we do something against Bayern Munich.'

Rovers sold out all of their 10,000 allocation of tickets. The excitement around Kirkcaldy on the Tuesday afternoon was palpable as supporters prepared to leave for the capital. There were reports of a jury trial in the town being adjourned at lunchtime after a couple of jurors said they had to leave for 4pm due to 'prior commitments'; 4pm just happened to be the time when supporters' buses were leaving for the game.

As the squad departed the Dalmahoy for Easter Road, they were relaxed. 'When we got near Easter Road you could see loads of Raith fans approaching the ground,' says Julian Broddle. 'The lads and everyone on the coach was buzzing and you could just feel it was going to be an amazing night. I had family up and most of the lads had their family and friends there, so it was a very special atmosphere.'

Jimmy Nicholl once again ensured that the whole club was included in such a special occasion, with youth players travelling with the squad and allowed to go on to the pitch to warm up, even though they would not be taking any part in the game. Everyone knew that this was an occasion to savour. 'You even had these fancy paper team sheets that were around the dressing room with all the names and the numbers on them,' says Robbie Raeside. 'I regret big time that I didn't stick one in my jacket pocket. I remember looking at one in the dressing room before the game and it had my name. I looked across at the Bayern team and my opposite number was Jean-Pierre Papin. I just thought, "I think Rovers have the slightly poorer deal there!"'

The team Nicholl selected to face Bayern was Thomson, Kirkwood, Broddle, Coyle, Dennis, Sinclair, McInally, Cameron, Graham, Lennon and Dair. On the bench were Crawford, Taylor, Rougier, Raeside and Fridge. There would be no place for Barry Wilson, and it was a devastating moment for the young winger. 'I remember Jimmy naming the team at Easter Road and I started crying,' he recounts honestly. 'I have never felt like it in my life, before or after with regard to football. Having scored in the round before the goal that got the tie, to not even being on the bench. It was probably the lowest moment of my career.

'I now know as a manager you have got to make hard decisions. But at the time it was horrendous. To be honest,

I'm not sure I got over it. That was, probably looking back, the thing that knocked the stuffing right out of me.'

There was also disappointment for striker Stevie Crawford, who had selflessly led the line in Iceland. 'Jimmy decided to go with Ally Graham up front,' he says. 'When you find out you are not playing, it is a difficult moment. When Jimmy dropped me in games before, I always felt it in my stomach. I used to get real knots in my stomach, tight, but I didn't disagree or complain. I was just, "Bag it, bag it. Bag it. Just get out and get the warm-up done and don't show anybody you are disappointed." That night, I knew that it wasn't about me.'

Having both worked as managers, the challenges around selection of players is something that Crawford and Wilson now have a greater appreciation of. 'Some players can cope with it,' explains Crawford. 'And some players can't. I am not having a go at that. It is hard, but that comes through experience and trying to deal with the negative emotions that you get in football. I think if players can deal with being dropped and respect the decision, then that is how you know you have got the dressing room.'

Back in the stadium, the crowd filtered into Easter Road and began to fill all four stands. One group of supporters produced a flag stating 'Rovers go to Europe. Pars go to Greenock. European Tour 1995', a cheeky reference to the fact that while Rovers were participating in the UEFA Cup, local rivals Dunfermline were having to make do with the Challenge Cup. 'Jim Morgan made that flag,' says supporter Graeme Meldrum. 'He had that all the way from Kirkcaldy to Munich. The thing was that after the second leg he left it at the Olympic Stadium. A couple of weeks later someone turned up and gave it to him. They'd retrieved it, folded it and everything. He said, "What do I want with this? I left it over there for a reason!"'

Opening the commemorative programme that had been produced for the match, Rovers supporters were met by the words of their manager. 'The night we've all been waiting for has finally arrived,' wrote Jimmy Nicholl. 'When we won the Coca-Cola Cup back in November, there were a lot of one-liners flying around about how funny it would be to see Milan at Stark's Park or have Franz Beckenbauer asking about training facilities at Burntisland. It was funny at the time. It's even funnier now because it's all come true. Enjoy the game, get behind the team and soak in the atmosphere. This should be a wonderful night for football.'

Scott Thomson and Stephen McAnespie ready for the European adventure (RRFC)

Colin Cameron gets to grips with a Faroese opponent (Fimister)

Jason Dair celebrates a historic first European goal (Getty)

Tony Rougier pushes forward against Gøtu (Fimister)

Fans set sail for the Faroe Islands (Ely)

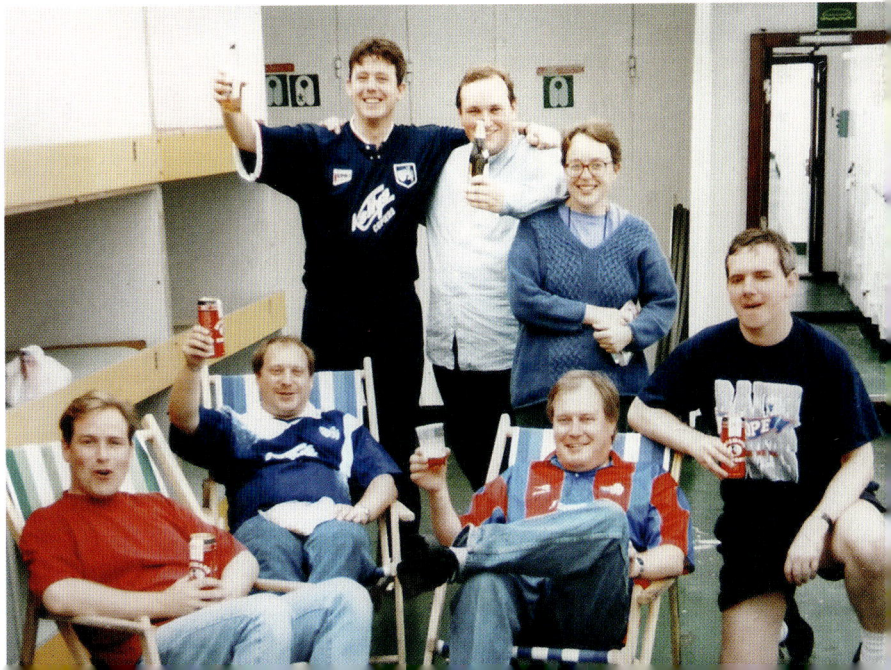

Steve Wallace and Niall Russell start the ferry party (Wallace)

Stevie Crawford puts his side ahead against Gøtu Ítróttarfelag (RRFC)

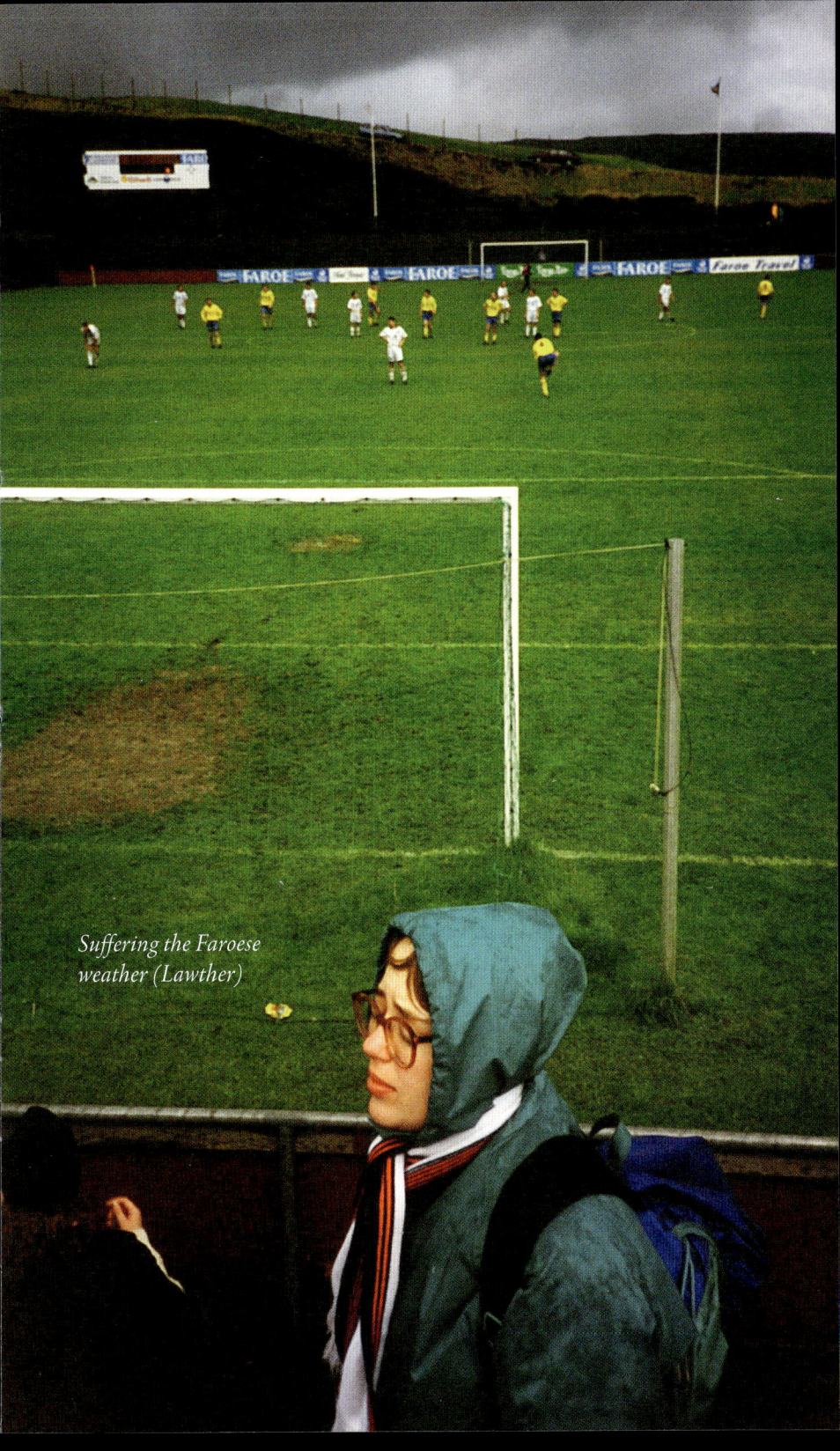

Suffering the Faroese
weather (Lawther)

On the attack at Toftir (Nicholson)

The squad to face Icelandic champions Akranes (Fimister)

Jimmy Nicholl watches from the sidelines (Fimister)

Rovers hunt for goals against Akranes (Fimister)

Shaun Dennis battles Arnar Gunnlaugsson (Brynjar Gauti Sveinsson)

Ronnie Coyle chases back (Brynjar Gauti Sveinsson)

21

Two Lapses of Concentration

JÜRGEN KLINSMANN peeled away from Shaun Dennis to give himself an extra yard of space and waited for Andreas Herzog to lift the ball into the no man's land between the defender and goalkeeper. With the German striker advancing on to the delicately chipped ball, Scott Thomson was left with no option but to try to get there first. Klinsmann narrowly won the race and lifted the ball up and over Thomson and watched it bounce, almost in slow motion into the net. There were just six minutes on the clock and Raith Rovers were already a goal down to Bayern Munich.

Over 12,000 supporters had gathered inside Easter Road to see if the small club from Kirkcaldy could fell their larger German opponents in the UEFA Cup second round match, and as the two sides emerged from the tunnel led by a single piper the roar of encouragement had been deafening. Now it was silent as Klinsmann raced away in celebration.

The Bayern side was packed with quality and a run-through of the team that night elicits names that even 30 years later are still remembered in Germany and beyond, none more so than Jürgen Klinsmann. The German striker had moved to Bayern the previous summer from Tottenham Hotspur for £1m after scoring 20 goals in the English Premier League. His football resumé was impressive: he had a World Cup winners' medal and had already won the UEFA Cup with Inter Milan four years earlier. Later that year he would add a second UEFA Cup, be the tournament's top scorer and be named as the runner-up for the Ballon d'Or, only losing out to Liberian striker George Weah of AC Milan. He also happened to be the 7/2 favourite to score the first goal against Rovers and his clinical sixth-minute strike at Easter Road punctured the atmosphere inside the stadium.

'I remember watching Klinsmann and his movement that night,' recalls substitute Stevie Crawford. 'He had obviously had that season in Tottenham before, played in World Cups and done it all and the way he peeled off Shaun Dennis, and for a big laddie, Shaun was quick, but he gets in front of him and the casual way he finished it.'

Crawford feared for his team-mates after losing a goal so early. 'When you are sitting on the sideline,' he continues, 'there is nothing you can do. You start to think that if this goes two, three, four, then all of a sudden, the romance of this tie is done. As much as we wanted to play Bayern, we didn't want to make a fool of ourselves. We wanted to give them a run for their money.'

Prior to the match, supporters and players had concerns about the quality in the Bayern side and the potential for a heavy defeat. 'Our big fear was letting ourselves and the town down,' says Shaun Dennis. 'We didn't want to get hammered in a match that the whole of Britain and much of Europe would be watching.

'We started nervously. We were still looking at the names on the team sheet rather than the players, but we didn't play against World Cup stars every day of the week. We lost a bad goal, and it took us about 20 minutes to get a grip, but gradually we began to realise we could trouble them.'

Scott Davie would later write in his match report that Raith looked 'frightened to death' in those early stages. It was undeniably a bad start, but crucially, there was no collapse. They gradually settled and began to work their way back into the match. 'I think we started to play,' reflects Ally Graham.

Rovers couldn't deploy their natural attacking game but focused on competing effectively and attempting to win individual battles with their opponents. 'The guy I had to play against was this big, tall German guy,' says Julian Broddle. 'He looked about six foot seven and I had to mark him. He was just this big, imposing guy and he never said a word to me. In Scotland you used to talk to players all the time, whether it was good or bad. You usually have some sort of banter. The whole 90 minutes he never said a single word.'

Rovers had to adjust their normal game to account for the sheer quality of opposition they were facing. 'You would have loved to get guys toward the byline to get crosses in for me to go and attack,' says Ally Graham. 'But you are playing Bayern Munich. They are not going to let you do that. I had to be unselfish, hold the ball up, try and get the guys into play, try and get my body in and try to get Cameron, Crawford, Dair, wee Danny involved.'

After 24 minutes, Broddle ventured forward and found space on the edge of the box, but his finish lacked direction. That the left-back was up on the edge of the Bayern box was a sign that Rovers had grown into the game and were competing more effectively. They were limiting Bayern, who were finding it difficult to create any clear-cut opportunities to score. Klinsmann put Scholl in on goal, but the midfielder controlled the ball with his hand and was booked. As the match drifted towards half-time, Rovers fashioned a final opportunity when Dennis found Graham at the back post, but the striker could only direct a weak header towards Kahn.

After conceding so early, to go in at half-time just one goal down felt like a small moral victory. Jimmy Nicholl was frustrated that he had approached the game too conservatively. 'I was too cautious in that first half,' he reflects, with an enduring sense of irritation. 'I felt we had to keep it tight, but I didn't think we would get that much possession. I probably did the players a disservice, but I didn't want us to get a mauling at home.'

The second half saw a more aggressive, attacking performance from Rovers. Playing up the Easter Road slope, they took the game to their opponents. That didn't mean that the German side were not still dangerous, and they almost doubled their lead on 53 minutes when a Dennis clearance cannoned off Klinsmann and Scholl found space on the left. Scholl rounded Scott Thomson and only a booted clearance on the goal line from Davie Sinclair saved the day.

The longer the game went on, the greater the confidence in the Raith team seemed and Jason Dair in particular started to demonstrate some dazzling wing play. On 65 minutes the moment of the match for Rovers arrived. A free kick was awarded on the left and Broddle caught the Bayern defence flat-footed when he took it quickly, whipping the ball perfectly on to the head of Cameron a few yards from goal. Cameron caught the ball perfectly and it looked a certain goal, until Kahn stretched out a hand to miraculously deflect it round the post. 'We get the free kick and Mickey Cameron looks at me and gives me the nod,' recounts Broddle. 'They are all just turning around and getting themselves sorted, so I think, "I should just whip this in now." So, I whipped it in, and Mickey gets a perfect header, or at least I thought it was perfect. What a difference it would have made if we had got that goal.'

'I was always looking to exploit something and do something quick,' says Cameron. 'The minute I have headed that I thought I had scored. I couldn't have headed it any better. Kahn made the save and that was that. I would have loved for it to have gone in, but it wasn't to be.'

Kahn's save had been astonishing. 'That was why he was Germany's number one, eh,' laughs Cameron, before adding ruefully, 'I don't score many with my head to be fair.'

It would be the last real chance for Raith in the game. They continued to play well, closing down the Bayern players and defending well, but with hindsight the moment was gone. As the night wound down to its conclusion, the effort that the Rovers players had put in began to take its toll. 'Midway through the second half I heard the substitute boards being banged together,' recalls Jim McInally. 'I looked across to see what change they were making and there was Jean-Pierre Papin about to come on and join Klinsmann. If one thing summed up the task we were facing that was it. I mean, they had one of Europe's top strikers sitting on the bench!'

Rovers made their own substitutions when Stevie Crawford and Tony Rougier replaced Jim McInally and Jason Dair in an attempt to find a late equaliser, but it would be the Germans who would score to double their advantage – Papin started a crisp move down the right and Alexander

Zickler cut the ball back from the byline for Klinsmann to score. Klinsmann was denied a hat-trick by a fingertip Thomson save moments later and in the last act of the game Papin rattled the bar with a thrilling 20-yard shot. 'I think we felt we deserved to keep it down to one,' says Dair. 'But it ended up in a 2-0 defeat. We were all disappointed at conceding that second goal.'

The match left many supporters with mixed emotions. It had been tremendous to see their favourites go toe-to-toe with such a stunning array of internationals, but there was a lingering frustration with how it had unfolded. Not that most supporters had expected to beat the Germans, but the closeness of the contest in the end left many feeling short-changed by a two-goal defeat. 'I don't think the team got as much credit as they deserved that night because they lost the game,' reflects Jim Clark. 'When you look at what Bayern were doing to other teams in that competition, they were hammering everybody, so to keep them to just two goals, especially after conceding so early, was a tremendous performance.'

Among the squad there was the same frustration, especially within the defenders. The nature and timing of the goals left some irritated. 'Two lapses of concentration were all it took to give them two goals and I could kick myself for what happened at the first one,' said Shaun Dennis after the match. 'I allowed Klinsmann to drift off me and that's criminal. If you are a defender, you are judged on the number of goals you lose. By that standard, we can't be happy.'

'The first leg at Easter Road was hard and we let ourselves down by the way we started,' reflects Davie Sinclair. 'We started off sloppy and if you play like that against quality teams, they'll punish you and they did when Klinsmann scored.'

There is now recognition that the Raith squad, despite being one of the strongest in the club's history, was no match for the talent available to Bayern. Even some of the younger fringe players at the time, who fans were unfamiliar with, would go on to establish themselves as regular internationals and household names. 'I thought Shaun and I played well at centre-back,' says Davie Sinclair. 'But we were playing some of the best players in Europe in Papin and Klinsmann. I managed to get Papin's top after the second leg, so that is a great souvenir to go with the memories.'

'It was disappointing not to have scored,' reflects Julian Broddle. 'If Mickey had got his goal and we held it to 1-1, then we could have gone to Munich believing we could do something. But we did well, and we never let the club down that night.'

'I think over the piece we gave our all,' says Scott Thomson. 'We never disgraced ourselves at any point in the tie. It was just the quality shone through in a team like that. They were a top-class side, and they were chucking on people like Papin and [Christian] Nerlinger, so what chance did we have really?'

And then there was Jürgen Klinsmann, still considered by many as one of the game's most lethal strikers. 'Klinsmann was the difference in that game,' reflects Ally Graham. 'His movement all night was phenomenal. He just never stopped. He was clinical.'

'Sinky and Shaun really tried to get stuck in about him,' says Stevie Crawford. 'But nothing ruffled him that night. I am not saying they manhandled him, but they let him know they were there and not once during the game did he let it bother him. He wasn't ruffled, and he wasn't losing his focus. When the chances come, he is not thinking about them and that was something I learned that night that probably helped me in my own career.'

Klinsmann was gracious about the Kirkcaldy side after the game. 'I thought the Raith players gave everything and fought for the entire 90 minutes,' he said. 'In the second half they put us under pressure, and it took an unbelievable stop from our goalkeeper Oliver Kahn to stop them scoring. I'm not saying if Raith had scored then that it would have changed the game, but if they had equalised then, they were right back in it.

'I could have had a hat-trick but for a great save from their keeper. But two goals is enough for me and enough for Bayern.'

The implication was clear, despite the complimentary words: the Germans felt that the tie was effectively over. If they had not scored in Scotland, then it was incredibly unlikely that Raith could score in Munich.

22

Give Them Something to Cheer

THE PLANNING of supporters for the Munich trip had begun well before the first leg. Those who had been to the Faroe Islands and Iceland now felt like veterans, and for those who had stayed at home there was a realisation that if they were ever going to follow their club in Europe, then this would likely be their last chance.

Dennis O'Connell was again helping fans get to the match, but he was now joined by Ramsay Travel and a Manchester firm, Universal Tours, as interest soared. Fans had the option of travelling by bus or plane. 'There was a more expensive flight option,' explains Steve Wallace. 'But by this point I was down to unofficially deferring payments of things like council tax, so the bus option was the only one I could afford. Having already been on a ferry to the Faroes and a plane to Iceland, I felt that I was at least ticking off all the modes of travel.'

Also opting for the bus through necessity was Shaughan McGuigan. 'I had been saving up and putting money aside,' he says. 'But I couldn't afford to fly. In terms of the bus, the hotel, and my match ticket, I think it was about £160 all in. That was pretty much all I could afford.'

The bus journey across to Munich would prove an 'experience' for all those who travelled. The buses departed Kirkcaldy bus station at 10am, arriving in Dover for the 10pm ferry to Calais. On arrival in France, it was back on the bus, reaching Munich at noon on the day of the game. 'I would love to say it was a great adventure as you journeyed through Europe on a bus,' reflects Shaughan, 'but it was absolutely miserable.

'On the way there somebody decided that they couldn't sleep in their seat. So he lay down on the floor to sleep in the aisle. There was this one wee old guy on the bus who decided to get up in the middle of the night to go to the toilet. It was pitch black and he couldn't see that there was someone on the floor. He took a step, stood on this guy's chest, let out an "Oh!" and then proceeded to fall on top of him.'

The incident at least helped Shaughan pass an hour laughing at the absurdity of it.

Gavin Quinn also experienced the journey to Munich on a bus organised by Dennis O'Connell. 'Dennis decided he'd had enough of the planes at that point,' says Quinn. 'So, he organised a bus to Germany, which seemed like a good idea at the time. Colin Cameron's dad was on the bus and Sinky's mum and dad, so it was not just a group of fitba' fans, but family as well.'

'My family all went over to the game,' says Cameron. 'The stories they tell of the trip, getting the ferry over and my dad getting lost in Munich and then getting found. Their stories are far better than my stories. I would have loved to have been there to see it all.'

Supporters travelling by plane would face a less arduous trip to Germany. Kenny Smith had originally decided on the bus, but some good fortune allowed him to upgrade. 'The Rovers had a thing called the Premier Club back then,' explains Kenny. 'A few weeks before Munich I won the draw. My friend Bodge came back from the Friday night event and said, "You lucky bastard. You won the Premier Club draw, first prize." I thought he was winding me up, but I phoned the club on the Monday, and they told me I had won £250. That paid for my Munich flight.'

On the flight across there was excited anticipation, though there would be a brief pause in the boisterous atmosphere when they eventually landed in Munich. There had been trouble on a ferry involving Leeds United fans in the previous round and with German authorities not appreciating the difference between Scottish and English football supporters, the plane was diverted away from the terminal building. Passport control was set up at the bottom of the plane's stairs and under the watchful eye of police and their dogs, supporters were put straight on to buses. Throughout the experience, supporters had remained subdued, but safely on their transport, the party resumed as they made their way into the centre of Munich.

Everyone who made the journey was desperate not to miss out on such an historic moment for the club. Supporter Graham Freeman found perhaps the most cost-effective way to the game, using the complimentary rail transport he received from his job working on the railways to transport him and his son all the way from Kirkcaldy to Munich and back for free. Regardless of how they got there and how long their trip allowed them to stay, every Raith fan was determined to make the most of their time in the Bavarian capital.

The buoyant mood among the support was helped by the fact that most believed that the tie was effectively over.

After losing 2-0 at Easter Road, it seemed like an impossible task to progress. They would have had to score three goals to win or score twice and hang on through the ordeal of extra time and penalties. The unlikeliness of that happening lifted the pressure on supporters, meaning that they were free to enjoy the trip with limited expectations. 'My thoughts were that we were already out,' says Shaughan McGuigan. 'It was almost like you were doing it for the experience and so that you could say you had done it, that you could say that you had seen Raith Rovers play against Bayern Munich. At that point we had no idea what was going to happen.'

'We went into one of the big beer halls the night before the match and saw Jimmy Nicholl with his wife,' says Steve Wallace. 'It just goes back to that sense of togetherness. It was the night before a big game, and we are all out and even Jimmy is there with his family just enjoying Munich.'

The players and management adopted an optimistic tone in their pre-match comments. 'I think we're going there with a wee shout, particularly if we get an early goal,' said Nicholl. 'We'll have a go all right because we don't want to accept that we're out of the tie yet. We owe it to the hundreds of fans who'll be in Munich not to have the attitude that the tie is over.'

'We are not just going over to Munich to enjoy a holiday or to just say that we played in the Olympic Stadium,' added Shaun Dennis. 'We are going over there to win the game.'

Privately, most knew that it would be a huge ask to progress in the competition. 'I don't think deep down we thought we could win the tie,' says Jason Dair. 'I think it was just a case of going to enjoy it. We wanted to make sure we put up a decent performance and hopefully give our fans something to remember.'

For many, simply getting the opportunity to compete in such spectacular surroundings against such illustrious opponents was enough. 'If you can't enjoy the Olympic Stadium and playing against Bayern Munich, then you shouldn't be in the game,' offers Davie Kirkwood.

The squad were aware that a large number of fans would be travelling to the game and there was a desire to reward them for the support they had shown throughout the whole UEFA Cup campaign. There was still frustration that they hadn't given supporters a goal to celebrate in the first leg. 'The fans had turned up in their numbers and made themselves heard in the first leg,' says Colin Cameron. 'They never at any point in that game stopped supporting us, even when we lost a goal. They kept at it and that helped us. We had wanted to score for them, but it didn't happen.'

The squad were in confident mood as they departed for Germany, having secured a 2-2 draw with Rangers at Stark's Park on the previous Saturday. Having arrived in Munich, they trained at the Olympiastadion the night before the match. The memory of that training session is still one that players cherish. 'At the training the night before there was just excitement,' recalls Stevie Crawford. 'Being in that stadium, zipping the new [Adidas] Tango balls they had given us about. It was just genuine excitement. It was probably the closest we got to how we felt at the cup final. It was really similar to that, and the attitude was the same, "We have got a free hit at these guys, and you never know what might happen."'

'They had to tear us off the pitch when we were finished training,' says Davie Kirkwood. 'No one really wanted to leave.'

'We had five to ten minutes to ourselves at the end,' adds Colin Cameron. 'Some of the boys were hitting free kicks and that. A couple of us walked right to the top of the main stand and when you turned and looked back the lads on the pitch were like flies. They were tiny, such was the size of the stadium. You just got a feel for the place and how big it was.'

There would be one final impromptu training session on the morning of the game. In a reminder of the days when the squad would head to Beveridge Park and look for a patch of grass free from dog dirt to train on, Jimmy Nicholl took his team to a public park opposite their hotel for a final session. 'We put the sweatshirts down, did a couple of set plays and had a wee kickabout,' says Scott Thomson. 'There we were. We are playing Bayern Munich that night, but we are having a kickabout in a park. People were walking across the park on their way to work just looking at us.'

Nicholl faced a difficult decision on who would face the German side. His squad was full of talent, and all were desperate to play, but there would not be space for everyone in his starting 11. He finally selected the players who would represent Raith Rovers in what would likely be their biggest ever match: Thomson, Taylor, Broddle, Coyle, Dennis, Sinclair, Rougier, Cameron, Crawford, Lennon and Dair. On the bench were Kirkwood, McInally, Graham, McMillan and Fridge.

The news was a blow to those not starting or left out completely. 'I wasn't named in the starting 11 for the game in Munich and I was devastated,' says Ally Graham. 'Totally devastated. I am not going to lie, that was probably the worst moment of my career.'

'It was me and Bobby Raeside sitting in the stand again,' says Barry Wilson, who had also been left out of the squad at Easter Road. 'After the first leg, Jimmy took me into his office and spoke to me. He said, "Look, this is why I left you out, but the next leg could be the one for you." That perked me up a little bit. I stuck at it in training and tried to prove a point but then he named the squad in Munich, and I was left out again.'

'I felt for Barry,' says supporter John Greer. 'I really felt for him. He had scored the goal that had gotten us through against Akranes, but he didn't even get stripped over in Munich.'

Wilson did at least have the opportunity to experience being in Germany. Young apprentice Graham Robertson, who had earlier travelled to the Faroe Islands and Iceland, missed out altogether. 'Annoyingly, I didn't go to Munich in the end,' laments Robertson. 'That was the one trip in Europe I missed. I got ill in the build-up and then it was a case of, "You need to stay away from the rest of the players just in case." When everyone got back, they were all just telling stories about what happened. I just wish that I hadn't got ill, but it is what it is. That is life, and what happens with football.'

With team selection finalised, there was nothing left to do but enjoy the occasion and the luxurious surroundings of the Olympiastadion. 'You went into the dressing room, and it was massive,' recalls Stevie Crawford. 'There was an en-suite area and lockers and everything like that. We all had these individual mirrors and individual hairdryers beside each seat. At Stark's Park we had this one wee mirror, I always remember it because as a YTS we used to have to clean it, and if any players had caught you with a hairdryer in front of it you would be slaughtered.'

'I had been in the dressing rooms at Parkhead and Ibrox,' says Tony Rougier. 'But at Bayern Munich there was a pool, an ice bath, there was fresh fruit in the dressing room and Lucozade Sports drinks and stuff like that. Things that you had never experienced at club level. The way they treated athletes, it was fantastic.'

The surroundings continued to impress when they walked out to warm up. 'The night before when we had trained at the Olympic Stadium,' says Scott Thomson, 'they had one floodlight on, no advertising in the stadium, but come the night of the game the lights were on, there was advertising everywhere, TV cameras everywhere, cameras on strings behind the goal. It was like someone had taken you to a different place.'

The players were taken aback by the size of the support that had travelled to watch them. Around 1,500 had made the journey across from Scotland, including many of their friends and families. 'It was great to run out and see the Rovers supporters behind the goals, with their banners and flags,' says Davie Sinclair. 'It was special for me too, as my mum and dad were over for the game. A lot of the fans had dug deep to get over for the match and it was heart-warming.'

'You were aware that people were paying money to come and watch you,' explains Stevie Crawford. 'Jimmy always made us aware of that. There was always that sense of, "Don't let yourself down," but then there was also, "Don't let people down." The money people had paid to come and watch you meant you wanted to give them something back.'

It had been an emotional journey for many of the players to get to that point, particularly those who were local to Fife. It was almost inconceivable to have gone from playing in Fife leagues to be standing in the Olympiastadion preparing to face Bayern Munich. 'I played with Stevie [Crawford] at underage football,' says Jason Dair. 'So, our families knew each other. They always had shots at taking us back and forward to games and when you get to senior football, it is just the exact same. Our parents were at every single game. Stevie's mum and dad were at every single game and my mum and dad were too.

'Munich was a continuation of that. Although it was a very different setting from Castlebridge through in Oakley on a mucky park to the Olympiastadion. The setting was different, but our parents' thoughts would have just been the same. Hoping that we do well.'

The supporters had arrived at the Olympiastadion in jovial mood. Most suspected this was likely to be the end of the line of their UEFA Cup journey, but there was no sense of despondency. To be in this city, at this stadium and playing a team like Bayern Munich was an exceptional moment. That afternoon they had sampled the delights the Bavarian capital had to offer. 'I remember a lot of Rovers fans had congregated outside this one bar,' says John Greer. 'They were standing in the street outside singing, "Are you watching Dunfermline?" I was standing there laughing and thinking, "Unless CCTV footage from Germany is getting beamed into houses in Dunfermline, then probably not."'

The excitement had gathered pace as the day had progressed and as they made their way to the stadium. For those enjoying the famous Munich bierkellers, as each beer had gone down, optimism grew. The Olympiastadion had been built as the main venue for the 1972 Olympics and after the Games were over it had become the home of Bayern Munich. It sat in the Olympic Park and had a distinctive, flowing canopy as a roof. 'Seeing the stadium for the first time was, for me, sensational,' says Jonathan

Tippetts-Aylmer. 'I have got this vivid memory of the stand covering that looked like a spider's web. The whole Olympic Park was like that. It was really, really cool. I don't think we could believe that we were there.'

If there was one slightly disappointing aspect to the evening for some, it was the eventual size of the crowd. The Rovers section may have been bustling, but among the home sections there were large gaps, with the stadium only a third full by kick-off. The Bayern crowd were used to hosting the great and good of Europe, so a relatively unknown Scottish team with no European track record was perhaps not an attraction. The lack of a large home support did not detract from the occasion, and the eager and enthusiastic atmosphere in the away end did more than enough to compensate.

Bayern Munich had selected a strong line-up, an indication that they were in no mood to underestimate Rovers. There had been rumours that Jürgen Klinsmann would not play as he had suffered a recurrence of an ankle ligament injury in their victory over Stuttgart the previous weekend. He had initially been left behind when Bayern departed for their training camp outside Munich on the Sunday night, but a scan showed it was no more than a sprain and he was named in the starting 11.

Jimmy Nicholl's final words to his squad were to go and enjoy themselves. This philosophy had been the foundation of all their success to this point. He just wanted his side to express themselves and have a go. 'Bayern were expected to win five or six nil,' says Nicholl. 'So, if we string six passes together or had an opportunity to cross the ball and get a bit of goalmouth action or get a save out of the goalkeeper, then they are not going to be happy, so I said to them, "Go and try and do something. There is no point just defending. Go and impose yourself on the game and make runs. Do it. We have got to cause some chaos and give the supporters something to cheer.'"

23

The Olympiastadion

'YOU CAN always tell from the first 10 or 12 minutes of a game how your side are going to be,' says Jimmy Nicholl. 'Whether they are on the ball or they look intimidated.' The opening stages of the match gave the manager encouragement. There were no signs of his side being overawed. 'The lads started knocking the ball about,' he continues. 'They were doing their thing, clearing their lines, and playing. I was happy.'

Bayern had started strongly and were attacking with intent, but Rovers' defence looked solid. 'The pace of the game seemed a lot quicker than it was in Edinburgh,' reflects Scott Thomson. 'I don't know if that was them dictating the pace of the game or they had those instructions, but I think they came after us early doors to try and get the game tucked away. It was so quick, and I was trying to catch a breath, but we managed to bed ourselves into the game a wee bit.'

At the heart of the defence and leading by example was Davie Sinclair. The central defender was working hard to deny the Bayern forwards space and time to control the game. 'In contrast to the first leg, we started the match well,' he admits. 'Mind you, if you can't play in a setting like that you shouldn't be in the game, but we took the match by the scruff of the neck.'

Sinclair had been selected as captain for the evening, a decision that had taken him by surprise. 'I was quite shocked,' he says. 'Jimmy just said to me, "Lead the boys out, you are captain," just before we went out. I felt a wee bit sad for Shaun [Dennis] as he was the skipper for the first leg, but it was the boss's decision. It was up to him to decide who he feels should be wearing the armband and we all had to do the job asked of us.'

Reflecting back on the decision now, Nicholl believes that it was an instinctive choice, but that Sinclair's character and attitude had played a part. 'I had no real thought about that other than the way he was,' he explains. 'Sinky was a better player than a lot of people gave him credit for and the way he went about his job, his determination. I maybe thought that with the responsibility of the captaincy it might calm him down a wee bit, but you couldn't stop his wholeheartedness and the way he was a competitor. You couldn't take that away from him.'

The first 20 minutes of the match were played out to the surreal background of bagpipes. The Claymores Pipes and Drums, a group of Munich-born pipers, had turned up to entertain the crowd. 'There were bagpipes playing in the background somewhere,' recalls Ally Graham, who was sat on the bench. 'It was in the main stand and every time a song finished, the Germans would clap. It was bizarre.'

Rovers' good start threatened to unravel after 22 minutes when Andreas Herzog sent Christian Nerlinger clear down the left-hand side. Ronnie Coyle attempted the tackle but misjudged his timing and brought the striker down. The Ukrainian referee immediately pointed to the spot. 'The boy was about to shoot and looked certain to score so I just dived in,' reflected Coyle later.

Most in the away crowd felt for the veteran defender. 'I think Ronnie Coyle was one of the best defenders we had at the time,' says Steve Wallace. 'His play and positional sense was way better than people gave him credit for. He was just prone to those occasional errors and tended to be unlucky and got punished for it.'

The penalty would be taken right in front of the away support, meaning they had the perfect view as Jean-Pierre Papin blasted it high over Scott Thomson's goal. The miss was celebrated like a goal. 'When Papin missed the penalty, it was incredible,' says Jim Clark. 'I was probably more relieved than anyone else in the away end because Ronnie had been the one who gave it away. After Papin missed, I turned to James Fowlie and joked that at least Ronnie's booking meant he was suspended for the next round!'

With the ball having sailed over the bar, Thomson had been denied the chance to repeat his penalty heroics from the League Cup Final the previous November, but he still credits it as a save of sorts. 'I was on a roll with penalty kicks at that point,' he says. 'I had thought, "It doesn't matter who is taking it, I am going to save it." Obviously, I didn't need to save it in the end because it went over the bar, but it is still another miss, isn't it? I'll take that.'

It was a hugely enjoyable moment for the Raith fans and the miss immediately gave some in the away end a sense of belief. 'When Papin skied that penalty, it was brilliant,' says Gavin Quinn. 'You did have a wee thought at that point, "This could be our night."'

It was a belief shared by those on the pitch. 'If they had scored then I don't think we could have got back from that,' reflects Danny Lennon. 'We would have been three down and it would have just been too much. For it still just to be two goals, you still had belief that with the players we had, someone was going to do something.'

Rovers seemed energised by their luck and immediately took control of the game. They had been playing well up to that point, but they found a renewed confidence and started to push forward more frequently. 'I was at right-back,' says Alex Taylor. 'It wasn't my natural position, but I can't remember waves of attack coming flying at me. I can't remember feeling too worried or thinking, "I can't breathe here," or anything like that. We had the ball and we knocked it about pretty well at times, OK maybe with no penetration when we got to the final third, but we were doing well and matching them.'

As the minutes passed, many started to think about getting to half-time not having conceded.

'The closer we came to half-time, we were thinking, "Get in level," says Lennon. 'If we had reached half-time at 0-0, not having lost a goal, we would have been delighted.'

After 42 minutes, Lennon was involved when Rovers were awarded a free kick just over 20 yards out after he had been fouled by Herzog. He and Tony Rougier stood over the ball initially, but Lennon had been on a run of good form with free kicks and had hit the post at Ibrox the previous Saturday. He was the natural favourite to take it.

Lennon had joined Raith in 1993 after eight years at Hibernian. Jimmy Nicholl had long been interested in the skilful midfielder and had tried to buy him several times before, with no success, but eventually he got his man. 'It just came out of the blue on the last day of the window,' explains Lennon. '[Hibs boss] Alex Miller phoned me and said that they had got an offer from Raith Rovers that they were prepared to take. To be fair to Alex, I had a short time to decide, and he helped me with the deal, what to ask for and he looked after me that way. I was very grateful for that.'

At that point in his career, Hibernian had been all that Lennon had known, having joined the Edinburgh club as a boy. 'Hibs had been a wee soft spot for my dad,' says Lennon. 'When my dad grew up as a youngster, everybody in his house supported Celtic, but he supported Hibs, so there was a nice wee emotional connection there.'

He had enjoyed his time at Easter Road but having failed to establish himself as a first-team regular, he knew that he needed to move. The decision may have made sense for football reasons, but on a personal level, it was more difficult. 'Hibs was just like your extended family,' says Lennon. 'The dressing room at Hibs had some great guys in it and they were like brothers to you. When you have been in each other's lives for seven and a half years and you see them every single day, it is hard to leave that, but I knew that I needed to play regularly.'

Raith had been only one match away from relegation from the Premier League when Lennon had signed, so he knew that he would be playing in the First Division, but it was a sacrifice that he was prepared to make for more game time. 'It wasn't really a financial thing at that time,' he continues. 'I just came to a stage in my career where I needed first-team football. Raith weren't going to guarantee that, but they were certainly going to give me a better chance of it than Hibs.'

On arrival at Stark's Park, he immediately knew that he had made the right choice. 'Jimmy Nicholl was infectious,' says Lennon. 'He was the total opposite from Alex Miller. Alex was a great coach to work for, very methodical and I learned a great deal from him, but Jimmy was just different in his approach, he was infectious, training was fun. You wanted to jump in there in the morning. You went in with a smile on your face and you came out with a smile on your face. I loved it.

'At Hibs the setup was very professional. Things were done differently at Raith. The Glasgow boys used to stop at a cafe in Dalgety Bay every Friday morning before training for a full breakfast. It was so good big Shaun used to drive from his house in Leven just to join them. I've never known a dressing room like it for wind-ups. Someone once did something unmentionable in big Ronnie Coyle's shoes and he simply washed it out, pulled them on and walked home.'

Lennon established himself in the Raith team and would go on to play a critical role in the success of the club over the next two years. Now, he stood over the ball in the Olympiastadion, facing the Bayern wall and the imposing figure of Oliver Kahn.

There were just three minutes left until the half-time break, and although the team had been playing well, there had been few opportunities to test the goalkeeper. Lennon knew that it offered the best chance so far to haul themselves back into the tie. 'I just remember thinking that we had an opportunity here,' says Lennon. 'I said to myself, "Right, come on. Make something happen."'

24

The Perfect Deflection

DANNY LENNON struck the free kick. The ball successfully bypassed the Bayern wall and, travelling at pace, it deflected off the head of Andreas Herzog. The initial shot looked to be heading directly towards Oliver Kahn but contact with the Austrian defender changed the trajectory, sending it hurtling towards the opposite side of the goal. Kahn watched motionless as the ball hit the back of the net. Incredibly, Raith had taken the lead.

At the far end of the ground, there was a momentary delay as the away supporters tried to make sense of what they had witnessed. 'You know what it is like even if you are watching from the opposite end at Stark's Park,' says journalist Scott Davie. 'Everything flattens out and you don't get perspective of distance and everything. Given that you were in the Olympic Stadium with the running track before you even get to the pitch, and it was up the opposite end from the Rovers fans. They would have practically needed a telescope to see the goals.'

'It was kind of like Hampden,' agrees Shaughan McGuigan. 'You were separated by a running track, and you were away at the opposite end. When it goes in, as much as we saw the net ripple, it felt like there was a delay. Almost a delay between your eyes taking in what happened and your brain trying to work out what had just happened.'

When they finally did, it was bedlam. 'Everyone lost the run of themselves,' says Shaughan. 'If I had to pick one football moment to stay with me for the rest of my life, then that is it. It wasn't just the celebration, but that split second before the explosion.'

Graham Hunter of the *Daily Mail* would later describe it as a 'heart-stopping moment of sheer joy'. It was that and more. It was a moment of elation and one that will be cherished for ever by any Raith supporter lucky enough to have been in the stadium to experience it. 'We've used the word surreal a lot talking about the whole European adventure,' says Graeme Meldrum. 'But that moment and that goal, honestly, for God's sake. I am actually getting goosebumps just sitting here talking about it.'

The away crowd erupted when they realised that their team had scored. The celebration was incredible and once the jubilation eventually subsided, it was replaced by astonishment that they had actually taken the lead against Bayern Munich. Many shook their heads in disbelief, while others simply laughed. If there had been a rush of euphoria in the stands when the goal had gone in, it was also felt by the players back down on the pitch. 'The moment it hit the net,' says Danny Lennon, 'I can't even describe the rush.'

It was an emotion shared by every single one of Lennon's team-mates. 'Oh my god,' says Davie Kirkwood. 'The euphoria just went through your body. Unbelievable, absolutely unbelievable.'

'That moment,' reflects Tony Rougier. 'Just to be able to score. Oh, my goodness. To be leading 1-0, for me it was just as good as when Trinidad and Tobago qualified for the World Cup in 2006. It was that type of excitement. We could have blown the game off and gone home right then.'

As the furthest player from the goal, Scott Thomson had initially been confused. 'At first, I wasn't even sure how it went in,' says the goalkeeper. 'The angle it went in from where he hit it from was totally where it shouldn't have gone. I was thinking, "Did it take a wee nick?" You couldn't really see from the position that I was in.'

His confusion was replicated around the Olympiastadion. 'At the time I was thinking, "How did he beat Kahn from there?"' says Ally Graham. 'He had completely wrong-footed him. I didn't realise that it had gotten a deflection. I thought he had put it in the top corner. Then afterwards when I saw it on TV I was like, "Jesus, what a deflection!" But it still counts, you know – even if you do hit it off a guy's heid!'

Julian Broddle's first thought as the goal went in was of the fans who had come to support the team. The English defender had been frustrated that they had not been able to give supporters a goal to celebrate in the first leg at Easter Road. This felt like payback. 'When Danny scored,' he recounts, 'I thought, "We have given the fans what they wanted." They had travelled everywhere to watch us and had been brilliant. They had been in the Faroe Islands and Iceland, remote, freezing cold places and now they are in the Olympic Stadium celebrating a goal. That was the moment. This was the dream.'

After scoring, Lennon was immediately engulfed by his team-mates. It was his fourth goal in the competition, making him Rovers' top European goalscorer, with the added distinction of having scored in every round that they had competed in. The goal may have meant everything to those associated with Raith in that moment, but for the young midfielder it held a very personal significance. When celebrations subsided, Lennon glanced upwards. 'I had lost my dad when I was 20,' he explains. 'I just remember looking up to the heavens and having a wee moment thinking about my dad.'

There is warmth in Lennon's voice as he speaks of his family and the huge influence of his father. 'Family has always been the most important thing in my life,' he says. 'My folks weren't well off, but I had a smashing time growing up. After four daughters, I was the first son, and I probably had an easy time of it.

'My dad was fantastic and used to watch me play football for Hutchie Vale. If I had a poor game there were a few well-chosen words, never harsh, but enough to hit home, but he would let me make my own mistakes. I was delighted that he had been there to see me make my debut for Hibs at the age of 17, and when I scored against Bayern, he came into my thoughts. I had a wee moment looking up and I certainly knew that he would be looking down.'

It remains an emotional watch, even 30 years later.

For his team-mates, the goal felt like redemption for Lennon having missed out on the League Cup Final a year earlier. He was a popular member of the squad and there is still delight that he found his moment. 'I felt great for the wee man,' says Ally Graham. 'He had missed out on a lot when he got his bad injury, so to do that, it was brilliant for him.'

'Danny was a great boy and a terrific player,' agrees journalist Scott Davie. 'He missed out on that cup final, but he has got his immortality, hasn't he?'

Reflecting back on the goal now, it remains a special memory. 'I can still play that from the minute,' smiles Lennon. 'The exact place on the pitch. How the free kick happened. The wall. The reaction of the Bayern Munich manager. They are all etched in the mind. I got a little bit of luck along the way, but scoring in the game against Bayern in the Olympic Stadium still puts a smile on my face.

'Any time that Bayern Munich goal comes up, my brother-in-law, who is actually my best friend from growing up as he married my sister, sends me a text saying, "Are you still going on about that?"'

As far as Raith fans are concerned, Lennon can reminisce about it anytime he wants. It was pure gold.

Rovers were able to see out the game to half-time and leave the field with a one-goal advantage. Leading after the first 45 minutes was beyond the wildest expectation of players and fans. The half-time break gave supporters the chance to decompress from the goal as most remained stunned by what had just happened. 'After the goal,' says Kenny Smith, 'I actually got a wee bit tearful. I am an emotional person and I had broken down in tears of joy at the end of the Coca-Cola Cup Final. In Munich it was disbelief. Just surreal disbelief. Then I got incredibly emotional. I was just thinking, "What is going on here? This isn't meant to happen."'

The atmosphere in the away end was electrified during the break. You could almost touch the disbelief. Rovers were now only one goal away from levelling the tie. Then there was that scoreboard. The giant electronic scoreboard behind the supporters wasn't exactly state-of-the-art and may have looked like a relic from the 1970s, but that didn't matter. What mattered was what was written on it. The most famous scoreline in the club's history – 'Olympiastadion Munchen, FC Bayern, Raith Rovers FC, 0:1'. Those with cameras rushed to capture the image.

Even for those who still thought that beating Bayern remained an outside possibility, the fact that the team had scored first and the Olympiastadion scoreboard showed them leading was enough. 'It was just a chance to dream,' says Jonathan Tippetts-Aylmer. 'We had 15 minutes of half-time to dream in our heads that we might win, and it couldn't have got any better than that.'

When the emotion subsided, supporters occupied themselves until the restart. Kenny Smith found public phones at the back of the concourse and called a friend who had been in Iceland, but not travelled to Munich. John Greer walked around the stadium with fellow fan John Litster and his video camera in hand to get a perspective of the supporters and his flag that had been soaked in the Faroe Islands. Others just stared at the scoreboard in disbelief, still not quite able to grasp what had just happened.

If there was shock in the stands, it was reflected in both dressing rooms. Interviewed as he walked off, Franz Beckenbauer delivered a harsh message to the Bayern team. 'You are in danger of losing this tie because Raith Rovers are outplaying you,' he said. 'You must change everything in attack because Raith have learned to cope with the style you are playing. This could be embarrassing for us.'

Among the Raith players, the shock of taking the lead was matched by a sense of satisfaction that they had managed to re-ignite the tie. 'We had talked about sneaking that first goal and seeing how they were going to react,' says Jason Dair. 'And we had managed to do that. That was always the plan. If we can manage to sneak that first goal, then we would be back in the tie. You thought, "We have got a wee chance here. A chance to go and do something special."'

'It was a wee bit surreal to be honest with you,' says Colin Cameron. 'It was, "Jesus, we are only one goal away from levelling the tie." You go in at half-time and you are actually pinching yourself.'

The events in the dressing room at half-time have now become legendary, a story that captures the surrealness and the sheer enjoyment of the moment. As the half-time whistle went, Jimmy Nicholl had rushed up the tunnel to prepare his team talk. The stadium was still reeling from the goal. 'I never even looked at the scoreboard,' admits Nicholl. 'People always say to me, "It must have been great looking up at the scoreboard," but I never even saw it. I was straight up the tunnel to gather my thoughts.'

On the way, Nicholl had spotted Beckenbauer and Uli Hoeneß heading towards the home dressing room looking unhappy. He knew that they would be expressing their frustration towards Otto Rehhagel and his players. 'We were 1-0 up at half-time,' says Nicholl, 'and there's no point going into our dressing room and saying very much. I wanted to keep the players' thoughts away from the fact that Bayern would come at them in the second half.'

'To get to the dressing rooms you went downstairs,' says Scott Thomson. 'We went to the left and they went to the right. You could see their coaches being aggressive to their team and then going off their head when inside. When we got back to our dressing room, Jimmy was standing there waiting. You could see he wanted to say something relevant to the game, but he just looked around, said something like, "Fucking hell lads, 1-0 up," then burst

Rovers defend for their lives in the final minutes in Iceland (Brynjar Gauti Sveinsson)

Hero Scott Thomson celebrates getting through (RRFC)

The away end welcome the full-time whistle (RRFC)

All smiles back at the airport (Wallace)

Supporters queue for precious Bayern tickets (Fimister)

Colin Cameron charges forward at Easter Road (Fimister)

Oliver Kahn thwarts another Rovers attack (Fimister)

Rovers' substitutes get ready (Fimister)

Stevie Crawford fully focused (Fimister)

The away support gathers in Munich (Greer)

Waiting on kick-off at the Olympic Stadium (Nicholson)

Tony Rougier holds off Jean-Pierre Papin (Imago)

Steven Lawther roars on the team (Lawther)

The dream is over as Raith concede a second (Imago)

The team salute the fans as their European journey ends (RRFC/ Herald and Post)

Danny Lennon re-lives his Munich moment with John Greer at Reminiscing Raith (Gray)

out laughing. It was a great way just to bring everybody back down to earth.'

'It was the most bizarre team talk I have ever been in,' laughs Danny Lennon.

Nicholl decided to use their opponents' frustration to his own advantage. 'All the boys came in and I was starting to talk and all I could hear was them in the other dressing room talking in German,' he recounts. 'You would hear some German then "Crawford", then some more German then "Cameron", more German then "Dennis". It was as if to say, "How are these boys beating you 1-0?"

'I let on to the lads that it was Franz Beckenbauer. I said, "Listen. That is Franz Beckenbauer who has played in World Cups and all, one of the best players ever, giving them all a bollocking. That's Franz Beckenbauer and he is mentioning all your names. Listen to it, lads." They were all sitting there or up on the benches trying to listen for their names. It turned into a laughing thing at half-time which was probably the best thing. It just cut the tension. After that, I didn't need to say anything. I suppose that was the best way for them to go out for the second half. All relaxed and not anxious.'

'Jimmy was just laughing,' says Stevie Crawford. 'He said, "Boys, they are actually getting a telling off." We all sat back down, and he said, "I don't know what to say to you. I don't know what to say." It was such a surreal moment. This could be the biggest moment ever in club history and there is nothing much you can really say.'

'We knew that they would come at us right from the start in the second half,' says Davie Kirkwood. 'But we were just sat in there having a laugh and a wee sing-song and they were getting absolutely torn into. You couldn't make it up.'

The Munich scoreboard showing Rovers ahead is so iconic that it can be easy to forget that there was a second half that night. As the game restarted, some fans weree beginning to believe that they could actually win. 'We started to think that the comeback was on,' recalls Gavin Quinn. 'There was a feeling of, "We might just do this." It was unbelievable.'

Graeme Meldrum shared his optimism, 'I was starting to think, "We can do them!" You go back to when I started watching the Rovers and the position we were in and now I'm in the Olympic Stadium watching them beating Bayern Munich. And thinking we could win!' That the team had taken their supporters to that point was a testament itself to how incredible their achievement had been.

There would be one final moment of hope in the match when Tony Rougier had a chance to equalise shortly after half-time. On 50 minutes, Lennon played the ball short to Dair, who whipped in a fierce cross. It isolated Oliver Kahn and and eluded the German defence, arriving at the feet of Rougier unmarked at the back post. With Kahn taken out of the game, the goal in front of Rougier was completely empty. The Trinidadian forward attempted to wrap his leg around the ball and strike it towards goal, but the angle was incredibly tight, and he only partially succeeded, firing it agonisingly into the side-netting. The move had unfolded directly in front of the Rovers supporters and some on the opposite side from Rougier momentarily mistook the side of the net rippling for the ball having hit the back, but there were gasps all around the away section. 'That Rougier miss just after half-time,' sighs Kenny Smith. 'I might not have been sitting here talking to you if that had gone in. That just might have finished me off.'

Over the years, memories of that chance have evolved. As the years have passed, the difficulty of the opportunity has increasingly lessened, and it is now widely considered to be the sliding doors moment which could have ensured that history changed, and Rovers progressed. Looking back now, with an objective eye, it was an incredibly difficult chance and would have required something quite remarkable from Rougier to steer the ball into the net. Even if he had, the tie would only have been level at 2-2, and who knows how the remainder of the night would have unfolded? 'If Tony had scored that might have just made them angry,' suggests midfielder Alex Taylor.

'It was never really a great chance,' says John Greer. 'It was a tight angle. The ball was on him quickly and he would have had to do something miraculous to have scored. You get goals like that where the myth grows over time, like Gordon Pettie when he scored against Berwick Rangers at Stark's Park. After a few years, he'd started down the Prom with the ball, beat five women, a traffic warden, and every player in the Berwick team before he scored.'

That doesn't mean that the player at the heart of the moment doesn't have a little regret. 'I do wish I could take back that moment,' says Rougier. 'I am glad that I can't recall it very, very well, but I do remember hitting the side-netting. It was such a difficult shot, and to have taken advantage would have been ideal, but it was such a dream come true to even be in that moment.'

Rougier now reflects on the whole match and feels that he didn't play to his true capabilities that night. He was a huge fan of German football, with Lothar Matthäus his hero, so to be playing at the home of Bayern Munich was a realisation of an ambition. The magnitude of the occasion felt overwhelming at times.

Alex Taylor shares Rougier's frustration when he looks at his own performance. 'I was just a bit disappointed that I was just not a bit more proactive in the game,' he says. 'I just didn't want to make a mistake and I didn't want to let anyone down. If you play thinking about not making a mistake, then you are never going to reach that next level. If I had my chance again, I'd like to think I'd go and get the trumpets out and lead the charge, but then I know I probably wouldn't, because that's just not me.'

Rougier and Taylor are being unduly harsh on themselves. It was an incredible team performance against some of the best footballers in the world and the two more than played their part, an assessment underlined by the fact that there is no sense of recrimination about that Rougier moment among fans or former team-mates today. It was simply part of the journey and part of the experience. It adds to the stories and allows Rovers fans' minds to drift to the 'What if?' In reality they know it is fanciful, but then, the dream was always what the European journey was about.

Two minutes later the tie was effectively over when Rovers conceded an equaliser after a Ronnie Coyle slip allowed Alexander Zickler to race in and provide the perfect pass to Jürgen Klinsmann to net with a tap-in. Twelve minutes after that, Bayern netted a winner on the night when Scott Thomson was only able to touch a Marcel Witeczek corner to the back post. Dietmar Hamann headed back into the danger area and after several unlucky ricochets, Markus Babbel poked the ball home through a wall of Rovers jerseys.

Ronnie Coyle would later speak to the press about Bayern's first goal. 'I got a shout that I had time on the ball when it came to me, so instead of clearing it I decided to control it and try and start another move for us,' he said. 'Just as it came to me, I slipped, and the ball broke away from me. I didn't even see Zickler until he had crossed for Klinsmann to score. When the incident happened, I just wanted the earth to open up and swallow me.'

'It was a shame for Ronnie that night,' reflects Jimmy Nicholl. 'They didn't have to work hard to score and looking back, that was the most frustrating thing about not just that night but the two games. They didn't have to work for most of their goals across the two ties, the first Klinsmann one in Edinburgh aside.'

There was one final chance for Rovers late on when substitute Ally Graham chested down a Sinclair cross inside the box, Kahn diving at the striker's feet to deny him a moment of glory. 'I came on and had a wee chance, but the tie was over by then,' recalls Graham. 'I swear to God, if it was an Umbro ball we were playing with I would have scored. I know it is a stupid excuse, but it was a lighter ball, and it just flew off my chest and bounced too far in front of me.

'If it was a rainy night in Kirkcaldy with an Umbro ball, I definitely would have scored.'

Moments later, the referee blew the final whistle to bring both the game and Raith Rovers' UEFA Cup run to an end.

25

Afterparty

AFTER THE final whistle, Davie Sinclair, encouraged by his manager, led the team over to the Nordkurve section of the stadium to take the acclaim of the large travelling support. They may have just lost the match 2-1 and the tie 4-1 on aggregate, but fans were appreciative of their efforts and wanted to thank them for that magical moment just before half-time and the whole European adventure.

On reaching the supporters, the players linked arms to thank all those who had made the trip. 'It was special going up to the fans at the end,' says Danny Lennon. 'I still have a great picture of it, the line of us with our hands in the air, giving the fans a bow. They were a part of everything that we had achieved. They kicked every single ball with us and what they went through to get to the matches. It wasn't just our success, it was theirs as well.'

Most of the Rovers players were adorned in Bayern Munich strips, having already swapped with their German counterparts. Sinclair stood bare-chested, his Jean-Pierre Papin's strip tucked into his shorts. 'It was my proudest moment in football,' he reflects.

Those Bayern tops would become treasured mementoes of a magnificent night, although not everyone had grasped the moment. 'My one regret,' reflects Jason Dair, 'was that after the game when everybody was outside swapping strips, I was sat with my head down a bit disappointed that we had got beat. Thankfully when we got back, we had managed to get a few spare ones, so I did get a Bayern strip in the end.'

The young winger was not the only one distracted at full time. 'At the end of the game, Ronnie was still dwelling on his mistake,' explains Jim Clark. 'His head wasn't quite in the right place. He said that when it came to shirt swapping, he missed the jerseys of the big names that he had been marking, but he did end up with Zickler's top, who at the time was just a kid. That strip now hangs in a frame in his house and has pride of place. The only time it has been taken off the wall was when we took it down recently to bring it to the Reminiscing Rovers event with his daughter Briony.'

Jimmy Nicholl had taken Coyle off with ten minutes to go, to allow a one-to-one with the defender to reassure him about his slip. It was a message reinforced by the rest of the coaching staff and his team-mates. 'Every goal there is a fault somewhere or a mistake at some point,' says Alex Taylor. 'You were never going to criticise Ronnie for that, not in the slightest. You see players like Steven Gerrard slipping and making a mistake at a critical time to lose Liverpool the league, so it can happen to anybody.'

Over time, Coyle came to terms with the events of that night and looked back with pride of having been part of such a historic occasion. It was a pride shared by everyone associated with the club. They may have exited the tournament, but they had gone toe-to-toe with

Bayern Munich over the two legs, given them a fright and at no point in either fixture been outclassed. 'There was definitely pride after the final whistle,' says Davie Kirkwood. 'Not just pride for the players, but pride for the supporters and the club and for where we had come from. We were playing in the First Division a year and a half earlier. Coming that far in just a year and a half and playing in the Olympic Stadium against Bayern Munich, it was a fairytale script.'

'Although we lost that night, we were still proud,' says Stevie Crawford. 'Jimmy looked at every one of us that night and said, "You know what? We have done ourselves proud." We knew that if we met anybody at the airport who had a Raith Rovers scarf on we could look them in the eye, and nobody would have said that we let ourselves down.'

For the young striker, the two games against Bayern provided a taste of what was possible in football and left him eager to experience similar nights again. 'That night definitely left me wanting more,' says Crawford. 'I wanted to go and try and test myself against that quality of player again. I was hungry for it.'

There would be one final reminder of the disparity between the two sides when some of the Raith players asked for a tour of the Bayern team bus after the match. 'Their big coach was there after the game,' recalls Danny Lennon. 'Shaun Dennis and I went down and asked if we could get on, just to have a wee look. We were walking on to the bus with a bottle of beer and these Bayern guys are reclined, they have got their tight pants and all that on for the blood circulation. They are getting vitamin injections to prepare for the game three or four days later. It was just a totally different world.'

After defeating Raith, Bayern would go on to win the UEFA Cup that season. Of all six two-legged ties Bayern played on their way to that success, only their 4-3 aggregate win over Barcelona in the semi-final had seen a narrower victory margin. Nottingham Forest had been humiliated 5-1 at the City Ground in their second leg against Bayern and French club Bordeaux were defeated 5-1 on aggregate in the final. It was an illustration of just how well Rovers had done, and Bayern manager Otto Rehhagel would later write that the two legs against them were 'the toughest we endured during the competition'. High praise for a little-known Scottish club making their European debut.

The two sides would reunite two years later when Bayern accepted an invite to be the opposition at the official opening of the newly renovated Stark's Park at the start of 1997. It was special to finally be able to bring the Germans to Kirkcaldy and even better to defeat them 1-0 thanks to a Peter Duffield goal.

There was nothing left to do in Munich but celebrate. The squad had been promised by those running the club that win, lose or draw there would be a party to end all parties after the game, but it never materialised, a situation that still irks Jimmy Nicholl. 'That was the promise given to the players,' he says ruefully. But it never happened. 'I just thought, "Look at the money that the players have brought in. Look at the memories we have created." That was the start of it.'

Some players sensed a frustration from the chairman and some of the directors that they had not managed to progress in the tie, but they were not going to let that get in the way of their last night in Munich. Rovers had made it through two rounds in their first attempt in European competition, something that Rangers, Celtic, Aberdeen and Dundee United all failed to do on their European debuts. It was an outstanding achievement and an incredible journey from start to finish. 'The UEFA Cup campaign was everything I wanted it to be for the club,' reflects Nicholl. 'We were never going to win the trophy, but we had a wee run, and it was great to go out on such a memorable occasion.'

The rest of the evening was spent celebrating. 'We got to meet up with the families and had a right old good time,' says Colin Cameron. 'It was probably the biggest party we have ever had considering we got knocked out of the competition!'

The fans who stayed also enjoyed their night. 'After the game we went back into the centre of Munich,' says John Greer. 'We were in this pub, and it was packed full of Rovers supporters. I look at pictures of that night now and one of my best friends was there, Alan Donaldson, and sadly he passed away two years ago, so it is really quite sad, but those times were great, and they are memories that I will have for a lifetime.'

The following day's press was extremely complimentary of how Rovers had performed and how they had frightened their German opponents. 'All of Scotland was proud of how supposed no-hopers played against the Munich millionaires,' wrote Iain Campbell for the *Daily Record*. John Greechan, writing in the *Fife Free Press*, was equally generous, 'In one of the most theatrical of venues in world football, the quite stunning Olympic Stadium, Rovers belied their bit-part status with a virtuoso performance, and for 22 glorious minutes, half-time interval included, the biggest shock in Scottish football's European history was definitely on the cards.'

Their headline writers backed up the praise. 'Brave Rovers' said the *Daily Mail*. 'Take a bow Rovers – You did us all Proud' said the *Daily Record*, and the *Courier* added 'Rovers bow out but not without a fight'. The consensus was that Rovers had performed above and beyond expectations. It had been a truly special night, and delivered an iconic picture of a scoreboard that still brings a smile today. 'When I came home after that tie and people heard I hadn't seen the scoreboard on the night, they were sending me all these pictures of it,' recounts Jimmy Nicholl. 'I was given a full-blown picture of it from the Novar Bar and had to go down and receive it. It was only when I looked at it, I thought, "Jeez, would you look at that."'

'I have that scoreboard picture in my house right now,' says Tony Rougier. 'It is a reminder and everybody that sees it says, "You guys played Bayern Munich?!" I am extremely happy that I was part of that moment. Just to be able to wear that strip on that day. It was a very special moment for me that no one can take away. No one.'

'The biggest thing for me was that they never weakened their team,' reflects Scott Thomson. 'If anything, they were even stronger in that second leg than what they had put out in the first leg. That was a wee pat on the back to say that Raith Rovers aren't a run-of-the-mill football team, they are potentially someone who could cause us trouble. That was a testament to the boys and where we were at that point. As a younger player I was involved in the Dundee United stuff, but I was always on the bench. There was never any chance I would be playing. To actually get out there and play in Europe with Raith Rovers was amazing.'

It is not just their own experience that the players are proud of. There is immense pride in the fact that they gave the fans something special, something to treasure and a moment to cherish. 'I sometimes look back and, in a way, I feel a wee bit jealous of what the fans were up to and the experience that they got,' says Colin Cameron. 'Booking the tickets, going together and the fun and games that they had, but then if you put the boot on the other foot the fans would have said the exact same the other way. They would have loved to be playing for the club and playing in that environment.'

'You knew that it was a night that was going to be remembered,' reflects Stevie Crawford. 'We could have gone there and been turned over. Thankfully it didn't come to that, but can you imagine if it was, "Aye, remember the UEFA Cup run where we got to Bayern Munich and got beat 7-0?" But that didn't happen. We gave them a night that will be remembered by supporters for a long time.'

'I think the fans got the reward,' says Ally Graham. 'Going to the Faroes, going to Iceland and then going to Munich. I don't think you get any better than that.'

Graham's summation is one that every fan who had been on the journey can agree with. Every single trip was special, and it was an unforgettable time. 'It was just such an adventure,' admits Kenny Smith. 'An absolutely unique experience.'

'If you were making a movie of this and you were writing the script,' says Steve Wallace, 'I don't think you could write it much better. OK, you could have had us beating Bayern and winning the UEFA Cup, but that was never going to happen. In terms of a realistic script bringing in different levels of experience and joy, I don't think you could have written it better. It was just the whole nonsensical nature of it that makes it so special.'

'You had all these ups and downs,' says Gavin Quinn. 'Bobby Wilson, getting relegated at Meadowbank, struggling in the old Second Division. You go to all those games in the hope that eventually the team is going to improve and maybe get to the Premier League, win a cup, play in Europe. And that is exactly what happened. We went from playing in the Second Division to playing in Europe in the space of ten years. That is some going, like.'

'The adventure was over,' concludes John Greer. 'But, God did we enjoy it.'

26

The Start of the Breakdown

AFTER THE high of Munich, things unravelled fast. There had been ongoing speculation around players and management at the club and manager Jimmy Nicholl was the first to leave. 'I was gone three months later,' he says.

When Mick McCarthy left Millwall to take up the role of Republic of Ireland manager, the south London club looked to Kirkcaldy for a replacement. Nicholl was already having difficulties with those running Rovers and his contract was due to expire in the summer, so it was not a difficult decision to move on. 'Millwall came in on the Monday,' he explains. 'The club OK'd it on the Tuesday or the Wednesday and I was in London on the Friday. It happened that quick.'

The loss of someone who had been the driving force of their success would always be difficult, but the speed of Nicholl's departure sent shockwaves through the whole club.

'If I am honest, it felt like the heart and soul of the club had been ripped out,' reflects Robbie Raeside. 'That is football, people move on, and it was a great opportunity for him, and he had to take it, but Jimmy was the beating heart and soul of the whole club at that time.'

'The season went a bit flat after Munich,' says Davie Sinclair. 'And it was difficult when Jimmy left in February. It was the same when Frank [Connor] left. It took the boys a while to pick up again. When Jimmy went, it was difficult for the boys who had been there when he started at Rovers, who had worked with him for years. I think we were on the slippery slope after that.'

'We were gutted,' says supporter Gavin Quinn. 'I sent a wee thank you letter down to him at Millwall, and I included my cup final ticket in it. I just said, "Thanks for all you have done for the club." He sent a letter back saying, "Thanks very much for your letter, but here is your ticket. You should keep it as a memento and a reminder of that time." Him and Martin Harvey had signed it for me.'

'After Jimmy left it was so strange,' reflects Julian Broddle. 'We felt numb. The training changed and all the old banter had gone. It was too serious, and the atmosphere disappeared. Then when the younger guys left to follow him to Millwall, we knew it was the beginning of the end.'

Once in post at Millwall, Nicholl moved to bring Stevie Crawford, Jason Dair and Davie Sinclair down to London. Along with Paul Hartley from Hamilton, they would form a Scottish cluster at his new club. 'I wasn't in a hurry to leave,' explains Crawford. 'I felt I was still learning at Raith Rovers, but people were putting in bids and there are only so many times that you can get asked. Motherwell offered £660,000 for me and Aberdeen also agreed a fee.'

Crawford did finally agree to move to Millwall, knowing that Nicholl would remain as his manager. For Dair, the presence of Nicholl also proved the deciding factor. 'It wasn't really an easy decision,' he says. 'I was still young at the time, 20 or 21. I think there were a few teams sort of sniffing about, but obviously Jimmy was a big factor in everything that had happened at Raith Rovers for me, and the fact that he was interested and wanted to take me down south. That was the pull.'

Crawford and Dair would be joined by Sinclair and, later, apprentice striker Graham Robertson. Nicholl had invited several young apprentices down to play in friendlies and see if they could secure a deal. 'The first week I stayed in Jimmy Nicholl's house with him and his wife,' laughs Robertson, 'I was coming in to training in the car with him, which was not a good look. But seriously, it was just the way he was as a man. He invited me into his house, his wife made me dinner every night and they just looked after me.' Robertson would eventually be offered a contract with the Lions.

The Millwall experience would prove a challenging one for players and manager. Nicholl's reign lasted for only a year before he was sacked after a poor run of results and a damaging FA Cup defeat. 'When I look back on it, I would do things differently,' reflects Nicholl. 'I had gone from working at Raith Rovers with the boys every single day, who were brilliant and were just enjoying their football. I went from that to Germans, Russians, different cultures, players walking off training on a Thursday morning. Then I had the directors upstairs telling me that I had a goalkeeper coming in that I hadn't even seen. In the end I fell out with everybody. I had more problems in a year than I had in six years at Raith Rovers and then when I came away from it, they went into administration.'

Eventually, all of the Scottish players would return north. Dair and Robertson would go back to Kirkcaldy, Crawford joined Hibernian and Sinclair signed for Dundee

United. 'Millwall didn't turn out very well for me in the end,' reflects Sinclair. 'I thought I had done well in the pre-season games. I got [named] man of the match against Liverpool, but I got injured in the first game of the season in a horrendous tackle from a young winger. It was a foot injury and after that I struggled to get fit. I don't think I got a real chance at Millwall.

'I didn't really want to go back to Scotland. I wanted to stay and fight for my place, but Nicholl said to me, "Get yourself up the road and make sure you're all right because things are turning sour here."'

Reflecting back on their London experience, all are philosophical about it. 'What I learned in that year was that football wasn't rosy and that we had been very fortunate at Raith Rovers,' says Stevie Crawford. 'It was a real learning experience. You were going into a different environment, a different dressing room and a different culture. You had all the London boys, who were decent boys, but it was proper cut-throat. They were all looking after themselves and it was a very different environment.'

'I enjoyed my time at Millwall,' adds Jason Dair. 'But I was young and naive and maybe enjoyed myself too much at times. We tried to just keep doing the same sort of stuff, but it was a tougher league. We ended up staying in the same house together, myself, Sinky and Stevie. That was only for six months and then you got your own place and that could be a wee bit lonely. I wanted to get myself back up the road and I was fortunate enough to come back to Raith Rovers.'

The dismantling of the Munich squad continued when midfielder Colin Cameron was sold to Hearts. 'The decision to leave for me was nothing to do with where the club was at or what we had achieved,' he recalls. 'It was the right time in my career to take the next step. Realistically with Raith Rovers, they were never going to be a team that was playing in the Premier League every season and the opportunity to join Hearts, a club I felt was one of the top four in the country, was an opportunity that was too big to miss.'

After Nicholl's departure the Rovers board had appointed youth coach Jimmy Thomson as manager, with midfielder Jim McInally as his assistant. The choice left many in the squad and supporters puzzled. 'Jimmy Nic was such a unique character,' says Barry Wilson. 'It was always going to be hard to replace him. They then promoted Jimmy Thomson from reserve manager up to manager and no disrespect to Jimmy but it felt as if the spark had kind of gone.'

For some senior players, the appointment marked the beginning of the end for their time in Kirkcaldy. 'Jimmy Thomson kicked me out in no time,' remembers Julian Broddle. 'He took me in and told me that East Fife wanted me. I was absolutely devastated. One minute I am playing and then he says, "We are letting you go." I am just sad, even after all these years, that it ended as it did for me.'

Ronnie Coyle was also a reluctant departee. 'Ronnie was really keen to stay on, but he got released in the March along with Julian Broddle,' explains Coyle's friend Jim Clark. 'The justification was that they would let them go then so they could get a deal, rather than having to wait until the close-season. It worked out for him in the sense that [Gordon] Dalziel immediately phoned him, and he went down to Ayr United, but he was still disappointed.'

Forward Ally Graham was next to leave. 'I sat next to Jim McInally in the dressing room,' recounts Graham. 'He would be telling me things about this player and that player. I was never interested in those sorts of things. The next thing I knew, he was telling me who was interested in me, and I thought, "I must be getting papped here." I ended up training with the reserves and getting left out with no explanation. Then it was a swap deal with Falkirk for Stevie Kirk.

'People move on, I know. That is football, it evolves, but just the way it was done. It wasn't professional and it could have been handled better.'

Barry Wilson would also depart the club at the end of the season. 'After Bayern, I was in and out of the team,' he says. 'They offered me a new deal on the same money with no sign-on fee. I thought, "Nah, I am not happy with that," and initially turned it down. Rather than offering me more, they just released me. I got married in the summer and came back to a letter saying that I was being released.

'I don't think my time at Raith Rovers was great when you compare it to the rest of my career. It might have just been too much, too quick. Latterly in my career when I was at Livingston and we qualified for the UEFA Cup, I really savoured it and probably did myself more justice.'

Robbie Raeside also believes that Raith supporters never saw the best of him. 'I wonder what my career at Raith could have been without my injuries,' he ponders. 'I had some great highs at Raith, but I had some bloody low times as well, but that is football. You just have to accept it. I was 23 or 24 when I left, and it was probably more of a mutual thing. I hadn't really established myself as a regular and I got an opportunity to go and play more at Dundee.'

The team that had taken to the field in Munich had been decimated in a short space of time. At the start of the following season, only a handful of players from the side that led in the Olympiastadion remained. 'A big core had been ripped out of the team,' says goalkeeper Scott Thomson. 'It was difficult, and it just wasn't the same kind of place. It was a team that you have played with and to see that team disbanded pretty quickly was hard to deal with. Football evolves and all the rest of it, but we never got the chance to build on what we had achieved. We had great momentum, but the ball just stopped rolling for us at that point.'

27

The Self-Destruct Button

'MAYBE IT was my less logical teenage brain at the time,' reflects Shaughan McGuigan. 'But I thought Munich might be the start of something. What I probably didn't realise was that this was going to be as good as it gets. 'It all kind of fizzled out. It felt like ultimately, we wasted the money that we got from the transfer fees, the European run, everything. Every year after that we seemed to get worse and worse and worse. After two or three years, I think we had all probably acclimatised to the fact that we were a fairly mediocre, second tier side again.'

Jimmy Thomson's tenure as manager proved short-lived. After seeing out the last three months of the season following the departure of Jimmy Nicholl, he was sacked after two matches of the 1996/97 season. His replacement Tommy McLean's tenure proved even shorter, lasting less than a week. 'I knew Tommy from my time in Dundee,' recounts journalist Scott Davie. 'I went up to Stark's Park on the Monday for his announcement as manager. Tommy McLean sits down beside [chairman Alex] Penman and Penman goes, "Right, well we are obviously here to unveil Tommy McLean as the new manager, but before that I would just like to say that I am resigning as the chairman, and I am leaving." Tommy McLean was looking at me like, "What the fuck is going on here?" By the Friday, McLean was away.'

It is a situation that still confuses those who were around at the time. 'Tommy had us all out on the pitch,' recalls goalkeeper Scott Thomson. 'We walked through what we were going to do for the game, and then he wasn't there the next day. We were all just, "What is going on here?" Why did he even take that job in the first place? I just don't understand that at all.'

McLean was replaced by Iain Munro, but the trajectory of the club had already been set in motion and Raith entered a period of slow decline, culminating in financial difficulty and eventual relegation. It would be their last appearance in the top tier by the time of the publication of this book. Many still question the financial decision-making in the period immediately after Munich. 'They had the money there from Europe and from Millwall to rebuild,' says Danny Lennon, who was one of the few who had chosen to remain. 'Was that money spent wisely? That's another story.'

'They chucked away money,' says Scott Davie more definitively. 'Look at the money spent on Paul Hartley and the boy [Paul] Bonar. That money was blown. Hartley cost a fortune and hardly kicked a ball. Bonar cost £100,000 and I think a couple of seasons later, I saw him on the bench for Albion Rovers at a game I was reporting on.'

There was also the impending need to build a 10,000-seater stadium to remain in the Premier League, a ridiculous criteria that was scrapped a few years later, but not before forcing Raith and several other clubs to invest in infrastructure that they did not need. 'When we sold the players to Millwall and got the money from Stevie McAnespie,' says Davie Kirkwood, 'if you had have put that straight back into the team then fine, but obviously they had to build the stadium and that is where a lot of the money went.'

For supporters, the decline was hard to watch, particularly after experiencing the numerous highs of the previous few years. Eventually, most of the players who had graced the field in Munich departed the club. Centre-back Shaun Dennis left for Hibernian in 1997 having been at the heart of Rovers' defence for almost a decade. 'I met [manager] Jim Duffy in Magaluf one summer,' he recalls. 'He told me that if he ever got a bigger job than Dundee then he would make me his first signing. And he did when he moved to Hibernian.'

'Shaun was exactly what we needed at the time,' reflects former Rovers manager Ian Murray, a team-mate of Dennis at Hibernian. 'Hibs were always seen as a soft touch, and it was guys like Shaun that would toughen us up. He was a big personality in our changing room. He was aggressive as anything; he would defend for his life. I was young at the time and came up against him in training and he didn't show you any mercy. A good guy and a great team-mate.'

Tony Rougier would also depart for Easter Road but remains thankful for his time in Kirkcaldy. 'My first professional contract was playing for Raith Rovers,' says Rougier. 'Every time I went on the pitch, I just wanted to give Raith Rovers the same that they had given to me. It was where it all started, and I thank the people of Raith Rovers for accepting me as one of their own.'

Another two players who departed the club in 1997 were Scott Thomson and Alex Taylor. The latter would finish his career in Angus. 'I was playing at Forfar,' recounts Taylor. 'I remember in training thinking, "Fuck, there is something not right here." My body didn't feel right. It was testicular cancer, but lucky they found it early and it was something they could take care of. That kind of finished me off playing-wise.'

Thomson, who had made the save to start the whole European adventure, also left the club at the same point as Taylor. 'I got promised a contract at the tail end of that season,' he explains. 'When I went to sign it after the season had ended, we had obviously got relegated and the contract I got offered wasn't there any more. I could see the way the club was going. It was kind of losing its wee bit of spark, so I thought it was probably the best time for me to go as well. I was 30 or 31 and as a goalie still in the prime of my career, so it made sense to move. I was sad to leave, because I had a great time at the club.'

Less than two years after Munich, only three of that team were at Stark's Park – captain Danny Lennon, Davie Kirkwood and Jason Dair, who had departed for Millwall, but returned to Kirkcaldy. Lennon and Dair would leave the club in 1999, for Ayr United and local rivals Dunfermline respectively. By then, the financial situation at Raith was acute. 'I am still friends with Kevin Fotheringham who was playing at Raith at the time,' says Jason Dair. 'He tells the story that he had to go and pick up the cheque from Dunfermline for my transfer then go back to Stark's Park and give it to the secretary so they could pay the wages that month. That was how bad it was when I left.'

If it feels that the legacy of Munich was wasted in the immediate aftermath of that achievement, the club has continued to journey through periods of success, periods of failure, and several moments of downright farce. 'I sometimes think that with Raith Rovers, anything that can go wrong, will go wrong,' says journalist and supporter Scott Davie. 'We seem to just stagger from one fiasco to another over the years. You can't point to one person, but there seems to be a self-destruct button at Stark's Park down the years.'

This is not the place to dwell on every mistake made by the club over the last 30 years, but it is worth remembering some of the more nonsensical moments that supporters have had to endure:

- Installing amateur DJ Claude Anelka as manager in 2004 when his only credentials for the job were that he had a famous football-playing brother

- Demolishing Livingston 4-0 at Almondvale on the Saturday, then three days later allowing them to buy Rovers' three best players for just over £20,000

- Owners whose approach to their custodianship of the club involved threats to raze Stark's Park to the ground and build flats

- Board members getting embroiled in a betting scandal on the last day of the season when they knew that the club would be playing a mix of fringe players and youths

- Not having a fit registered goalkeeper on the books and having to play a centre-forward in goals for a league match at Somerset Park

- Signing a player in 2022 who sponsors, volunteers and supporters had all warned against bringing to the club, resulting in supporters walking away and the reputation of the club reaching one of the lowest points in its history

- Sacking a manager after just one league game when he had just taken Rovers as close to the Premiership as they had been since 1997.

All of these events have sought to test the patience and loyalty of fans, but if there was one on-field decision that encapsulates the propensity for self-inflicted hurt, then it was the 2016/17 season. Playing in the Championship and managed by Gary Locke, Rovers loaned striker Lewis Vaughan to Dumbarton, a bizarre decision given that Vaughan was widely regarded as one of the club's more gifted forwards and Dumbarton were in the same division. Dumbarton were in a relegation fight when Vaughan made the move and Rovers sat towards the top end of the table, but as the season progressed the two clubs swapped places, largely due to Vaughan's contribution for the Sons.

Vaughan was left in the uncomfortable position of winning games for his loan side on a Saturday and returning to train at Stark's Park during the week with colleagues who were aware that his vital goals were putting them in greater and greater danger of relegation. Locke was eventually sacked and replaced with the equally inept John Hughes, who proceeded to manage Rovers into ninth and a relegation play-off with Brechin, which they lost on penalties, consigning them to League One. 'I was up at Peterhead the day Rovers were playing Brechin at Stark's Park in the second leg,' recalls Scott Davie. 'I was covering Peterhead's play-off and after the game I went into their manager Jim McInally's office. He put on the radio, and we listened to Rovers losing the penalty shoot-out and getting relegated.

'I headed back to my car and listened to the radio on the journey home. Darren Dodds, the Brechin manager, came on. The interviewer says, "What about that goal you scored from the free kick to take it to penalties?" and Dodds replies, "You know, that is the first time this season we have scored from a free kick." I just laughed and thought, "They have never scored a free kick in 30-odd games, but they put one in the top corner at Stark's Park." It could only happen to the Rovers.'

Yet despite numerous moments of farce, it has not all been doom and gloom. There have been great sides, great players and magnificent days since Rovers played in the UEFA Cup. Supporters have enjoyed promotions, title wins, and memorable cup victories over Premiership opponents. The Challenge Cup has been added to their list of honours, most memorably defeating Rangers 1-0 in 2014, allowing older supporters the boast of having seen their side get the better of both sides of the Old Firm in a cup final.

Raith may not have qualified for Europe again or returned to the top league in Scotland, but that doesn't mean that fans have lost hope. For many who were in Munich the optimism remains intact despite all the ups and downs and has been fuelled by recent changes at the club. 'There seems to be an overall sense of ambition around the club now,' says Graeme Meldrum. 'It looks as if we now have guys who know what they are doing. There seems to be more of a plan behind it. Hopefully that may allow us an opportunity to take the step sometime in the next few years.'

This optimism is shared by many of the club's former players. 'Raith Rovers have been so close to promotion in the past,' says Tony Rougier. 'You have got to keep believing and keep going to find the right tools and the right environment to make sure that we get over that line.'

'I think the current board have the right intentions and are trying to build the club in the right manner,' says Stephen McAnespie. 'It is great that there are people within the building that get the club and understand past success. You don't want to dwell on the past, but it is good to know how it happened.'

'Can it be done again?' asks Jimmy Nicholl. 'Of course, it can be done again. I don't see any reason why it can't.'

28

The Bond is Back

A WEEK after being appointed manager of Raith Rovers in May 2022, Ian Murray sat in his office and thought to himself, 'What have I done?' He had left Airdrie, well run and transparent, and found himself in Kirkcaldy, at a slightly chaotic club still reeling from recent off-the-field troubles. After a successful playing career representing Hibernian, Rangers and Norwich, the former Scotland international had built a strong management track record at Dumbarton, St Mirren and Airdrie. Raith presented a different challenge, but after gathering his thoughts, he started the process of rebuilding bridges around Stark's Park. 'I just thought, "Let's get on with it and see what we can do,"' he says.

In his first season in charge, Rovers finished mid-table and lost out in the Challenge Cup Final to Hamilton, but a change of ownership would provide the spark necessary to deliver one of the most thrilling campaigns supporters had witnessed since the 1990s. Over the summer the dressing rooms and other infrastructure around the club had been transformed to provide modern facilities for the players. Murray had built a strong squad, selling them on the environment and the changes that were happening around Stark's Park. 'We knew we had good players,' he says. 'If you have got players like Lewis Vaughan, Dylan Easton, and Aidan Connolly in those forward positions, you are always waking up thinking, "I wonder what we will get today. Who is going to do that little bit of magic today?" More often than not, one of them did.'

Rovers started the season in blistering form, matching title favourites Dundee United game by game until December. It was not just the results that were satisfying, it was the manner in which they were winning. The squad developed a reputation for late winners and comebacks, creating some truly thrilling moments. The excitement peaked in December when Rovers travelled to Tannadice and beat United 1-0 with an outrageous Dylan Easton goal to go five points clear at the top of the Championship. The club had laid on free buses to take fans to the game and handed out free Santa hats, so at the final whistle the team were greeted by an ecstatic wall of blue-hatted supporters celebrating the win.

Watching events unfold was Grace Fowlie, a long-time supporter from Edinburgh, who had started working for the club as their digital marketing executive at the start of the season. The role afforded her a front-row seat to how the season was developing. 'It was really exciting,' she says. 'We were getting so many last-minute winners and there were so many good things happening. The players genuinely believed. Even if there were just three minutes to go or whatever, the players always believed that they could turn it around. That collective belief and momentum, that togetherness just kept pushing it forward.'

Grace had started supporting the club years earlier when, aged seven, she had asked to accompany her dad James on his Saturday afternoon routine of watching Rovers. 'I don't remember the first game I went to,' she explains. 'But I remember getting those Million sweets, the little balls. I spilt them and for three seasons straight those Millions were still on the floor at my feet in the Main Stand.

'I loved the whole day out. The journey on the train, getting there and seeing all these people you recognise, and they are starting to recognise you. It was that feeling of stepping into somewhere and genuinely feeling like you were a part of it. You instantly felt like you belonged.'

Grace would take her love of Rovers one step further when she played for the club. Playing football for Boroughmuir Thistle in her home city of Edinburgh, her coach Pete Shaw knew she was a passionate fan so organised a match against Rovers. 'We played a friendly against Raith and I went away from that thinking, "I wonder if I could play for them?" I was about 16 and I messaged one of their players on Facebook and said, "Hey, this is really random, but what do you have to do if you want to play for Raith?" She said to just come along to training, so I did.'

Grace would go on to represent Raith's women, memorably scoring a goal in a derby against Dunfermline. 'You went to the boardroom at Stark's Park,' she recalls. 'They took a picture, and you signed a contract. As a 16-year-old Raith fan I absolutely loved it. There was an extra incentive playing for the club you support, playing in derby games, scoring against Dunfermline. It genuinely felt meaningful.'

After a period in the USA for university and several volunteer roles with Rovers, the chance to work fully for the club presented itself as the new ownership sought to refresh their social media presence by bringing in a new digital marketing executive. 'I was reading the job description and was thinking, "That is literally me, I would love this job,"' says Grace. 'When I was offered the position, I honestly thought I was going to start crying, I was so happy.'

It is a role that even after a year in post still thrills her. 'The players play a massive part in making you feel like you are part of it,' says Grace. 'I had idolised Ross Matthews and Lewis Vaughan and now I see them every day, and they know my name! Last season I asked Shaun Byrne to sign his top for me at the end of the season. Laura [Andreucci, the club's commercial manager] was, "Oh my god, you're such a fan girl," and I was, "I know, but it's Shaun Byrne!" I am still just excited by everything.'

After the win at Tannadice, and sitting five points clear, some supporters started to believe that Raith could actually have an opportunity to win the league. It was still an outside chance, but it was a chance. Ian Murray admits that he started to feel the same. 'I think that was the game where we kind of went "OK",' he says. 'We never went overboard or said we were going to win the league, but we thought that we might have a chance. If you are a manager, five points isn't that much. You can be behind five points and think you can catch up or you can be ahead five points and still looking over your shoulder. But it was certainly a moment where we thought there is a bit of an opportunity here.'

Murray was particularly delighted that it had been Dylan Easton, a player he had brought from Airdrie, who had scored the winning goal at Tannadice. 'I had Dylan at Dumbarton when he was 17,' says Murray. 'But it was a completely different Dylan we got at Raith. He had to go away a bit and find his feet in life and in football. His ability on the ball is phenomenal and he will bring that moment of magic, like he did at Tannadice. There is no other player in the league that could have done what Dylan did that day. Unbelievable.'

There would be another memorable win over United in February, when Scott Brown fired in a thunderous shot from 30 yards in the final minutes to keep Rovers in touch at the top. 'I had tried to sign Scott a few times at Airdrie and couldn't get him,' says Murray. 'When I got to Raith, I looked at the finances and what we had, and I thought, "This guy's perfect for us." His work rate, his training, the way he was in the dressing room. My first two signings at Raith were Dylan and Scottie and I probably couldn't have picked two better ones.

'We struggled a wee bit in the second half that night. Dundee United were very good that night, but the last 15 or 20 minutes we had a wee go and brought fresh legs on. Scott came on as a substitute. My mantra all season long had been that just because you aren't starting today, doesn't mean you are not a good player. It is just that this is the team that is going to start. You guys are going to be the ones who are going to finish.'

And how Scott Brown finished it. The Rovers fans in the sold-out stadium erupted as the ball hit the net. 'For that Dundee United game, I was sitting in my normal seat,' recalls Grace Fowlie. 'But we had said if we win that we would need to go down and get instant footage of the celebrations. The goal got scored and I was sitting thinking, "Oh my god, that's probably the best thing I've ever seen at Stark's Park," and then I had to go down on to the pitch and video the players as they celebrated. Being down on the pitch looking up at everybody in the stands celebrating, it is such a surreal feeling. You almost wanted to just lie down and take it all in.'

The team spirit, enthusiasm and sense of enjoyment within the Raith camp was reminiscent of the Jimmy Nicholl era, with the same feelgood factor around the town. Rovers were being talked about again. If there were last-minute winners and victories over title rivals to savour, there was also the small matter of beating Dunfermline five times – Rovers won all four league games and knocked the Pars out of the Scottish Cup. 'That was the absolute highlight for me,' smiles long-time supporter Gavin Quinn.

In the end, Rovers didn't win the league. They finished second, six points behind Dundee United. A damaging loss to Arbroath and a 2-0 defeat to United in the second fixture at Tannadice sealed their fate. 'We just came up that little bit short,' says Colin Cameron, Rovers' assistant manager that season. 'But I think what we achieved was massive because if you think of our budget compared to Dundee United's budget and it was only the last half-dozen games that we kind of fell away that wee bit. It was a great achievement by the boys. They gave everything.'

There would be an interesting postscript to that season when the clubs eventually posted their financial accounts. Dundee United had lost £2.8m, while Raith recorded a profit of almost £50,000. The gulf in how each club was operating underlines how winning the league was always going to be an incredibly difficult task. In the circumstances, to have run United so close for so long was a triumph.

Rovers would face Partick Thistle in the Premiership play-off semi-final. They had beaten Partick twice during the regular season and drawn the other two games, but each one had been close, so it would not be an easy task. For the first half of the first leg at Firhill, Rovers threatened to run away with the tie, racing into a two-goal lead with Scott Brown and Lewis Vaughan scoring the goals. 'People had told me for years how talented Lewis Vaughan was,' says Ian Murray. 'But I hadn't seen it up close. When he came back from rehab [after a long-term knee injury], I couldn't believe how good he was. His finishing was outstanding and the way he finishes in different ways. I have seen him dink goalies from four yards out. I have seen him hit the ball as hard as he can. He gets on the end of crosses in the box which for a guy of his size he should have no right to. His movement is just outstanding.

'To get him back to where he was before his last injury, scoring goals and a mainstay in the team, was brilliant. The biggest credit I can pay to Lewis is that when we went to Thistle in the play-offs, and we played 4-2-3-1. It was a tough choice who to play up front. We also had Zak Rudden, Jack Hamilton, and Calum Smith as options. I said, "We are playing Lewis," because we might only get one chance and who is going to score from the one chance? And he did it, and it was an incredible goal.'

The second-half performance didn't quite match the first and Rovers conceded a sloppy goal towards the end of the match. It frustrated Murray and introduced an element of doubt into his mind about the second leg. The doubt was to prove well founded as Partick Thistle won 2-1 at Stark's Park to take the tie to extra time. Brian Graham had a chance to break Rovers' hearts late on in the game but scooped the ball up and over the bar to the relief of every home fan in the ground. When the match went to penalties, Rovers were the first to miss. 'When Scottie

[Brown] missed, I started to think about what I would say to the players,' says Murray. 'When you lose like that, you have to try and pick your words carefully to make sure that they are all right, especially the person who missed.'

There would be no need for Murray to worry about his team talk as Thistle went on to fire wide twice, handing Lewis Vaughan the chance to win the tie, which he did in style. After Vaughan's penalty hit the net he stood magnificently, arms outstretched as fans started to invade the pitch. If ever a Raith player deserved such a moment, it was Vaughan.

The final against Ross County would prove a step too far for a team running on empty after a long, emotionally draining season, with the physicality and strength of the Dingwall outfit too much to deal with over two matches. 'We knew we had a good chance,' says Scott Thomson, now a goalkeeping coach with Ross County. 'We just needed to keep ourselves in the tie after the first leg and did really well on the night to win 2-1. In the second leg, we got the goals at the right time. The Rovers actually started the game better, but then Simon Murray scored and you could see the stuffing getting knocked out of them a wee bit. The experience of playing in the play-off the season before probably helped us. It was new to the Rovers and the magnitude and pressure of the game; it is a different level.'

Thomson's split loyalties between his old team and his current employers were exacerbated by the fact that his son Robbie was part of the Rovers coaching staff. 'I had said to Robbie for months, "Don't even think about us meeting in the play-offs,"' says Thomson. 'I just had a feeling that it was going to be Raith. I didn't even speak to him before the game. I just gave him a quick handshake and it was, "On you go." Someone caught us for a photo, and it was two of the most serious two faces you have ever seen!'

For Ian Murray, the play-off would prove the high point of his time at Raith. Just one league game into the following season he was sacked, but there is no sense of bitterness from the former manager as he reflects on his time in Fife. 'I loved being at Raith Rovers,' he says. 'I loved the camaraderie we had with the players. I loved the rebuilding of the club with the supporters and making it better. I felt like I did at Dumbarton and Airdrie, that I left Raith Rovers in a better position than when I first walked in. Now, that is not just down to me. You need the backing from above. You need the players to play on the pitch and you need the supporters to come and support you. The way I ended wasn't the way I wanted it to happen, that's for sure, as I genuinely felt like we were building something, but I look back with fond memories.'

For the away fans who travelled up to Dingwall, it was a disappointing end to what had been a hugely enjoyable season. The team may have been defeated, but as the fans stayed behind to applaud the team the overriding emotion was pride and appreciation of what had been achieved. It was yet another echo of that night in Munich 30 years before. 'There was that bond again between the team and the fans,' reflects Graeme Meldrum. 'It was back again just like those times under Jimmy Nicholl in the 90s. Which was brilliant because I think that was lost for a long time.'

29

Inspiring the Next Generation

THIRTY YEARS on from Munich, many of the team who took to the field in a Raith shirt are still involved in football and making an impact on a new generation of player. Two former Rovers currently doing so in the USA are Stephen McAnespie and Tony Rougier, in New Orleans and Boston respectively. 'I have got an academy of 3,500 kids here,' says McAnespie.' We started it from scratch, and I have kids from four years old all the way up to going off to college. They can get a college scholarship, or they can go into the professional game.'

It is a rewarding role that McAnespie loves, although watching some of the young players arriving at training in large SUVs and limousines is a far cry from stepping off the bus in Kirkcaldy back in the 1990s. He does admit to occasionally bringing a little bit of Fife to southern USA. 'The kids sometimes ask, "Did you play?"' He says. 'I have shown the video of the cup final a few times, but it is mostly "Your hair is weird!" That is what they care about, but it is fun to show them.'

Further north, Rougier is also working hard to pass on his knowledge coaching in MLS Next, the youth academy league of Major League Soccer. Alongside his work, he has established the Anthony Rougier Foundation, a non-profit organisation to help those from underprivileged backgrounds to be able to play and progress in the game. 'The reality is that Diego Maradona didn't come from money,' says Rougier. 'Messi didn't come from money. Cristiano Ronaldo didn't come from money, but it is getting to the point here in the US, if you can't pay then you won't be able to play at that level. Not everybody has money and that is where my foundation comes in. We raise money to help kids play soccer in the US. To buy a pair of cleats [boots] and sometimes to put food on the table too.'

It is a mission that he is passionate about. 'My wife Trisha tells me to slow down,' he laughs. 'But you can't stop because there are kids that need help out there. There is another Anthony Rougier out there that needs help to become a player to help his family, to help his community and I am blessed to be able to use the skills I have to help others.'

Stevie Crawford shares Rougier's passion for making football accessible but is making a difference closer to home. His Fife-based academy is open to all. 'I am not making my academy an elite academy, far from it,' he explains. 'It doesn't matter how good a player is, whether it is a boy or girl, what age they are, what is important is "Are they better than what they were when they first walked in the door?" Kids get judged too quickly today and they end up not enjoying the game. In academies, you have got to go and let them be in love with the game and play with a smile on their face.'

Crawford carries the learning from his apprenticeship at Raith with him to this day. 'A lot of what we do in my academy is based on what I was lucky enough to inherit from

Jimmy [Nicholl] and Martin Harvey,' says Crawford, who went on to manage Fife rivals East Fife and Dunfermline. 'I have always tried to have conversations with young players, giving them that wee bit of love and guidance, because Jimmy gave me that in abundance.'

At times in his managerial career, Crawford worked alongside former colleague and friend Jason Dair, another player who has successfully navigated the tricky Raith Rovers–Dunfermline divide. 'It was an easy role for me to fill,' jokes Dair. 'I was from Cowdenbeath, so I was halfway between anyway.'

Dair had spells at Motherwell, Livingston and latterly at East Fife when he was a player and assistant manager to Crawford, before having to retire through injury. For Rovers supporters, the talented collective of Cameron, Crawford and Dair that emerged under Jimmy Nicholl remains one that is frequently mentioned in the same breath, although Dair often makes light of the fact that he was the only one of the three not to go on to represent his country. At a recent Rovers reunion dinner he opened by saying that he was proud that together the trio of young players had amassed 53 Scotland appearances, pausing for comedic effect, before joking that unfortunately this was all down to Cameron and Crawford. His self-deprecation belies the fact that he was a remarkable talent. Since retiring from playing, Dair has coached non-stop all across Fife. His family remains steeped in football with his brother Lee, who also played for Rovers, often coaching alongside him and his nephew Brodie, currently retracing his journey to London by signing for Fulham. 'I phoned him last week and was saying to him I was 20 when I went down to London,' says Dair. 'It was 30 years ago, so I don't think it will be the same as it was back then, but I said to him if he ever needed anything just give me a shout. Football is just a huge part of our lives and hopefully that is the way it stays.'

Making the move into coaching and then management has been a common theme for many of those who featured on Rovers' European adventure. Davie Kirkwood, like Jason Dair, also suffered an injury late in his career that encouraged him into coaching. Of all the players who featured in Munich, Kirkwood remained at Raith Rovers the longest. It was while playing for the club that he suffered the ACL injury that ended his career. He would go on to become under-18 coach at Raith and would later manage at Wick Academy and Brora Rangers, even facing Rovers in the Challenge Cup while with the former. Kirkwood has now left management, and is content to be away from the demands that football brought. 'I left Brora in the summer,' says Kirkwood. 'I am happy to be out of it. I had been coaching for nearly 27 years and it is great to have a Saturday to myself. I am 57 now and have been in football since I was 16. It is time for a break.'

The paths of former Raith players from the 1990s can frequently cross and when Kirkwood left Wick Academy, he was replaced as manager by Barry Wilson. After his disappointment of not featuring in either of the Bayern Munich games, the young winger rebuilt his career at Inverness Caledonian Thistle and latterly at Livingston. 'I was 40 when I stopped playing,' says Wilson. 'I actually scored my last goal about a week after I turned 40, so I could not have squeezed one day, one training session, one game, one anything out of it. I think most people think I ripped the arse out of it for far too long!'

He would go on to manage Wick Academy and Elgin City, before returning to Inverness first as a coach, then assistant manager with Billy Dodds. His last game in that position would be in Kirkcaldy. Just a few months after being in the Scottish Cup Final and only five games into a season, Dodds and Wilson were sacked by the Inverness club after losing 1-0 to Rovers. If it was a bad day for Wilson, it was a more enjoyable one for the Raith supporters as Jamie Gullan's goal ended a 23-year winless run against the Highland side in the league that had stood since October 2000.

Like Davie Kirkwood, Wilson is now just enjoying a break from football. 'I have been a player or a coach for 35 years,' he says. 'Now it is just a case of getting on with my shop and my business and other aspects of life. I have probably only watched about four or five games in the last year, which is crazy, but it is time for other things now, which is something I never thought I would say.'

If the Raith influence is being felt here in Scotland and across in North America, it is also being felt in Asia. Gordon Forrest, who took to the field as a young apprentice in the Faroe Islands, is currently coaching in the Chinese top flight with Shenzhen Peng City, a City Group stablemate of Girona, Melbourne City, New York City and Manchester City.

Forrest's coaching CV is perhaps the most global of the Stark's Park alumni, having previously worked under Stevie Crawford at East Fife, coached the New Zealand women's team at the 2012 Olympics and been in MLS with Vancouver Whitecaps, as well as winning consecutive Scottish Championship titles at Dundee United and Hearts. 'I came back to Scotland from the USA to work at Dundee United with Robbie Neilson,' explains Forrest. 'We won the Championship and then Hearts came in for us. We won the Championship again and then finished third in the Premiership. Robbie got moved on and I stayed on as assistant with [Steven] Naismith. We finished third, fourth, third, had three European campaigns and two Scottish Cup finals, losing both of them to Rangers and Celtic and then you lose your job. That is football.

'I got sacked on the Sunday, and the sporting director at Shenzhen phoned me and asked me if I would come out on the Wednesday, because they had just moved the manager and were trying to keep their team in the Super League with three games left. I flew out to China on the Wednesday and came in to work with a head coach who was assistant to [Roberto] Mancini at Man City. We kept them in the league, so they wanted us to stay on.'

Forrest believes that it was his former experience around the world that helped secure the role. 'I think they see me as a fit because I have coached around the world and moved,' he says. 'That has been the beauty of moving, it has opened doors for me, you are willing to try a different country and they know you can adapt and adjust. We have five foreigners, and the rest of the squad are Chinese, don't speak a word of English, so it is a different challenge. I have my own interpreter, when I speak, he speaks!'

His success is not a surprise to his former manager, having witnessed him helping coach Derek Smith with the under-13s and under-15s at Raith. 'When you saw wee Gordy Forrest, and how he was with the kids, talking to them, joking with them, making them comfortable,' says Jimmy Nicholl, 'right away you knew he had something.'

The environment at Raith in the mid-1990s has remained at the front of Forrest's thoughts throughout his coaching career. 'How Jimmy Nic and Martin Harvey were as people and how they were as characters, just sinks right into me as how I would like to be as a coach,' he says. 'That is hopefully how I am as a coach. Always available, always helpful, always had a smile, and so much energy.'

Also currently working in Asia is the man who scored that goal in Munich, Danny Lennon. He credits his time in Kirkcaldy for starting his coaching journey. 'I was always keen on coaching,' Lennon says from his current base in Malaysia. '[Former Raith player] John Millar and I went down one summer to do our [UEFA] B Licence when we were at Rovers and that is where it started.'

Lennon was appointed Cowdenbeath manager in 2008, leading them to two successive promotions. His success led to an appointment as St Mirren manager and the pinnacle of his time in Paisley was leading the club to their first League Cup success, defeating Hearts 3-2 in the final at Hampden in March 2013. 'That is something that nobody can ever take away,' smiles Lennon. 'I had so many people coming up to me and so many letters from people who said that they had been there in 1987 with their fathers when St Mirren won the Scottish Cup and then when we won the League Cup, they were there as fathers with their kids. That sort of thing makes the hair on the back of your neck stand up.'

He would go on to have periods in charge at Alloa, Airdrie and Clyde before moving to Malaysia to run an academy in Penang, although he still harbours ambitions to return to management closer to home. 'It is a nice place and a great lifestyle,' says Lennon. 'I am making a difference here, but if an opportunity arises back home then I still dream to this day that I can get back to that level of managing teams, developing great players and winning cups.'

If the class of 1995 are making a difference around the globe, one player who made an impact right here in Kirkcaldy was Colin Cameron. The former midfielder went on to have a fantastic career after leaving Raith, finding success most notably at Heart of Midlothian, Wolverhampton Wanderers and as a Scotland international, winning 28 caps for his country. After coaching roles at Berwick Rangers and Airdrie, Ian Murray had no hesitation inviting Cameron to be his assistant at Rovers. 'I knew his relationship with Raith, and I thought he was the perfect fit,' says Murray. 'He is from Kirkcaldy, he knows a lot of people in Kirkcaldy, his connection with the club, but he is also a great coach. He was a great person that you trust to have at your side. I can't speak highly enough of Colin.'

Cameron was brought up in the shadow of Stark's Park so his eventual return to the club felt like part of a natural cycle. Alongside Murray, he formed the successful management team who took Rovers to the brink of the Scottish Premiership, the closest they had been since he himself had graced the Stark's Park pitch. After Murray's exit he stayed as a stabilising force for successive managers, before departing in the summer of 2025. He may no longer be at the club, but he remains adored by supporters and a Rover at heart. 'Some of the players couldn't get their head around that I am a Raith Rovers fan,' reflects Cameron on his time as assistant manager. 'I am born and bred in Kirkcaldy, and it is the club I supported as a kid. I still support them now. Even when I finish my coaching career, I'll still support them. I always will.'

30

Legacy

'WHAT I love about Raith Rovers Football Club is that you know how to celebrate achievements,' says Danny Lennon. 'This is one of the best clubs I've ever seen that celebrates its people and greatness. Europe was a pinnacle point in my career. Playing at that level, scoring against such illustrious opponents. It is a reminder that dreams can become a reality, with hard work and belief. It put Raith Rovers on the map and gave us all an achievement that we all still carry today.'

'The history of the club is really important,' agrees Grace Fowlie, currently working to strengthen the connection between fans and club. 'We are thinking about our season-ticket campaign and one of the things we have been thinking about is that the past builds a foundation and helps show you where you could potentially go.'

And as a moment in time, leading Bayern Munich in the Olympiastadion is up there. 'As the years go by the memories actually get stronger,' reflects Jim Clark. 'I think social media has a lot to do with that as you see other photographs and footage of those games. You talk to people who were there, and you talk to people who wish that they were there. I went to Munich for the weekend a few years ago with my wife, Rachel. On the Saturday morning we went out to the Olympiastadion. It all came flashing back, just standing there, and I had a wee tear in my eye.'

Fellow supporter Graeme Meldrum is in full agreement. 'As you get older,' he reflects, 'you look at it and realise what these achievements are. If we stop celebrating these moments, then what are you going to celebrate? It was like that season we went close under Ian Murray. Fans of other clubs were complaining that we were over-celebrating all the late winners and stuff, but you know that those are finite moments. There will come a point where things turn, so always enjoy the highs and Munich was as good as it gets. That was our moment.'

If the supporters felt privileged to have been there, the same is true for the players who made it happen. 'No one will ever forget our European run nor that night in Munich,' says Davie Kirkwood. 'Raith Rovers playing in the Olympic Stadium is right up there. It means everything. I have my medals, I have got my strips and I have still got that Bayern Munich top, but the most important thing I have is the memories.'

Kirkwood is not the only former player who treasures the memories as well as the physical reminders of that time. 'I still have my Rovers memorabilia up in my house and it is framed with the strip and the medals,' says Stephen McAnespie. 'When I walk past it, I am not going to lie, I get goosebumps every now and then.

'I went on and won championships with different teams. But they don't mean anything like Rovers. They are just another medal, but when we did it at Rovers, it meant something to the community, and it still does. That is what makes it amazing to us as players being part of that. It was not about the cup itself or the games, it was being a part of what it meant to the people of Kirkcaldy and the community.'

If there is personal satisfaction in the contribution they made, the success they secured and the level that they reached, there is also pride for the legacy they created for the football club and for the supporters. 'We created those pictures on the walls,' says Julian Broddle. 'We helped create those two new stands. We created that history and fantastic memories that people will never forget. My Raith Rovers days were amongst the happiest of my football career. They provided me with a lot of great memories, great friends and a couple of winners' medals which I am incredibly proud of. It was just a fantastic time where everything we touched turned to gold.'

'It is just pride when I think of that time,' agrees Barry Wilson. 'You were part of something that was huge. You were part of a squad that won the championship, won the League Cup, who were playing Rangers and Celtic at the time and part of the squad that helped that run to get to Bayern Munich. That is something that people can't take away from you.'

'The feeling I have got for the Rovers will never leave me,' says Stevie Crawford. 'The opportunity, that journey, what Jimmy created, the fans, the European journey. That will always stay with me.

'Jimmy wanted us to play a household name. He wanted someone who would always be something to look back on. He wanted us to experience it for ourselves, but for it also to be something for Kirkcaldy and for Raith Rovers as a football club. He said, "I want kids who have been at the game telling their kids about it and grandads can tell their grandkids." And he was right.'

That is the legacy that the UEFA Cup run created. To have brought a moment that we can all share and that we can all celebrate. If the Munich moment was the pinnacle, for many just the experience of being at Raith Rovers in the 1990s brings a smile. The warmth, the togetherness and the fun made it a special time to represent the club. For many it was the peak of their career and their happiest time in football. 'It was a great time to be a Raith Rovers player and I'm sure it was probably a great time to be a Raith Rovers supporter as well,' says Jason Dair. 'I was just lucky enough to be in the right place at the right time.

'My time at Raith is up there at the top of my football career. My debut was huge, the cup final was huge, winning the league and getting promoted was huge, being lucky enough to score the first European goal was huge and playing Bayern Munich was huge. It was one of the defining moments of my career. I had a decent career and had bits and pieces wherever I went, but all those things that happened at Raith Rovers are at the very top.'

'I was there for four years, but it was the quickest four years of my life,' reflects goalkeeper Scott Thomson. 'It was just a whirlwind in terms of what we went through. A lot of success, a lot of good times, a real lot of good times. It is a period in my career that I am really proud of. For most people success is spread over a career, but for me it was spread over those four years at Rovers and for it to come together at the one time in that way. That is why you play football.'

'Raith Rovers are the reason I had the career that I had,' says Colin Cameron. 'That was the foundation for the rest of my career, and it was the main reason that I was able to achieve what I did. Jimmy changed me from a striker as a young kid into a midfielder. He gave me the confidence to go on and with my hunger and desire, I managed to get that little bit further. It was just incredible, really. At that stage of my career to have been able to have been part of something like that. I don't think any player, or any fan connected with that whole European adventure will ever forget it.'

'You guys know how I feel for my God,' says Tony Rougier. 'To put me in that moment, in that particular moment to be a part of this Raith Rovers journey. It was heaven-sent. The timing could not have been better. It was fantastic. Being able to travel, being able to represent the team and Scotland, not just Raith Rovers, it was fantastic. I mean this really from the bottom of my heart and on behalf of my family, to all at Raith Rovers, thank you very much for everything that you have done for me.'

The bond developed in the Stark's Park dressing room has endured, whether it is in the many reunions that have followed or supporting each other in their subsequent careers. The friendships and camaraderie remain to this day. 'You are still in connection with all these guys which is unique,' says Gordon Forrest. 'We are all different ages, but I have always kept in touch with Jimmy. I have kept in touch with Robbo [Graham Robertson]. Stevie Craw asked me to be his assistant at East Fife with Jason Dair as well, I see Mickey Cameron, I see Sinky out with the kids, I spoke to Jock McStay at Celtic Park recently. I have had a lot of big games in my coaching career, Scottish Cup finals, winning the league, and on those occasions these guys still keep in touch and wish you all the best which is fantastic.'

'The reality of being involved in that team was that we all worked for each other,' admits Stevie Crawford. 'Whether it was good times, bad times or indifferent times, we genuinely all worked for each other. I was very lucky. I was fortunate to do it with people that I still have a lot of feelings for. That probably for me is more important than anything. To experience stuff with people you like being around and being in the trenches with them. I always enjoyed that togetherness.'

'I saw Mickey Cameron at an event earlier this year,' says Ally Graham. 'I said to him, "By the way, what a fantastic career you had." He said that he owed a lot of it to us, telling him to do this, do that, helping him, and I feel quite proud of that. For him to turn around and say I played a part in his career. That is a fantastic thing. I used to love working with him. I mean, I had Mickey Cameron, Jason Dair, Stevie Crawford and then Daz [Gordon Dalziel] alongside me. It was a dream come true. I used to just run into guys, put the centre-half off and let one of those guys latch on to it, and they did it superbly.'

Jimmy Nicholl created such an inclusive atmosphere at the club, that it no longer matters whether someone played in the games, scored the goals or carried the kit, they were all part of what happened and part of the story. 'For me, there is just an overwhelming sense of pride that I was at the club at what was the pinnacle of Raith Rovers,' says former apprentice Graham Robertson. 'I was at the club when it had its best time ever and there will never be anything other than just pride about having been part of all of that. I don't talk about having played football very much, but when it does come up and I tell people that I was at Raith, they ask me when, and when I say it was when Jimmy Nicholl was there and they won the cup and played in Europe, the reaction is always "Wow".

'Even when you walk in today and see that tiled Raith Rovers badge on the ground. I mopped that every day for three years. It is just the memories, the flashbacks and even the smell of the place when you go back in. I have taken my boys along and they love it. We were up at Tannadice when they beat Dundee United 1-0 just before Christmas and I took them to the play-off game against Partick. That was a really nice moment for me, seeing them cheering on the Rovers and dancing about in the main stand when they won on penalties.'

That sense of togetherness is not just felt by the players who walked on to the pitch together. It is felt by the fans who were lucky enough to witness them ply their trade every Saturday. 'Over the years, many people have said to me, "Why do you go to watch Raith Rovers?"' says John Greer. 'In many respects it is not about being successful. I'd go to see the Rovers at whatever level they are playing at. It is as much about friendships, who you sit with, the banter. It is about more than results.

'We could be having a poor season, but we'll still go to Hibs and beat them in the Scottish Cup, or Grégory Tadé will score a winner up at Aberdeen or winning up at Tannadice to go five points clear. Even if it was just fleeting that we were top of the league for a wee while, there's always moments like that that get you through.'

If the players and coaching staff moved on to the rest of their careers, the people who remained were the fans. Those who travelled by ferry, braved the flights, and endured 24 hours on a bus to watch their team play in the UEFA Cup. Thirty years later, they are all still part of the Raith Rovers fabric, loyally supporting and doing whatever they can to help the club that they love. The intervening years and all of the ups and downs have not dimmed their passion for their football team. If anything, it has deepened.

John Greer works hard to ensure that the players and the history of the club are not forgotten.

'The history of any institution like a football club is very important,' he says. 'And that is why things like Reminiscing Raith and the Hall of Fame matter. Ally Gourlay [Rovers' media officer, club historian and former players' association chairman], who is sadly no longer with us, always said that the Rovers were important to the fabric of Kirkcaldy and the one constant in the town from the Victorian times. That is why we need to make sure that we keep the history alive.'

Jim Clark currently volunteers for Raith TV, an incredible initiative that has been broadcasting matches for years, the quality and professionalism of its output outstripping many larger rivals. The fact that it is run by a team of volunteers including David Codd, Ian Grieve, Neil Ingebrigtsen, and Kirsteen Wright, makes it all the more remarkable. Jim frequently co-commentates on matches with club treasure Davie Hancock. 'Davie is the voice of Raith TV,' says Jim. 'He would put professional broadcasters to shame with the amount of research he does and the hours he puts in every week. And he does it all travelling with his wife Linzi and daughter Molli, arriving at games early and leaving long after fans have gone home. All for the love of Raith Rovers.'

Davie has his own unique Munich story. A student at the time, finances were tight and to make sure that he and Linzi made it to Munich, he made the sacrifice of a treasured record collection. An avid lover of music, he had forensically curated a collection of vinyl by The Smiths including white labels, promo copies, acetates, mis-pressed recordings, and foreign and original artwork. It was all sold for £1,500 to allow the couple to make it to the Olympiastadion. Having checked record collector listings recently, Hancock estimates the collection would now be worth around £20,000 but he has absolutely no regrets. Some games are bigger than others after all.

Steve Wallace sits on the board of the Raith Supporters Trust, working to give fans a voice. 'You are there to try to keep the club going and make our voice heard,' he says of his role. 'It wasn't that long ago that if you looked at ticket prices for kids, we were the third-most expensive child ticket in Scottish football, with only Rangers and Celtic charging more. The supporters' trust campaigned on that, and we've resolved that now, which I'm incredibly proud of. I'm also proud that as a trust we were responsible for putting up the murals in the South Stand that celebrate moments in our history, including the Munich scoreboard.'

Graeme Meldrum fundraises for the club and is a regular contributor to the *OhNoNoNo Podcast*, a weekly production picking over matches and the highs and lows of following Rovers. 'I like it because there are folk like Duncan Cameron and Robbie Weir on it who are knowledgeable and serious about formations and selections,' says Graeme. 'Then there's me who just goes on to blether nonsense!'

Gavin Quinn continues to take his place in the Stark's Park stand and has been responsible for one of the longest-running fundraising initiatives at the club, Rock the Rovers. The event, a one-day festival of music to raise funds for the football club and local charities, has been running for over 20 years. 'At the very start it was done as a one-off to help save the club,' says Gavin. 'A friend of mine, Marsha Tarvett, who was involved in bands, came to me and said, "I've got an idea for doing a gig. An all-day thing with 20 bands, ten on each stage and all the money would go to Reclaim the Rovers." We just kept it going and are not far away from over £100,000 raised over the years. We have done all right.'

And if these fans and others who were part of the European adventure remain at the heart of the club, the club remains firmly in their heart. 'It has been my life,' says Gavin. 'Right from since I was a wee boy running on the pitch to get autographs through to nowadays. Always following them, always being there. It is just my club. Rovers mean everything to me.'

'So many memories in my life are linked to Raith Rovers and that is the highest compliment I can give to them,' adds Kenny Smith. 'Looking back and reflecting on it, the European trips were just some of the happiest times of my life being a supporter. The three trips were just all so unique. That ferry trip and a week in the Faroes. A jam-packed day in Iceland and then going to Munich. I am so fortunate to have these memories.'

And that is what Raith Rovers and other football clubs can provide – memories. Memories and connections with others. 'My wife once said to me, "You don't know how lucky you are, going up and down the country going to watch Raith Rovers,"' continues Kenny. 'At first, I was, "Lucky? You should try going to Dingwall on a Tuesday night when we get beat 4-1!" but she makes a really good point. My son and daughter, we have been to all these places together, Dumbarton, Berwick, Stranraer, Wick. It has shaped our relationship and I have such a strong bond with both of them. You spend time with them, and it is a great thing.'

'I think as you get older and maybe lose a parent you understand it more,' reflects Graeme Meldrum. 'I think back to my dad, off work and thinking, "How do I bond with my kids? Let's go to the fitba."' And to be able to do that now with my own kids is just brilliant. It was at the Dunfermline game in the cup. We had beaten them 3-0 and after Lewis Vaughan's free kick, the camera cut to the crowd. It was just me and my son Cammy having a hug. That is just priceless.'

These are the next generation of supporter, signing up for the journey, preparing to embrace the good and the bad, learning to cherish those spectacular moments to sustain them through extended periods of mediocrity. And listening to our stories of how we travelled to the Faroe Islands, celebrated in Iceland and watched Raith Rovers lead the mighty Bayern Munich in the Olympiastadion.

That moment is one that still gets supporters through the more difficult times. It still has the power to bring a smile to the faces of supporters 30 years later. 'It brings a warmth to my heart,' beams Steve Wallace. 'I can't think about that scoreboard or look at the scrapbooks I have of that time and not smile. It was a time when you couldn't script it. You were just part of it, and it was fantastic. To lead Bayern Munich 1-0 in the Olympic Stadium. How lucky were we to have seen that? That period from winning the cup, winning the First Division, playing in the Premier League and playing in Munich. If you take that as a two-year snapshot, fucking hell, it was just absolute gold dust.'

Steve is correct, it was golden. And if there is one legacy above all that has endured since the 1995 UEFA Cup run, it is hope. The hope that even in the most challenging times, that things might get better. Jimmy Nicholl and his squad proved that the incredibly unlikely and seemingly impossible can happen. They gave us memories to treasure for ever, deepened our love for our club, and instilled in us a belief that one day, no matter how unlikely it seems, it might just happen again.

It couldn't, could it?

Afterword by Steven Lawther

SPEAKING TO players and supporters has brought home the surrealness and joy of Raith Rovers' European adventure. I'd known it was special of course. I'd travelled to Tórshavn on the 25-hour ferry, flown to Iceland and made my way to the Olympiastadion in Munich. The astonishment that Rovers were playing in Europe never left me through the whole journey. Part of me still can't quite believe it.

I'd stood at the top of the concourse of the Olympiastadion at half-time, wide-eyed and incredulous that we were actually leading. Around me, fans laughed in wonderment, equally unbelieving about what was happening. An older supporter approached me, grabbed my arm, looked me straight in the eye and earnestly proclaimed, 'We can beat these bastards.'

In my heart of hearts, I probably didn't share his belief. I knew we were 1-0 up, but I also knew that there were 45 minutes left to play and that those 'bastards' were still Bayern Munich. But it is a moment I cherish and still think about from time to time. I loved that he believed. That despite the seemingly insurmountable odds, there remained the possibility that we'd score again, hold on through extra time and sneak through on penalties. We didn't of course, but for just over 20 minutes it was possible.

Among the excitement of that night, I managed to lose my camera somewhere in Munich. Like everyone else in the away end, I'd taken a picture of the half-time scoreboard, but my own personal photographic evidence was gone for ever. A few weeks later at Stark's Park, I was approached by Tom Phillips, who we'd met on the ferry to the Faroe Islands. He had a photo from Munich. It was me, perfectly framed, arms aloft in the Olympiastadion. He'd been visiting a friend who, showing his photos from Munich, had turned over this photo and said, 'I've no idea who this guy is.' Tom immediately recognised me and had promised to pass it on. I'll never know why his friend had decided to take a photo of the random big guy standing behind him, but I'll be for ever grateful that he did. It is the one picture I have from inside the Olympiastadion and being handed that photo felt like the perfectly surreal conclusion to a surreal journey.

I returned to the Olympiastadion with my brother last summer, the day before Scotland opened the 2024 European Championship in Munich. Unfortunately, AC/DC had played the night before and the stadium was closed as they dismantled their equipment. We tried our best to persuade one of their crew to let us stand at the top of the concourse to reminisce, but sadly got nowhere. I was more fortunate when I returned to Akranes a few years ago. The football season had finished so we were able to wander on to the snow-covered pitch at the Akranesvöllur, sit in the dugouts and once again stand in the away end. The memories flooded back of that surreal and sunny afternoon in 1995, singing our hearts out and praying for the final whistle. I've not yet returned to Toftir Stadium in the Faroe Islands but hope to one day – although if it does happen, I'll definitely not be taking the ferry.

Writing this book has allowed me to relive an unforgettable period in the club's history and recapture the magic of the three away trips. I left every conversation smiling and thinking how wonderful it had all been and how lucky I'd been to have experienced it. To have shared those moments with fellow fans and to have the privilege of re-experiencing them with the players who made it happen. Most of all, I reflected on how lucky I'd been to have chosen Raith Rovers as my team.

Speaking to fellow supporters, it seems that most had a moment when they could have taken an alternative path. If Shaughan McGuigan had chosen his grandad's other team rather than his local team; if Gavin Quinn had been allowed on the bus to Parkhead; if Jonathan Tippetts-Aylmer's parents hadn't offered him the option of football rather than Saturday afternoon shopping; it all could have been so different. I experienced my own personal sliding doors moments as a boy. Our family had relocated from Belfast to Fife during the height of the Troubles and although my dad never really liked football, his background brought the loose tribal allegiance to one side of the Old Firm. It took the father of a friend, Rob Anderson, driving me to Kirkcaldy to transform my outlook and show me that there was an alternative. Once inside Stark's Park, I never looked back.

Raith Rovers may frustrate and disappoint on a regular basis, but what they have given me over the last 40 years can never be repaid. That sense of togetherness, that sense of belonging, that sense of home. This is my place and my club. And over the years, it has become my daughter Grace's club. To have been able to pass that love to her is joyful.

I always joked that I'd drag her along until she realised that there were far better ways to spend a Saturday, but she's persisted. Travelling to games together, listening to music, laughing, celebrating the highs, consoling each other during the lows and generally revelling in the absurdity of following Rovers is perhaps the greatest privilege of all.

And as we head towards our seats in the South Stand every second Saturday, just before ascending the stairs to row MM, there's a poster. It's a poster that Ali More and I worked on as part of a wider project to celebrate the club's history. It's a photograph of the scoreboard. The scoreline on it, reminding me, as if there was ever any chance I'd forget, that we led in Munich.